I0081744

RETURNED SOLDIER

Published by Melbourne Books
Level 9, 100 Collins Street,
Melbourne, VIC 3000
Australia
www.melbournebooks.com.au
info@melbournebooks.com.au

Copyright © James Prascevic 2014

All rights reserved. No part of this publication
may be reproduced, stored in a retrieval system,
or transmitted in any form or any means
electronic, mechanical, photocopying, recording
or otherwise without the prior permission of
the publishers.

National Library of Australia
Cataloguing-in-Publication entry
Author: Prascevic, James
Title: Returned soldier - my battles : Timor, Iraq,
Afghanistan, depression and post traumatic
stress disorder
ISBN: 9781922129413 (paperback)
Subjects: Prascevic, James.
Post-traumatic stress disorder--Australia.
Depressed persons--Australia--Biography.
Soldiers--Job stress--Australia.
Soldiers--Australia--Biography.
Combat--Psychological aspects.
Psychology, Military.
Dewey Number: 355.0092

www.differentchallenge.com.au
www.facebook.com/Jamesprascevic

RETURNED SOLDIER

My Battles: Timor, Iraq, Afghanistan, Depression
and Post Traumatic Stress Disorder

JAMES PRASCEVIC

M

MELBOURNE BOOKS

Dedication

This book is dedicated to my parents, my sister, my ex-wife, my family, my friends, all who have suffered from a mental illness, and to everyone who has served in the ADF, past and present.

CONTENTS

INTRODUCTION	IRAQ, OCTOBER 2005	7
ONE	GROWING UP	14
TWO	TRAINING	24
THREE	POSTING TO 1 RAR	36
FOUR	TIMOR	48
FIVE	BETWEEN TIMOR AND IRAQ	62
SIX	IRAQ: FIRST BLOOD	73
SEVEN	IRAQ: THE EMBASSY AND THE COB	89
EIGHT	BETWEEN IRAQ AND AFGHANISTAN	100
NINE	AFGHANISTAN: THE BATTLE BEGINS	107
TEN	DIARY ENTRY: THE SANDBOX	112
ELEVEN	ROCL	128
TWELVE	DIARY ENTRY: CONTACT	130
THIRTEEN	SPECIAL FORCES: THE TEST	158
FOURTEEN	REHAB AND MARRIAGE	174
FIFTEEN	SINGLETON	180
SIXTEEN	PTSD AND DISCHARGE	194
SEVENTEEN	PREPARING FOR THE CHALLENGE	212
EIGHTEEN	THE CHALLENGE	236
NINETEEN	THE BREAKDOWN	246
TWENTY	THE ROAD AHEAD	264
	A NOTE FROM JAMES' PSYCHIATRIST	270

INTRODUCTION

IRAQ, OCTOBER 2005

I had been deployed on the eighth rotation of the Security Detachment (SECDET 8). Our main task was to provide security for the Australian Embassy, which included Australian Very Important Persons (VIPs), who were personnel that worked at and visited the embassy, located in the Green Zone. The Green Zone is an area in Bagdad, the capital of Iraq, where most of the Coalition forces, as well as civilians, live and work. It is an area bordered by the Tigris River, flowing north from the mountains of Turkey through Iraq, and is about 1850 kilometres long and protected by huge T-shaped blast walls, concrete walls in the shape of an upside-down letter 'T'. The Green Zone is just over six kilometres square, with large checkpoints for entry from the Green Zone to the unprotected area known as the Red Zone. To the side of the Australian Embassy is a Landing Zone (LZ) for helicopters, and adjoining the embassy is the American hospital, at the time occupied by the 10th Combat Support Hospital (10th CSH).

Here, war was tangible. It wasn't what I had seen on TV programs or played in video games. This was where I saw the results of the fighting, especially the devastation of the Improvised Explosive Devices (IEDs). An IED is a bomb that can be made relatively easily,but can cause major injury and death. It is very efficient and cheap to make, and is one of the main weapons used against the Coalition forces and the civilians of Iraq.

Seven months earlier in Australia I had been driving to work at 1530, 3.30pm, to do a Special Forces Entry Test (SFET) which, if I passed, would enable me to attempt the Commando Selection and Training Course (CSTC). I worked at the 1st Battalion, Royal Australian Regiment (1 RAR), Charlie Company (C Company), 8 Platoon (8 PL).

I was changing the station on my radio, searching for music to pump me up for the testing. When I looked back to the road I saw, 100 metres in front of me, a truck crashing into the rear of a car that was turning into a driveway. The car the truck hit, a red hatchback, was pushed into a white Magna.

I pulled over immediately, went over to the Magna and supported the driver, a woman in her fifties, as she got out of her car. She was in shock and had very little balance. I yelled out to a younger lady, who had run out of the house where the red hatchback had been turning into. She was screaming and crying, and I instructed her to support the lady from the Magna. I checked the Magna to see if there were any other occupants and luckily there was no-one else in the car. I then went over to the hatchback.

The first thing I noticed was that the driver had been thrown from her seat and was lying halfway out of the smashed back window. She was a large woman, probably in her late twenties, and was saying that her back was hurting and that she was worried about her passenger. I instructed another person who had arrived on the scene to support the driver's head and talk to her while I checked on the passenger.

As I approached the passenger, I noticed that she was an older lady, probably in her late seventies or early eighties. She had her eyes closed and was not breathing. She had a look on her face like she was at peace. She had been killed instantly. Another thing I noticed was that her body was positioned in her seat as though nothing had happened.

Her left leg from the upper thigh had been skinned all the way down to her foot so there were rolls of skin, like when you push your socks down. There was no blood, which surprised me, especially with that type of injury. As I was checking her pulse another lady arrived on the scene and identified herself as a nurse. She also could not find a pulse and confirmed that the lady was deceased.

I then returned to the driver and checked her over for any non-visual injuries other than the pain in her back. She had only minor cuts and scratches, which once again surprised me because of the seriousness of the accident. I supported her head and talked to her, trying to keep her calm until the ambulance arrived.

A major concern for me at the time was that the fuel tank on the hatchback had ruptured and a lot of fuel was pouring out onto the road at my feet. After what felt like an eternity the ambulance, police and firefighters arrived. I gave the medics a handover of the three victims, told the police what I had witnessed, gave them my details and went back to my car to go to work for the test. As the road had been blocked, I had to go the long way. As I drove off I noticed the damage to the truck's front end and wondered how only one person had been killed. I did not turn the radio on for the rest of the trip.

I arrived five minutes late for the testing and was questioned by the Special Forces (SF) staff running the SFET as to why I was late. I explained and they asked me if I was okay to do the test, to which I replied that I was. A note was made about the incident in one of the staff's notebooks (I was worried that it was about my late arrival) and the testing began.

The test involved a 2.4-kilometre run in camouflage uniform (known as cams) and sneakers. We were required to carry our webbing, which holds our ammunition, water and other items that we were required to carry on our person at all times. For testing purposes, our webbing would be a minimum weight of eight kilograms, and we also carried a plastic training rifle weighing nearly four kilograms. The run was to be completed within 12 minutes. After the run, wearing cams and sneakers, the testing continued with a minimum of 60 push-ups within two minutes, a minimum of 10 heaves or pull-ups in your own time, and 100 sit-ups to a cadence. Next was a 400-metre swim in cams and sneakers in under 18 minutes, a practical navigation test and a 15-kilometre pack march with 30 kilograms of weight, which included webbing, a pack and a training rifle. This pack march was to be completed in under two hours and 40 minutes. Boots in this case had taken the place of sneakers. The testing was conducted over a five to six hour period.

At midnight, the testing was complete and after a cool down, some stretches and some food I drifted off to sleep in my bivi bag (a thin waterproof sleeping bag with a zip at the top to prevent bugs from biting you while you sleep) satisfied that I had passed all the tests. I felt relatively good, apart from having sore shoulders and legs.

Two days later, I was having lunch at the 1 RAR Other Ranks (ORs) mess hall. Different ranks within the Australian Defence Force (ADF), and in this case the Army, have different messes. Privates (PTE), Lance Corporals (LCPL) and Corporals (CPL) share a mess, which is the ORs mess. Sergeants (SGT), Warrant Officers (WO), and Second Lieutenants and higher have their own messes.

The Commanding Officer (CO) of the Battalion was having lunch in the ORs mess to mix with the 'subordinates'. He approached me and congratulated me on passing the SFET, and said that he had heard about the vehicle accident and my involvement, from the note the SF staff had made, and that I was to be put on the two-week long Combat First Aid Course (CFA) starting in one week.

The aim of the CFA course is to prepare and qualify personnel of PTE to CPL ranking to perform advanced first aid techniques in the field. This includes the administration of drugs and fluids intravenously. There is usually only one qualified medic per Company, so it is very important that there is at least one CFA per Section (eight personnel, nine when I first joined, plus attachments). If a member is injured or becomes ill and is away from the Company medic, there are members able to give first aid. CFA members can also assist medics when required. This is how I wound up working in the 10th CSH in Bagdad's Green Zone in Iraq.

...

And so the experience of working in the medical side of war began. The intention was for CFA-qualified soldiers like me to work in the hospital so we could have exposure to the injuries we would come across as infantry soldiers. I enjoyed the fact that Australians such as myself would be assisting our Coalition partners (the Americans), enabling them to see what it was like to work with Aussie soldiers.

The first day, I and another CFA-qualified PTE walked into the hospital. It was supposed to be a day of getting to know the American staff and to see where the main areas in the hospital were, such as the emergency room, where we would spend most of our time. Other areas we were shown were the X-ray and Magnetic Resonance Imaging (MRI) room, the surgery and a room set up for blood testing, so if blood was required for incoming wounded the right type would be ready. Even though all soldiers wore dog tags indicating their blood type, along with their regimental number, religion and date of birth, blood type had to be confirmed prior to administration.

While we were being shown by the American Captain the locations of items, such as bandages, needles and other equipment, a nurse entered and stated that an Iraqi civilian who had been involved in an IED incident was coming in. The Captain turned to us and said, 'Put your gloves on.'

I could hear the medical evacuation (medivac) helicopter in the distance, then heard it land at the LZ. I was starting to feel very nervous. When we were being told to put our gloves on, two American medics had left for the LZ in a small vehicle that could carry two stretchers. The vehicle was similar to the ones you see when injured footballers are taken off the field when they cannot walk. The vehicle had arrived back at the hospital with the injured civilian, the two medics and the medic from the helicopter, who was giving a handover of the patient. The handover was similar to what we had learnt on the CFA course and can be remembered by an acronym, because the Army has an acronym for everything. This one was MR MIST, which means the MR (person injured), M (method of injury), I (injury), S (signs and symptoms) and T (treatment). For example, (MR) John Smith (M) fell from a ladder, (I) he has a broken lower left leg, (S) there is swelling and a bump in the lower left leg area and he is also telling me of severe pain, (T) I have placed a splint on his legs and I have given him 15 milligrams of methoxyflurane.

The Iraqi civilian was taken off the vehicle, carried on the stretcher and placed in one of the three beds in the emergency room. The first thing I noticed was that his clothes were red all over. His left leg had been completely blown off just above the knee.

Before I could comprehend what I had just seen, everyone started doing their part. I was given a pair of scissors and told to cut off his clothes. The most serious injury he had sustained was the loss of his leg, however he had also received numerous shrapnel wounds to his body. He had a tourniquet on, which is a strap about three centimetres wide and when tightened around a part of the body, in this case the leg, it stops the blood flowing from the body by clotting the blood. It is placed about six centimetres above the wound, though if it is left on for too long it can cause more damage, meaning the leg may have to be amputated even higher. Anything can be used as a tourniquet, such as a piece of rope, a bandage or a piece of clothing. Though it is a good device, it is usually a last resort. In this case, the tourniquet had worked. As the blood had clotted on our patient's exposed arteries and veins, we were able to slowly remove the tourniquet.

While this was going on the rest of the staff were stabilising him to get him ready for surgery, as he was in and out of consciousness. Blood samples were taken and rushed off to the blood testing room. He was hooked up to fluid bags and the required drugs were given to him. Once he was stable, we took him into the X-ray and MRI room to see where the shrapnel was, in case it was near any of his vital organs.

He was then taken off to surgery, and that was the last we saw of him. If he was an American, a Coalition soldier or a civilian worker, after surgery and when stabilised he would have been flown either to Germany, where the Americans had a hospital, or straight back home.

After the patient was taken to surgery, we cleaned up the emergency room and the equipment and wiped up the blood, with the help of some locally employed civilians (LECS). We replaced all the equipment used, ready for the next patient to come our way.

Once I had finished at the hospital, I returned to the Australian Embassy for my 8-hour guard shift. Once my guard shift was finished, I headed to the American mess (the DFAC, short for 'dining facility') for dinner at around midnight. The DFAC had four mealtimes, as someone was always working and for some people dinner might actually be breakfast. After the midnight dinner I returned to the embassy to get some shut-eye, so I could be ready for my next stint at the hospital and my next guard shift.

Lying in bed, I was finally able to process the day's events. I had just spent three hours working in a modern-day M*A*S*H. For the first time I had seen the results of war in a way that had never seemed real to me until now, and it was only going to get worse. What also went through my mind was the American staff still at the hospital and how they had really impressed me. They did shifts of 12 hours on and 12 hours off for 12 to 14 months. I could just leave the hospital when I was tired or it got too much for me. I was also going home in six months.

ONE

GROWING UP

On 6 November 1979 (which happened to be Melbourne Cup Day) I was born in Colac Hospital, in country Victoria, about two hours south-west of Melbourne. When the doctor came in to deliver me, he stated to everyone in the room that the gates were about to open for The Melbourne Cup, 'the race that stops the nation'. The people in the room didn't care about that so-called important race; they were all excited about who was about to come into the world: me.

The exact time I was born was at 1459, weighing in at 8lb 6oz. I was named James Edgar Prascevic. Edgar had been my maternal grandfather's name.

Two years and two months later I was joined by a sister.

My father was born in 1953. His official birthdate had changed a bit when he was growing up, but in the end it was put down to 28 December. He grew up on a farm in Monbulk and then Gerangamete, and eventually Colac in Victoria. My father worked a lot of jobs in between going to school, just to help feed the family. His jobs ranged from paper deliveries, working in a butcher shop, to working at a sawmill.

My mother was born on 7 August 1954 in Colac. She was the youngest of five children and left school at age 16 to work in a pharmacy. She worked in that industry until she retired, 35 years later.

I was raised in a house in Gravesend Street that my parents had bought very cheaply, as it was very run-down. It was on a large block ,and at the rear of the property was a laneway and a park where my sister and I spent many hours playing. My parents renovated the house to be one of the nicest houses in the area, which also had the best garden thanks to Mum.

My sister and I went to Colac South West Primary School, which I really enjoyed. I had a lot of friends, and thinking about it now I enjoyed that school a lot compared to my next school. This school was where I got my first nickname. One day in class we were reading a book called *Monster in the Bathtub*, when one of the kids said, 'Bames in the bathtub!' So for the rest of my school days, and even now when I visit or catch up with friends from the old days, I am known by the nickname of Bames or Bamer, not Pras as it is known to my Army mates and to everyone I meet from now on.

Every day, I looked forward to playing AFL football at lunchtime. We would go out every lunchtime, regardless of the weather, and play until the bell went. We would come into class covered with grass stains, or we were covered head to toe with mud.

I didn't own a pair of football boots, which during the winter months made it hard for me to grip on the muddy oval. I found a pair in a shoe shop for $30. They were red and black, the colour of the football team I barracked for: the Mighty Bombers. I begged Mum and Dad to buy them for me, but they decided this was an opportunity to teach me how to appreciate money. So dad organised for me to wash cars two afternoons a week for three weeks. I wanted the boots so badly that I took up the job offer, though I thought the boots would be gone before I got the money. Secretly, Mum and Dad had already bought the boots and had them hidden at home. When the three weeks were over, I went to the shoe shop and noticed the boots were no longer in stock. I went home in a bad mood, but was pleasantly surprised when Dad brought out the boots in the box. The next day at school I felt like I was my favourite AFL player, Paul Salmon, playing at the MCG in the Grand Final.

As I now had my boots I decided it was time to start playing AFL outside school, so I joined the local under-10s football club. I played in a forward pocket for the Magpies. During the first game I played, I received a very hard hip-and-shoulder in the first quarter and had to be carried off the ground. I came back in the third quarter and kicked my first goal, which I was very proud of. We ended up winning the Grand Final and I decided to play another season, as I enjoyed it so much. The next year we won the Grand Final again.

For some reason I stopped playing AFL and went out on a high. I regretted this decision later, as I was not doing as much physical activity and put on a lot of weight.

...

Our family had a holiday house in Lorne, where we went most weekends. The house was reasonably small at that time. The toilet, bathroom and laundry were located outside, around the back. Eventually, Dad rebuilt the house so all the areas were connected. Dad also built a deck that went around the house and met up with the driveway each side. Having the Lorne house was a fantastic getaway for us all. We would usually pack on Thursday nights and Mum would pick my sister and I up from school on Friday, and we would head straight to Lorne. Dad would come down as soon as he finished work. Each weekend we would go fishing, swimming and boogie boarding, we'd play on the beach and look for shells, in particular the cowrie shell, our favourite.

The house had a fantastic view of the ocean and was only a couple of minutes walk to the beach. The walkway from our house to the beach ended right next to the swing bridge, which was across the Erskin River. On the opposite side of the swing bridge were the paddleboats, which we loved going down to so we could paddle up and down the river.

...

When I finished grade 6 at Colac South West Primary School, my father encouraged me to go to Colac Technical School, as it focused more on vocational training. He thought I might use these subjects to gain an apprenticeship in the building trade and I agreed. However, a lot of my other friends from Colac South West had decided to go to Colac High School, which left me feeling a little alone. The worst part, as a lot of people know about starting at a new school, is that you are on the bottom of the food chain again. I had put on a lot of weight over the Christmas break and, as we know, kids can be cruel. Although in some classes I had a few people to connect with, when it came to recess and lunchtime I felt like I was on my own all the time.

When I turned 15 I got a job at the local supermarket. As I had good money coming in, at recess most days I would buy a few sausage rolls and some chocolate milk. This diet, along with smoking and a lack of physical activity, really affected my weight and confidence, and by year 10 I was weighing approximately 100 kilograms. My unhealthy lifestyle led to a lack of school friends, so when recess came I would get my food as quickly as possible and go to the library, as I felt it was the safest place.

Sometimes while walking around the school grounds by myself, I would come around a corner, see a bunch of people and hear them say, 'There he is, let's get him!' My initial reaction was to run but I was always caught, my shirt ripped, I was called names and taunted until they got bored. There were even times when I would be walking along the corridor and a bully would just walk past and punch me for no reason. One time while walking home from school, I had a bully run up behind me, push me to the ground and punch me in the face over and over, saying that I had said something about him. Some days, I rode my bike to school and when I went to get it at lunchtime someone would have taken it without asking me. When I'd go to get the bike at the end of the day it would be on the bike shelter roof. I really hated school and wanted out.

My job at the supermarket had changed and I was now working most days. I was making good money, though people were threatening me at school and telling me to buy smokes for them or they would bash me the next day. But I enjoyed the work because I felt like I had a place and was worth something.

Year 11 came around, which I did not want to do, but after long talks with Mum and Dad, I eventually said that I would. It was agreed that if a plumbing apprenticeship came up I would begin that, with the aim of eventually owning my own business.

The subjects I was doing in year 11 were woodwork, sheet metal work, English and basic maths. The five spares I got per week was time that I was supposed to spend in the library working on my homework but instead I would go home and watch movies, as I couldn't stand being at the school any longer than I had to. At this stage I was working 36 hours a week at the supermarket. At the halfway mark of year 11 I was failing most of my subjects, so it was decided I would stop working at the supermarket for a couple of months and focus on my schoolwork, which I did. Once I had caught up to where I needed to at school I went back to work at the supermarket.

Close to the end of year 11, one of the local plumbers was looking for an apprentice. Along with a lot of other people, I applied for the job. I felt like I had an advantage, as I had done the work experience with this same plumber the year before. It got down to me and another bloke. I wasn't given the job, as the other bloke was six months older than me and he would get his licence that little bit sooner.

I finished year 11, passing all my subjects. They weren't all As, but I had passed and no-one could take that away from me.

...

I bought my first car with the cash I had saved up from working at the supermarket. It was a VL Commodore station wagon. It was a great car and was perfect for my needs at the time. I could fit all my tools in the back, I could lay down the back seats and sleep in it when I went away on the weekends, and it would also fit my fishing rods.

I applied for a job as an apprentice plumber in Melbourne through Master Plumbers Group Training Scheme. They hired apprentices out to individual employers for periods of time, ranging from one week to four years. I got the job and moved into a house in Elsternwick, Melbourne, with a family who had previously been our neighbours in Colac. I did my first year of schooling.

Once I completed the first year I was put on the job. My first job was in Dandenong and at the time I was living in Ascot Vale, which was on the other side of the city. Having to depend on public transport as I was only 17, I had to be at the train station at 0500 hours to catch the first train into the city so I would be able to catch the first train out of the city to Dandenong. The earliest I would get home was around 1900 hours. It was hard because I was living with four strangers and sleeping on a mattress in the lounge room, and had to wait for them to go to bed before I could.

After a while a friend of my father's from Colac, who had been renting a small bungalow behind a shop in East Malvern, let me know that he was moving out and gave me the relevant contact details to apply for the bungalow. I was successful in the bid and, after nearly a year of living in Melbourne and moving from house to house, I finally had my own place. It was a bit rundown and didn't look very nice, but it was mine. Dad came down one weekend, and we painted the inside and cleaned up the outside area to make it look a bit more homely.

Just before I turned 18, my parents suggested that maybe I should invest in a property in Colac. I thought it would be a good idea because houses in my price range, and in a good area, would potentially increase in value over the years. We found a place that was close to the hospital and main street, and central to all the schools in the area. I purchased it at a fantastic price. There was a fair bit of work to be done to the house prior to it being rentable, so every weekend for the next month I came home and worked on it. I was lucky that my father was experienced in renovating houses, and he put in many hours working on the house throughout the week. Dad found a fantastic tenant to move in and she looked after the house as though it was her own until it was sold for a profit five years later.

...

I met some great people during my apprenticeship, though I only stayed close with one of them. As I hadn't had many friends while growing up, I was a little afraid to call him up and see if he wanted to hang out with me. When I did summon the courage to call him, we had a great time.

We would sometimes go to South Yarra and get a souvlaki and a pizza, then drive to St Kilda and observe the sex workers that were standing on the streets waiting for the next customer or a delivery of drugs. We used to see a lot of the girls being dropped off at a particular phone box. There they would make a phone call and a couple of minutes later someone would arrive, a transaction would be made, the car would leave and she would walk up an alleyway or a dark street. We also noticed that most of the girls had a male sitting near them who would write down the numberplate of the car she got into. This was her boyfriend, pimp or both.

Sometimes we would drive out to the airport and park right at the start of the runway, and watch as the planes flew in just above us. These parking areas were also known as places for people to smoke drugs. One evening, the police came into the car park and talked to us, asking us what we were doing there. We explained that we were watching the planes, but they didn't believe us and requested to search the car. I had no issues with this, as I didn't do drugs. I was more concerned that the car may have not been roadworthy. They found nothing in the car and left.

My friend and I had a lot of fun together and still remain close friends today.

...

During my apprenticeship, I worked on a lot of union sites in the city. This meant that it was all new work and I would get site allowance, which was an average of $2 to $3 per hour extra on top of my normal wages. This was very handy, as apprenticeship wages are low compared to a fully qualified plumber. This also helped with my mortgage.

I used to go home most weekends. I would leave work on Friday and head to Colac for a home-cooked roast that Mum would make. Then I would meet a friend at the bowling club across the road, drink beer, play free pool and go to the pub. During the week I did not eat well at all, and most nights I would order a large pizza and a bottle of Coke for dinner.

One weekend in Colac I was at the hospital for some reason. While Dad and I were waiting he said, 'Why don't you jump on the scales and see how much you weigh?' When I saw the number 130 staring back at me, I knew I had a problem. I knew I had been overweight previously, but to see 130 kilograms was very scary, to say the least.

As soon as I got back to Melbourne, I started investigating local gyms and pools. I went to one of the gyms and noticed they had a boxercise class, which I went to. I didn't have any runners or sporting clothes. All I had were my work boots and a pair of tracksuit pants. I really enjoyed the session, although I was absolutely exhausted after 10 minutes. The trainer was a boxing coach who was opening a gym in Collingwood that had been closed down for a number of years. I decided there and then that I would focus on my fitness. I started going to all the sessions he was running and also started going to the pool every other day. I began eating properly and I gave up alcohol. After six months I was weighing 100 kilograms, and was feeling extremely fit and very proud.

When I finished my apprenticeship and was a fully qualified plumber, I wanted to remain in Melbourne and continue working on the union sites I had been working on. I applied for a couple of positions, however nothing came of it so I decided to move back to

Colac. As soon as I got back to Colac I found a job working on the new hospital. I applied for the job and received it straight away, and got to work.

A few months into working at the hospital, I felt like maybe plumbing was not what I wanted for my future. One Sunday evening while watching television with my parents, I said to them that I wanted to do something different in my life but had no idea what. On cue an ad appeared advertising jobs for the Army and straight away I thought that could be what I was looking for.

The next day I rang up and inquired in regards to joining the Army as an infantry soldier and was sent out an information pack. I told them that I was a qualified plumber and they said that it would be best for me to join as a plumber. However, I had no intention of doing so, as I wanted something different. I was told there would be a six-month wait until positions were available for the infantry. So all I could do was wait and maintain my fitness.

After the hospital work was complete there was still no call from the Army. I was over plumbing big time, so I applied for a job to work at the Lorne pub. I received a job as a bartender and worked there over the summer of 2001 to 2002. After the summer period started to wind down, all the staff that had been put on during the summer period were then put off. However, I was offered a job in the kitchen washing dishes so I thought, *Why not?* There was no pressure on me; all I had to do was rock up to work on time, wash the dishes and go home.

Around this time a lot of bills started to come in, such as insurance and registration for my car and motorbike. The money that I was receiving at the pub would not cover any of that. So I made a regrettable choice and sold my motorbike, but the bills kept piling up. I applied for a job as a plumbing subcontractor for a local plumbing company in Lorne. I received the job and started back in the plumbing trade. I began to enjoy plumbing again and I was making really good money. This was where I regretted having to sell the motorbike. If only

I could have held out one more month I could have paid the rego and the insurance in a week.

After about two months working as a plumber again I received a phone call from the Army to say that positions were available and that I was to come to Melbourne for a fitness test. The fitness test included push-ups, sit-ups and a run called a Beep Test, where you run back and forth between two witch's hats located approximately 25 metres apart within a certain amount of time. Once a beep goes off you run back to the other witch's hat. The beeps start to get closer together and you have to increase your speed, until you reach the minimum pass mark or until you can't keep up with the beeps.

I passed all the requirements and then I went inside to have a medical check-up by the military doctors. I passed all medical tests, however I had put on approximately five kilograms and was told to be very careful, as according to the official body mass index charts I was getting close to the overweight point. Due to my height of 186 centimetres, the official body mass index charts would have me weighing in the 80 to 85 kilogram range, which I felt would be unrealistic and unhealthy for me.

I returned to Lorne, and for the next couple of weeks I watched my weight and focused on improving my fitness. I received in the mail my approved forms, stating that I was fit to join the Army and that the enlistment date was 23 April 2002.

On 23 April, with all my bags packed and ready to go, Mum and Dad took me down to Melbourne, where I signed the paperwork and read out the oath to my country and to the Australian Defence Force. I said my goodbyes, boarded the bus and headed for my next destination: the 'Home of the Soldier' at the Army Recruit Training Centre within Blamey Barracks in Kapooka, New South Wales. I was so excited. It was a different direction in my life, a different challenge. Little did I know where I would be in eight years time.

TWO

TRAINING

As we approached Blamey Barracks, our home for the next six weeks, a quietness fell over the bus. I remember wondering what was going to happen to us in the next two minutes. Was it going to be like in the movies, where the instructors are yelling at you and in your face all the time? I figured that question would be answered very soon.

There was a CPL who had jumped on the bus in Melbourne dressed in his polyesters, or parade dress. He sat up at the front of the bus and did not say a word to anyone the whole trip. When the bus stopped and the door opened, he stood up and walked out. You could hear every noise that he made, but as soon as he was out of the bus there was silence again. Were we to get up and get off the bus? Did we have to stay where we were and wait for instructions?

After about 10 seconds of silence I heard footsteps walking up to the bus along the concrete path, and then a military policeman (MP), who would have been about 190 centimetres tall and weighing about 110 kilograms, stepped into the bus and started yelling, 'GET OUT OF THE BUS, HURRY UP, GET OUT OF THE BUS, HURRY UP!'

We were instructed to get our bags out from under the bus and to form two lines. We were then rushed to our accommodation area. At the front of our accommodation our names were called out in regards to where we would be sleeping. After everybody's name was read out we were told to go to the rooms, put our bags down and get changed into an Army-issue tracksuit that would be hanging in our locker. Mine did not fit at all — I could not do up the front of my jacket and my pants barely came up halfway past my arse. There were about 40 of us and after we had changed we were moved into the common room at the end of the corridor, where we sat down on the floor and had the rules read to us. They went on forever. The basics were to follow the rules, do what the staff said to the letter, and never ever question them. Over the next six weeks we were to be taught the basics of the Australian Defence Force, which would progress us to our Initial Employment Training (IET), which for me was infantry.

We were then sent back to our rooms and were given instructions about how we would be woken up. We were in Delta Company and our Platoon number was 33. So whenever we heard the words 'hallway 33' we were to yell out 'hallway 33' at the top of our lungs, which was called the echo system. This system would take some getting used to, and for a long time we were not in unison. However, after a while we got used to it and when the staff yelled out 'hallway 33' everyone would yell it back at the same time. When we yelled this, we had to stand in front of our rooms in the corridor at attention, waiting for the staff's next order. That was how we would be woken up in the morning. On our bed was one bed sheet at the bottom, one top sheet along with a cover and, if required, a blanket. In the mornings when 'hallway 33' was yelled out we were to grab our bottom sheet, throw it over our shoulder and run out into the hallway, standing at attention to await orders to begin the morning routine. Then we were to clean the PL area, our rooms and ourselves, all within a certain time period. If these tasks were not achieved in this time, we would have to start again. After making our beds to inspection order they would yell out 'hallway 33' again, and we were required to rip our beds apart and begin the routine again. We did this over and over, until we were able to get it done within the staff's time limit.

...

'HALLWAY 33, HALLWAY 33, HALLWAY 33!' was what I was woken up to in the morning on that first day. The staff were yelling it over and over again. They were running into our rooms and coming right up to our faces and yelling it until we yelled it out again.

I sat upright and started to yawn. That was when the staff member yelled again, 'Hallway 33, hallway 33, hallway 33!' I yelled it in reply but it did not convince the staff member, who yelled it at me again. I grabbed my bottom bed sheet, threw it over my shoulder and ran out into the hallway. The next two hours we were put back into bed and 'woken up' again, over and over, until we finally got it right.

After that was completed and we had finished morning routine and breakfast, we were taken down to the quartermaster store, better known as the 'Q-store', to be issued with our equipment. It was like getting a showbag on a massive scale. There was a camouflage uniform, boots, webbing (containing all your essential needs when outfield), our pack and all the things that would go in that, such as sleeping bags, warm weather gear, waterproof equipment, and so on. We were also issued with our ceremonial dress, which included brass pieces shaped but not shined. The brass would fit on our pants, which would sit at the top of our belt. The belt was joined together by two pieces of brass and held on with another two pieces. During our spare time, we were required to sand down the rough edges of the brass and then polish it until we could see our faces in it, then polish it some more. The brass did make our ceremonial uniforms look good, however the amount of work that was required to keep them up to standard was unbelievable.

After we dropped our issued equipment at our lines, which was our accommodation, we were given a haircut. Everyone was given the Army haircut: a number four all over, unless your hair was already shorter. The idea was that we would all look the same; we would have the same haircut, we would wear the same uniform and we would do everything the same. Our PL would become as one by the end of our six weeks here. We would be in unison.

One thing that was considered to be important when learning to be 'as one' was that we marched and conducted drills in formation. So everywhere we went, we would practise. The staff would call out the steps, saying, 'Left, right, left, right, left, right, left.' All we had to do was make sure that a particular foot hit the ground when it was called out. At the beginning, if the staff didn't call out the steps when we were marching, within a few steps we would be out of synch. As I would come to learn, drill would be a challenge for me for a long time. It was only when I was required to conduct extra drills after I had forgotten to lock my locker while I was away that I believe I passed the drill test.

As I had joined the Army on 23 April, which was only two days prior to Anzac Day, I felt very proud because this was my first Anzac Day as a trainee of the Australian Defence Force. I also wanted to see how important it was for the members who had been in the Army longer, like the CPLs and above.

We got up early and went down to the undercover area next to our lines, where we were given a coffee with a nip of rum, the same as the Anzac Diggers had prior to leaving the ships to storm Anzac Cove on 25 April 1915, 87 years prior.

After we finished our coffee and rum (both of which I dislike), we marched over to the headquarters of Blamey Barracks, where the memorial service would be held. The last post was read out, along with the playing of the bugler, and our minute silence began. The Australian flag was lowered to half-mast.

Those famous words sent chills through me as I stood below the flag:

They shall grow not old,
As we that are left grow old,
Age shall not weary them,
Nor the years condemn.
At the going down of the sun,
And in the morning
We will remember them.

After the service was finished we were taken back to our lines, where we were left alone for the rest of the day to work on our equipment, while the staff enjoyed the day's celebrations.

...

The next day we got back into training and were broken up into Sections and given a Section Commander by the rank of CPL. They would be our direct point of contact. He or she would teach us all the things I would later learn on the promotions course.

First off was drill, where we would go off to our allocated areas and practise all the different turns and halts. As I said previously, I was shockingly bad at drill. I would be out of step at all times. When my CPL would call the direction to turn, I would turn in the opposite direction. I just could not get it right. We would go out and do a 40-minute session, where we were taught a particular move, such as how to halt or stop in a format of step-by-step. These sessions were the longest sessions at Kapooka for me, apart from the high wire confidence course.

The high wire confidence course was a set of obstacles at the approximate height of the average power lines. You are harnessed up and required to attempt all obstacles in order to pass. I did not have too much of a problem with heights as I was a plumber prior to the Army, working on roofs all the time. However, I had an incident not long prior to joining the Army, where I almost fell off the roof but was saved by the harness that I was wearing. This had shot my confidence completely out of the water in regards to heights. Apart from the drill I had been pretty confident with everything else, but the high wire confidence course did put me back in my box big time. I struggled with it a lot, as I did not trust the equipment we were using. If I had trusted it, I would have enjoyed the day so much more because at every obstacle I fell off.

Next thing we were taught, which I enjoyed, was weapons training. We were taught how to correctly handle and conduct the stoppage drills of the F89 machine gun and the F88 Austeyr rifle. The F88 is a very popular weapon used in movies, such as *Die Hard* and *Harley Davidson and the Marlboro Man*, as it looks like a weapon from the future. Once we were confident and competent with this weapon, and had been tested by our staff, we were taken to the range and were able to fire the two weapons. We were required to fire 20 rounds at a target. All rounds had to be within a 200-millimetre radius.

I remember the first time I fired. We were all lying down ready to go and were given the command, 'In your own time, go on.' But no-one wanted to be the first person to fire, so everyone just lay there waiting for someone else to fire first. After what felt like forever, one of the staff yelled out that it was okay to fire for a second time. On the F88 there is a button that can be pulled out below the trigger, which will turn the weapon from an automatic to a semiautomatic weapon, meaning you can fire one shot at a time or a full magazine of 30 rounds at a time. You can still fire single shots while it is set for fully automatic, it is just down to how hard you pull the trigger in. If you pull the trigger in halfway it will fire a single shot and if you pull the trigger past the halfway point it will fire an automatic burst. When the first shots were fired there were many fully automatic bursts, as a lot of us had forgotten to pull down the button below the trigger. This completely ruined our chances of a first time pass, as when you fire an automatic burst the weapon tends to move upwards and to the left.

The F89 machine guns were also a lot of fun. We were given belts of 20 rounds and when firing it was all down to trigger manipulation as to how many shots you would fire. A good burst is approximately three to four rounds, as the more you fire, the more the weapon tends to go off target and as per the F88, up and to the left.

...

On Sundays we would do our own thing, which was usually polishing our brass or working on our ceremonial uniforms. However, if you were a churchgoer (which previously I was not) you were able to attend the service, and afterwards given lamingtons, tea and coffee. To us this was a luxury we had not had for a long time. With the choice of either clean your brass and iron your uniform, or go off to church and get away from the PL area for the morning, by the end of the six weeks everyone on the course believed in God.

One morning while rushing out of my sleeping area, I forgot to lock my locker and left it open. The lock was there but I had not pushed it closed. Once I returned to the lines, I found my locker had been emptied out onto the floor in my room, which I shared with three other people. I was then called to the office utilising the echo system. This was when the staff yelled out, 'Recruit Prascevic to the staff's office!' and once I arrived at the staff's office I was required to halt and yell out, 'Recruit Prascevic to see Corporal xxxxxx!' I was asked if I knew why I had been called to the office, to which I replied, 'Yes.' I was told that, along with another person who had done the same thing, I would be seeing the disciplinary officer that afternoon.

Later that afternoon, I was marched into the disciplinary officer's office and given two days of restriction of privileges, meaning that when it was time to relax and work on our equipment during the night I was to be doing jobs, such as drill and other tasks like sweeping the parade ground with a hand brush. During my restriction of privileges, while wearing marching order (when you have your pack and webbing on) I was told to drop off my marching order in my room and return within 60 seconds. I ran inside and one of the blokes who was ironing had his locker open. The locker's wooden door was blocking the entrance to my area. As I had my pack in one hand and my webbing in the other, I kicked the door closed to get through, as I was running out of time. I didn't realise my own strength and the weakness of the door, and I put my foot straight through the wooden door. I went outside and told the staff what had happened, and I was read out the charge sheet. This went something along the lines of 'anything you say can and will be used against you'. I was shitting myself by that time.

I continued with the evening's activities in regards to restriction of privileges, which finished that night. About two weeks later while we were at the range, I was called up to see the Corporals and the Platoon Sergeant. The Sergeant said, 'Corporal xxxxx has a turtle and Corporal xxxxxx has a turtle. These two turtles are going to have a race. If Corporal xxxxx's turtle wins you will be charged, but if Corporal xxxxx's turtle wins you will be charged.' In other words, I was stuffed either way.

I walked back to my area and continued cleaning my weapon. About five minutes later I was called up again and told to disregard the whole incident and that it was over. Those five minutes were the worst five minutes in my Army career up until that point, other than the high wire confidence course. But the CPLs enjoyed seeing me suffer for those five minutes. They must have got a kick out of it.

It felt like they were trying really hard to make life difficult for us. There was a line marked on the ground with black tape just before you got to the doorway of the toilets/showers. Every time we went into the toilets/showers, at the line we were required to conduct a drill movement that we had been practising at the time. For example, if at the time we were practising a right turn on the march I would march up to the line, conduct a right turn, then an about-turn and a left turn, and go into the toilets/showers. It was a lot easier doing a turn while stationary. This was a pain, as it took up a lot of time that we did not have. However, it was a good way to practise our drills, especially as we had to pass an individual drill test prior to marching out (passing the course).

Physical training (PT) was a big part of our six weeks at Blamey Barracks, and every day we would conduct PT with the Physical Training Instructors (PTIs). They would teach us how to correctly conduct pack marches, webbing runs, how to carry heavy items such as ammunition boxes and stretchers, and how to maintain and improve our fitness and strength as a member of the Defence Force. By the end of the six weeks we also had to pass a Basic Fitness Assessment (BFA), which comprised of a 2.4-kilometre run in a set amount of time, and a set number of push-ups and sit-ups, which varied between age groups.

For the last week we did a field exercise in which we were taught the basics of patrolling and setting up all-round defence (or as we call it, a harbor). This is used when having longer breaks, i.e. while the commander is in planning stage, when eating and for extended periods, including overnight. We were also taught the basics of a Section attack and by the end everybody knew the role that was conducted by the nine people in the Section. On the last day of the field exercise we were required to attempt a combination of what we had learnt, which comprised of a pack march, a stretcher carry, patrolling, a Section attack, the obstacle course, the bayonet assault course and a shooting task. This was called 'The Challenge'. It was the hardest thing, mentally and physically, that I had done in my life so far, yet this was nothing compared to what my Army career was going to give me.

Once all the assessments were complete, for the last few days we conducted drill training for a march. My parents drove up from Victoria to watch my promotion from a recruit to a PTE. The recruit training required us to display leadership, work as an individual, display self-knowledge, interpersonal skills, display soldierly conduct, courage and initiative, conduct a daily routine in the barracks, comply with the customs and traditions of the Australian Army, perform drills with a service weapon and participate in administration. I had met all these requirements. I was now ready for my next challenge. My IETs for the infantry at Singleton, New South Wales.

...

We arrived at Singleton, at the School of Infantry (SOI) on a Sunday evening. We had the Monday off so were able to settle in until everyone got back on Tuesday. There were only two or three people still around. They had only arrived a couple of weeks prior to us. They were in a holding PL waiting for us to arrive to enable a full PL, which at Singleton was four Sections, three in the Battalions, to start the training. We were told by one of the blokes that, 'This is not recruit training here and that if you gob off to anyone here you will get bashed.' This bloke had been here two weeks and was trying to act like the tough guy, but this didn't work on myself or the other person with me, who was from a rough area of Frankston in Melbourne.

On the Tuesday we were allocated our Sections, and for the next four days we went over what we were taught at recruit training and issued the equipment we would need to conduct the IETs. Recruit training had been the overall training we would come across within our careers within the Army, but the SOI was directed at our job as an infantry soldier. The role of the infantry is 'to seek out and close with the enemy, to kill or capture him, to seize and hold ground, to repel attack, by night or day, regardless of season, weather or terrain'.

Over 10 weeks we were taught numerous skills. They included: understanding enemy tactics; how to perform as a rifleman in a Section and PL defensive position; perform in a PL withdrawal; construct field defences, such as digging and building sleeping and fighting pits; setting up wire obstacles and trip flares; how to conduct a Section and PL ambush, patrol and attack using live rounds. Also during these 10 weeks, we were taught how to use the Grenade Launcher Attachment (GLA), which attached to the underneath of the F88 and would fire a 40-millimetre grenade to a maximum distance of 400 metres. We were also taught how to use the M72 disposable rocket-launcher that fired a 72-millimetre rocket, as well as the Claymore mine, used in a lot of ambush situations. It contains 300 metal ball bearings that are propelled towards the enemy. We were taught how to use the F1 hand grenade and smoke grenade. We were also taught how to operate the night vision goggles (NVG), the night aiming device (NAD) and the night weapon sight (NWS). Utilising this equipment would allow us to operate successfully by day and by night.

Other things we were taught while at the SOI were how to operate radio equipment and how to talk using the phonetic alphabet, for example: A=Alfa, G=Golf and K=Kilo. We were taught navigation in regards to route planning, map reading, and then we put this into practice moving from one place to another. We also concentrated more on field exercises and battlefield skills, such as understanding the conventions of armed conflict, handling prisoners of war, performing individual field craft, which included field hygiene. This is because if you did not look after yourself, you would be a liability to your Section and PL. We also conducted basic first aid. While at the SOI we focused heavily on fitness because as infantry soldiers we were required to be fit due to the tasks we performed.

To complete and pass IETs and to be posted to a Battalion, we were required to finish a combination exercise on everything we had been taught. It started off with five days outfield, digging in a defensive position and fighting off an 'enemy'. Due to the tasks in regards to setting up a PL defensive position, we had minimal sleep as throughout the day we patrolled and set up wire obstacles and at night we dug our defensive pits. After a large attack by the 'enemy' and five sleep-deprived days, we were pushed off our position by conducting a PL withdrawal, which started an exercise called 'hardcore'. Hardcore was similar to the challenge at recruit training, but this went for five times the distance and you actually had to finish it, not just attempt it, to march out. This started off with a pack march, which led into a stores and stretcher carry, then an obstacle course and the bayonet assault course. After that we went out and conducted a shooting task in which we were required to shoot a certain amount of balloons from distances ranging from 300 to 100 metres. All this was done after five days of barely any sleep and constant work, which was both mentally and physically draining.

Once we finished, all we had to do was clean our gear and we were ready for our posting to either one of four Battalions that we had to choose from. The other posting was to the Training Support Platoon (TSP), which supplied the 'enemy' and infantry demonstrations for us while conducting our IETs at the SOI. I had chosen, in order, the 1st Battalion Royal Australian Regiment, or 1 RAR, then 2 RAR, both of them in Townsville. My third choice was 6 RAR in Brisbane. I was lucky to receive my first preference, and my best mate at the time was posted to his second preference at 2 RAR, so we were both heading to Townsville. My other good friend, Jacob Bruce Kovco, was posted to 3 RAR in Sydney.

THREE

POSTING TO 1 RAR

As we flew over Townsville, the capital of North Queensland, on that first day I looked down to see lots of hills and mountains in the area. I could see the heat in the air. I thought, *I'm going to hurt here*, as I did sweat very easily. As soon as I got out of the plane I was right in regards to the heat. It was so much different to summer in Victoria. The heat was more humid and as it was coming into summer I knew I was soon going to feel the full brunt of it.

We were picked up by a mini-bus and taken to Lavarack Barracks, where 1 RAR, 2 RAR and many other units are located. We were given a short brief by the Guard Commander about where things were and where to report in the morning, then we were allocated rooms. Being allocated our own room was good, however they were old-style rooms, with the majority of new rooms being taken by those already on base. The new rooms contained a small kitchen, a bathroom of your own and an area large enough to fit a queen-sized bed and a chair. These rooms included a carport and small shed. You shared a washing machine, dryer and a balcony with the person next door to you. To anyone who was living in the new rooms, it was like living in a palace because in the old rooms there was a bathroom with four showers and four toilets that was shared by about 10 people, and four washing machines and dryers to be shared by about 40 people, with no shed or carport. The rooms were quite small and they would only fit a single bed, a small chair and desk. The only good thing about these rooms was that there was a large wardrobe in which you could fit all your equipment quite easily. In regards to cooling, there was a fan and glass louver windows to allow the cool air into the room. There was also a door that led out onto a small balcony.

...

The next day when we reported for PT we were taken for a run around the Battalion area, which ended up being a run that included the entire Brigade area (the whole base). It was not a bad way to get used to the heat and humidity, as by 0700 it was already above 30°C.

After PT I had a shower, then walked to the mess and had breakfast. While walking to the mess the humidity hit me again and I became wet from sweat, as though I had just finished the run. As I found out over the years, this would be the same regardless of how fit I was and I would have to get used to living with sweat. Throughout the rest of the day we did administration and got all our equipment sorted out because on Monday, in three days time, we were to start a one-week confirmation of what we had learnt so far in our short careers in the military to ensure we had been taught properly and not just rushed through training. It was also time to go over things that we had not practised for a while.

We were dismissed for the day and told the next parade was Monday morning at 0730. We stood there for a little bit, confused as we hadn't been given too much direction in regards to what we could do. Since becoming members of the ADF, we had always been told where we could go and what time we had to be back. We asked the CPL in charge and he said, 'It doesn't matter where you go, as long as you're back here by 0730 on Monday morning.' I was excited, as I had finally finished my training and was actually posted to a Battalion. I was only a week off from being posted to a Company, ready to do whatever was required of me, even deploy. The good thing about Townsville was that after we were knocked off, we could put on a pair of board shorts, a T-shirt and a pair of thongs and feel like we were on holidays. I loved the place then, and even miss it and the people there to this day.

As my best mate throughout training had been posted to 2 RAR and they had the same time off, we all got together and went out for a massive weekend. We didn't have to be home at a certain time. We didn't have to stick to any curfew. We could do whatever we liked.

After a great weekend and lunch on Sunday, at a place where we call the chicken parmigianas 'pelican parmigianas' due to their size, I returned, ready to go. By the end of the week we had all got through okay, apart from a few blokes who failed the Battalion Fitness Test (BFT). The test was twice up and down the ropes at a height just below power lines, without touching the ground when coming down the first time, wearing cams, boots, webbing (seven kilograms) and with a rifle (3.6 kilograms).Then it was a two-kilometre run in under 10 minutes. Only a few passed. I did, which I was very happy about, as it was my first fitness test at the Battalion. I didn't want people thinking I was unfit.

...

The next week I was posted to Charlie Company, 8 Platoon, 6 Section. Most of the PLs had a nickname and 8 PL's was 'The Bodysnatchers'. The name came from when they were deployed to Vietnam — the three PLs from Charlie Company, 7, 8 and 9, were told the PL that had the most enemy bodies by a certain time would be given extra leave. I will let you figure out the rest of the story of how the nickname came about.

Charlie Company had just got back from Hawaii, where they trained alongside the Americans. A week later, it was their turn to go to the Jungle Training School at Tully in Queensland, said to be the wettest place in Australia.

I had been lucky throughout Singleton to be trusted with the position of 2IC, or number one rifleman, for most of the time. However, I was the newbie and the newbies always got the machine gun, so I was allocated to be the main gunner in the Section. The worst thing about being a gunner in the Section was that you had to carry 800 rounds at a minimum (compared to 210 rounds for a rifle), an extra barrel, a night weapon sight (along with the NVG and the NAD), as well as things like gun stakes (used in ambushes). The gun was also an extra three kilograms heavier than the rifle. In Australia and overseas, we were required to have a weapon with us at all times. Compared to carrying a rifle, to put it bluntly, the gun was a pain in the arse.

…

The following Monday we went to Tully, which always starts off with a 'walk-in'. We were dropped off at an airstrip, and loaded up with ammo and rations. We were then required to walk along a route that ends with a walk up a hill called 'Heartbreak Ridge', which didn't seem that bad to me the first time I walked up it. However, I would remember it the second time. The first time I walked up I, along with another couple of members, went back down after getting to the top and dropping off our packs, to assist other members who were struggling.

Once we arrived at the accommodation, we were allocated areas to set up our stretchers and given a brief on the next few weeks. There is a sign just outside the mess at Tully that reads:

The oath to serve your country did not include a contract for normal luxury and comforts enjoyed within our society. On the contrary, it implied hardships, loyalty and devotion to duty, regardless of your rank. This battle school is here to remind you of that oath.

In other words, Tully is not a fun place to be. Tully, along with Canungra (located west of the Gold Coast, Queensland) is the closest environment troops get to training in an East Asia atmosphere. During training at Tully we were taught, and re-taught, everything about jungle warfare. There were people playing 'enemy' who kept us on our toes at all times. There were villages set up in a similar style to those in Vietnam or Malaysia, which we were required to search and clear. Throughout the villages there were multiple booby traps that were very simple and very effective.

In Vietnam, a simple hole filled with sharpened sticks that had been dipped in human faeces and then covered with leaves and light brush was an effective booby trap. If someone stood on one of these traps, firstly it would be very painful, but also the person would not be able to walk, meaning it would take three-quarters of the Section to move the injured person. Thus the enemy's goal was achieved, which was to maim, not kill. Lucky for us, the traps at Tully were fenced off.

The worst part about Tully, along with the mosquitoes, was the fact that due to the enclosed vegetation the humidity would make you sweat, meaning it was hard to keep hydrated. As soon as you started walking, the jungle heat would make you sweat.

At night it would get dark very quickly due to the vegetation, allowing minimal natural light through. When it was dark you could barely see your hand when you held it in front of your face. A couple of hours prior to dark we had to find a night harbor, mark out our track plans in between the pits and set up hutchie cord (a strong green string), so we would have something to guide us along. In front of the pits on the hutchie cord, we would tie a small stick so we would know where we were. For example, one stick meant it was the gun pit, two sticks meant it was the rifle pit and three sticks meant it was the commander's pit. Most nights when we were outfield we would also have to conduct ambushes, meaning that prior to it becoming dark, we would set up just off a track or road that was a 'known enemy movement area'. We would lay there, getting eaten by mosquitoes and with pins and needles, being unable to move for hours on end.

After the ambush was conducted, we would walk back to our night harbor, which we had set up prior to the ambush, and conduct the night routine. When we returned we would conduct a three-hour picket (two people keeping watch while the others slept) prior to us all getting up 45 minutes before first light to be on watch, which meant about three to five hours of sleep. This was because statistics show the enemy would attack at first or last light.

Once our morning routine was finished (shaving, cleaning weapons, eating, planning the day's events, etc.) we would conduct patrols all day, conducting PL and Section attacks over and over. By the end of the two weeks, we had so many injuries that the three PLs had to be condensed into one large PL. I was moved to another Section for the final stage of Tully, which was three days of what we had learnt the previous few weeks.

...

On the final morning we conducted a hardcore exercise, which started with a pack march that included a walk up Heartbreak Ridge. This was my second time up that hill. I had not kept my fluids up as well as I should have on the previous days, and just prior to the obstacle course I apparently walked off the track. I was dazed and completely dehydrated. I was laid down, covered in water and rehydrated with two bags of intravenous fluids. As the Sections themselves were timed in this exercise, this meant my Section was forced to wait for me. However, I don't think many of my Section members cared, as it was a good chance for them to have a break.

After I was rehydrated, the Section, including myself (even after I was told I did not have to continue and that it would be unwise) completed the obstacle course, the bayonet assault course, a Section attack and a short walk to the accommodation area, where the exercise finished.

That evening, after all of our weapons and equipment were cleaned, we were taken over to the boozer (bar) on base. We were spoken to by the CO of the school, who did two tours of duty in Vietnam, one as a PTE and one as a CPL, and had been in many real-life ambushes. During one ambush, he did not fire at the enemy because the number of them that walked by had been underestimated. During this ambush, an enemy soldier had brushed past his body.

He said that I had done a fantastic job, and that in his years at the school he had not seen someone finish the exercise after being in the state that I was in. He also announced that our Section had come dead last (cheers to you know who).

That night, everyone was able to relax and have a few drinks. I was feeling a bit under the weather still, so I had an early night. This was my first exercise in an RAR Battalion. Though I had learnt a lot, there was still much more to learn.

...

Not long after we had returned from Tully, an announcement was made that the 1st Battalion, minus one Rifle Company, would be deploying to East Timor in May 2003. Alpha, Delta and Support Company (Support Company was made up of Mortars, Direct Fire Support Weapons [DFSW], Pioneers, Signals, Recon and Snipers) confirmed to be going. It was just a matter of who would be the other Company — Charlie or Bravo?

At around the same time, my car and all my personal belongings had been shipped up from Victoria, which made me feel a bit more independent as now I didn't have to rely on taxis or other people to get around.

The Battalion's birthday celebrations were on 12 October each year and, a few nights before, a Battalion boxing night was planned. As I had trained in boxing for a period of time, I volunteered to fight. It was arranged that I was to fight a CPL from Signals PL, who had been in the Army almost 10 years. The good thing about doing the boxing training was that for the week the Battalion practised their drill for a parade, I was exempt from that. It was probably good for the Battalion, as I was still very bad at drill.

The closer the boxing night came, the more nervous I got. I thought this was a chance to prove myself, and to show I was not just some new bloke in the Battalion who had nothing to offer. If I needed to I could, and would, be able to stand up for myself and my mates. As

I was weighing around 100 kilograms at the time of my fight, I was one of the last competitors of the night, the heavyweights. I sat in the back room of the main gym for the night while all the other fights were on, waiting for my turn. It seemed like everyone was having a good time except for me.

There were about 500 people there on the night, however when it was my turn to come out I could not hear or see anything; all that mattered was that ring and the other bloke in it. It didn't matter whether the bloke I was fighting was a CPL or the Chief of the Defence Force, we were even as we stood opposite each other in the ring.

The fight went for three rounds, and in the final round every time I hit him he would spit his mouthguard out. This went on for the entire round, which annoyed me as I wanted to knock him out. In the end I won on a unanimous points decision, so I was happy with that.

...

A couple of days later at the Battalion Ball, I pulled my seat out to sit down and bumped into the person behind me. I apologised, and he turned around and said, 'No dramas.' That was when I realised it was the CPL I had fought. He asked me how I was feeling. I replied that I had no issues at all. When I asked him how he was, he pointed out his two black eyes and his fat lip, and also stated that his ribs were sore from all the body shots.

After that I felt satisfied, as I wasn't sure whether the punches I was getting through were doing any damage. Now I knew. Even though I had been at the Battalion a short time, I felt the boxing had earned me some respect. I hoped that when people saw me walking around they knew I would fight for what I wanted, that I wasn't some newbie with nothing to offer.

...

After the Battalion's birthday celebrations we were put into our

Sections, so if we were to deploy to Timor we would be ready. We would start getting used to how everyone worked and get some Standard Operating Procedures (SOPs) worked out. Training included patrolling, contact drills, PL and Section harbors, ambush drills and setting up Observation Posts (OPs), which we would monitor for days and nights at a time. We also did a lot of urban patrolling at the High Range town named 'Line Creek Junction'. This was a mock-up of a town that had all the things a small town would have, such as a main street with a bank, post office, motel, church, pub and shops. It even had a sewer system through which you could gain access to most of the places in the main street. It also had a number of houses and even a train station.

...

By December 2002, there were about 40 of us left. The rest of the Battalion had gone on leave and the only people left were the new people, who had not accumulated any leave. Some infantry officers were doing jungle training at Tully and nine people were required to go there and play 'enemy'. We would also be required to conduct infantry tactics, which had been demonstrated to us at Tully. We were asked if anyone wanted to go, but as it was very easy being on rear details no-one volunteered. We were told that nine people were required to volunteer by the next day or nine people would be randomly picked. As I was still living in the old lines and temperatures during summer were ridiculous, I decided that I would volunteer.

Three days later, I went up to Tully with eight others for two weeks. I enjoyed the two weeks I spent up there, as it was non-tactical for us when we were outfield, and we were just required to do scenarios while the officers did all the work. We were able to go up to the boozer and drink and watch TV, which was a luxury and a side that we had not seen at Tully when we were there as a Company doing our training.

By the time I returned to the Battalion, the majority of people were coming back from leave, so we began our training again. It was at this time that I was allocated a new room. A lot of the blokes wanted to live off base (an allowance would be added to their pay to help pay for this every fortnight), however I could not see the point of moving off base as I had everything I needed where I was. I had access to two different gyms, an Olympic-sized pool and it was only a two-minute walk to work.

When the entire Battalion returned, rumours were circulating and after a few weeks of suspense it was announced that Charlie Company would be the third Rifle Company to be deployed to East Timor. Bravo would supply personnel if anyone was injured or if blokes stuffed up, either in training or in the civilian world. We were always being watched.

We were required to pass all our fitness, weapons and shooting tests, and the Companies that were going to Timor went outfield for a few weeks of training. Once the commanders were satisfied the Companies were ready, the group being deployed to East Timor conducted a final exercise, called 'Timor Dawn'.

We 'deployed' to a location where a base was set up and we conducted simulated missions. We were watched by directive staff (DS), who would assess how we handled a situation and then report back for a summary of the whole Battalion's results. We conducted PL patrols and interactions with the 'locals'. If the Battalion from Timor Dawn was deemed suitable and correctly trained, we would be ready to deploy on AUSBAT 8, meaning 'Australian Battalion' and we would be the eighth rotation.

...

After the success of Timor Dawn, I hit a snag. While playing AFL for PT I received a cut on my left elbow, which became infected and developed into bursitis. This made my arm swell from my elbow to my hand. I was told to go on to pre-deployment leave and that it would go down with antibiotics. However, when I returned a week later the swelling was so bad that the skin on my arm had started to crack and tear.

I was admitted to a civilian hospital and the next day I had surgery. I was told that the infection would be cut out, and when I woke up it would be stitched up and I would be able to check out the next day. I could still be deployed to Timor after the stitches were taken out. When I awoke I was in agony, and when the doctor came in I knew by the look on his face that something had gone wrong. He told me that the infection had spread and he was unable to stitch up the wound. There was a hole in my arm about 13 centimetres long and about eight centimetres wide, packed with antiseptic pads. I asked him how long until my arm could be stitched up and he said it depended on how quickly the infection healed.

That night when I had a shower, I took out the antiseptic pads and could see the bone in my arm. At that time I thought there was no way I would deploy to Timor. I was visited by my boss and my Section Commander a few times. We stressed to the doctor that I was supposed to be deploying to Timor in 14 days. Every day I would try and explain to the doctor how important it was for me to be ready to deploy.

An easy way to explain how a soldier, or at least I, look at a deployment, is that it is like a professional footballer playing in a Grand Final. Every day, the footballer trains for their weekend games. We as soldiers train every day for a specific exercise, which we do outfield for up to three weeks every few months, fighting against an 'enemy' who we must track, capture or destroy. These exercises are repeated over and over, in preparation for a real-life situation overseas. For a soldier, deployment is a major achievement in your career and nothing can beat it.

...

After a week in hospital, and with only seven days until deployment, the doctor said that he would attempt to stitch up the wound in my arm. However, he could not promise the skin would stretch, or that it would heal in time. When I woke from my second surgery, the doctor came in and told me that the surgery had gone well and it was now a matter of whether the stitches would hold. I returned to work straight away on light duties.

Amazingly, I was still on the list to deploy. The reason I found this so amazing was that there were over 100 fit and able people from Bravo Company ready to take my spot. My staff, especially my Section Commander, knew how important it was to me to deploy, and had faith that the wound would heal in the remaining week before deployment. My Section Commander organised that I would carry a rifle for the first week or two, until my arm was strong enough to resume my job as the main gunner.

Seven days after the surgery, the stitches were removed. That afternoon, we were required to gather on the parade ground. We had our final rollcall, loaded onto buses and were driven to the airport, with the 1 RAR band playing as we left. It was a proud moment. I had been given the responsibility of representing my country overseas.

FOUR

TIMOR

We arrived at the Dili airport, in the capital of East Timor, where we were picked up by mogs (Army trucks) and taken to an Army base just outside of town. We did not have any weapons at all, and the only Australian soldiers who were armed were the transport personnel who had their pistols on them, as well as a rifle and spare magazine in their truck. It was a weird feeling because we, as infantry soldiers, train for the worst but hope for the best-case scenario. We have to be able to adapt to any situation, whether in a peacekeeping role or a combat role. The non-infantry personnel did not seem to have a care in the world. This was a UN mission, so we had to be on the ball at all times. Anything could happen at any stage, and we had to be ready for it. Not having our weapons when we first arrived was not exactly our plan. I felt naked and exposed.

We had a 20-minute drive to the base, where we picked up all our equipment. The next day we moved to Forward Operating Base (FOB) Maliana. This would be our home for the next three months. From there we were allocated tasks, such as security on the FOB and manning and providing security at Junction Point Charlie (JP-C was a border crossing from East Timor to West Timor). Other tasks were local patrols in the immediate vicinity, and patrols that would go for up to 10 or more days in the surrounding countryside. We also provided security at a re-trans, a location used to pass on radio communications. In this case, it was located on top of the highest hill, which we named Everest. On Everest, radio equipment could pick up all radio communications in Timor, regardless of where you were. For example, if a local patrol was out and they were unable to get communications via radio with their immediate base, they would contact the re-trans location on Everest and ask them to relay a message onto a specific call sign.

We were first assigned with security of the FOB and local patrols, which allowed us to settle into our accommodation. Three rooms, a little bigger than your average lounge room, were allocated to the PL. My Section was given the smallest room, which was to sleep nine people. We also had a small entertaining area that included a TV and a few fold-up chairs and a table. During the day and night we would conduct a picket on the front gate. On every other day and night we would conduct a patrol around the local area, usually walking through the markets.

One thing I did not like about being where we were, especially sitting on the picket box, was the way the locals regarded dogs. I loved my dog as though he was my own child. However, in Timor they are a source of food and money. I can understand this somewhat, but Timorese people believe if a dog dies under stress it means the meat is more tender. The owners would tie up the dogs, break their legs and beat them for days at a time before killing them, skinning them and walking them straight past our picket box in a wagon to the markets. Hearing the dogs suffer like they did was one of the worst sounds I've ever heard. But what could I do? That was their culture, and how they made their money and what they ate. I know I had hundreds of thoughts running through my head as to what I would do if I ever caught someone doing that to a dog back in Australia.

...

The patrols we initially conducted were presence patrols, so the locals would see that we were in the vicinity. During our time off we would do PT in the small gym on base and we could also go for runs, as long as we were at least in pairs outside the base and always carried our weapons with us. We also watched a lot of DVDs. We could buy the latest releases over there for around one US dollar.

After a couple of weeks, it became our turn to conduct area patrols. We would load up our packs with five days' worth of rations and a minimum of 15 litres of water. With our packs weighing in at approximately 50 kilograms, we would be dropped off in the middle of the bush by an Armoured Personnel Carrier (APC), where we would set up a PL harbor. From there, the Sections would conduct daily patrols around the area, sometimes going out overnight. We would then be resupplied by the APCs with water and food and then, as a PL, patrol to villages in remote locations where they had never seen Australian soldiers before.

A lot of the adults had red teeth, as they were always chewing a substance called betel nut, better known as Aceca nuts. They chew the nuts in a similar way to chewing tobacco, which produces a mildly euphoric and stimulating effect, and can help reduce tension. In some cultures, the red-stained teeth can be classed as attractive. I must admit, however, that I felt otherwise.

Our second PL patrol, which I can remember very well, was when we had to do a joint mission with the Indonesian Army. Border surveyors would go along the river and mark out the border between East and West Timor. It was our job to provide security for the surveyors, and the Indonesian Army was there to make sure we did not cross the border. I remember the stares the Indonesian soldiers gave us from the other side of the river, which was the survey route. We could tell that we had to be even more on the ball at all times for this patrol.

It was the first time I suffered from prickly heat. Due to the fact that you are sweating all the time, dirt gets into the sweat pores and creates a feeling of pins and needles. The visual part of prickly heat is a red rash all over the affected area. It was the worst feeling to have, made even worse because it began on the second day of a 10-day patrol. In my case my back was affected, and the only thing I could do was keep the area as clean as possible and put on clean clothes whenever I could.

The best solution was to stop sweating, though this was impossible in that hot and humid environment.

After an excruciating eight days, I began to wear an undershirt and carry spare ones as well. Although it was a little bit warmer with an undershirt, there was an extra layer between my skin and the dirt.

At about day eight, the surveyors decided that they had done enough and the rest could be done via air. They were picked up by APCs and we were required to patrol up to a village that had never been seen by the Australian troops. I was looking forward to it, but discovered why it had probably never been visited by troops — it was located on top of one of the largest mountains in the area.

Throughout the patrol we had been wearing our UN hats and armbands. Now we were told to take these off and cam up (paint our faces and exposed skin with camouflage cream), because we didn't know what to expect. This made the walk up the hill a little easier, knowing that there was something up there that no-one had seen before.

After about six hours, we arrived at the village. It turned out to be a non-event. There were a few children with small cuts on their hands and feet, which our Combat First Aider put some antiseptic and bandages on. After the boss had a chat with the village elder, we were picked up by the UN helicopter, which was an old Russian machine. We wondered how it was still flying as it took us back to our base. When we arrived, we didn't really care how old the helicopter was because at least we didn't have to walk back to base.

A few times we went down as Sections and did OPs on areas at the border. We were required to watch out for personnel crossing without declaring goods bought from West Timor. I used to enjoy these patrols, as we would be able to get away from everyone and go out as a Section to do a task for a week or so. As long as the weather was good I would really have a ball, as we were doing what we had been trained to do. Also the fact that we were doing it in secret (watching people cross the border without them knowing) was pretty cool. We would be dropped off at night and walk anywhere from five to 10 kilometres into the OPs to avoid detection. We would then watch the area to see when and where the popular crossings were for people who were avoiding declaring the goods.

...

The hardest PL patrol we did was when we went into an area where, once again, troops had not been for a while, if at all. We walked up and down the undulating terrain, going from village to village, being resupplied by the APCs every five days.

On this particular patrol we had plenty of rations. However, the lack of water was a big issue due to the terrain we were patrolling in, and the fact that a lot of the locals had been burning off trees in the area, which made it hard to breathe. This required us to drink more, to the point where we were a long way from resupply and only had an average of one litre of water per person. It was decided that the patrol be cut short and that the other PL at the FOB would be sent out to resupply us. When we met up with them we were given boxes and boxes of water, which I drank until I could not fit any more in. I had never ever in my life had that much desire for water.

The PL was annoyed, as we thought we had finished the patrol until it was decided that because we were close to a village we would do one last patrol prior to leaving. The thing that annoyed us was the fact that the other PL sat back while we did the patrol. Because we were so buggered our patrol turned out to be a walk with our heads down, us not even caring. This was very unsafe, upon reflection, because that is when things can go wrong. We were lucky that time.

...

When we returned to FOB Maliana, a few blokes from another Section were going on Rest Out of Country Leave (ROCL), when they could return to Australia for a 14-day break. As one of the blokes was the main gunner, I was assigned to that Section. The Section was being sent up to Everest to provide security for a week. This was a good chance to get away from the hierarchy, as the highest rank at Everest was a Signals CPL.

It reminded me of a camp that would be set up in Vietnam. It was all green tents and sandbags and signal towers. I loved it there. We were required to do a roving picket a couple of times during the day and throughout the night. However, other than the odd job of burning faeces and filling up the generators with diesel, the rest of the time was ours. There were no showers, power (other than the generators) or cooks and all our meals were made from ration packs. When we had time, however, we could make up some decent dishes from ration packs. We would mix the condensed milk with our fruit ration and shortbread biscuit ration. It tasted beautiful compared to nothing at all.

The toilet looked north towards Dili. It was just a toilet seat on top of a quarter 44-gallon drum, which needed to be burnt every day or two with diesel. I got stuck with that job once, however it was not as bad as I thought and the view was unbelievable.

In the early evening, pretty much at the same time, a cloud would come south over the mountain and cover the top of it, so visibility would be down to less than 10 metres or so. Throughout the day, while not on the picket, I and a couple of others went exploring around the area. We found some caves and did some rock climbing. When I look back at the photos I wonder how we didn't injure ourselves, as we did not have any ropes or safety gear. Due to this excess cloud cover, we were required to stay on the mountain an extra two days, as the helicopter could not get in to pick us up. When it finally did come I was a bit disappointed, as I had enjoyed it there so much.

...

When I returned it was my Section's turn to do a stint at JP-C.

Throughout the day we were required to provide security in assistance with the East Timorese Army and police on the border crossing. A lot of East Timorese personnel would go over to West Timor to buy their goods, such as food and cigarettes, as it was cheaper there. During the night we were required to operate a picket box that watched over the border crossing.

One night, while I was on picket and the bloke I was on with was waking up the next person for their shift, I was looking through the night weapon sight and noticed three to four people pepper potting (also known as bounding, when one person moves at a time while the others keep watch) across the other side of the border, moving from right to left, to a position where they could cross over to East Timor. The position they were bounding to would not be visible from the picket box. I was on my own and trying to use the communications back to the control and sleeping area, which was approximately 75 metres away, but I couldn't raise anyone on the phone. I watched them bound all the way across to a position where I could not see them. My concern was that they were not trying to cross the border to sneak goods in, but that they were moving towards our position for a possible attack.

Finally after what felt like an hour, but was probably only 10 to 15 minutes, the next bloke arrived and I explained to him what had happened. He rushed to the control area to alert the others. He then returned with my Section Commander, who took a group out and patrolled in the vicinity of where I thought the group had crossed, and in and around our area as well. Nothing was found, so everyone stood down and returned to night routine. By that time my picket was well and truly over, so I was able to hit the hay.

The next morning another patrol was sent out and human faeces was found in the area, but nothing else. It was reported and we were told to be aware of suspicious activity around the border, especially at night.

...

After that, it was my turn to go on ROCL. We were required to wear our uniform and UN beret while travelling. When I was at the airport in Melbourne and walking around the train station, a lot of people were staring at me. In Victoria, you don't see as many Army personnel in their uniform as you do in cities such as Townsville and Darwin. I felt pretty proud when I was picked up from the train station and my family and friends saw me in my uniform. I had a good couple of weeks rest and then returned to Timor, ready to get back into it.

When I returned, our PL had moved base and was posted to FOB Moleana. We were the Quick Reaction Force (QRF) for the Battalion. FOB Moleana was where Support Company was located, along with the rest of the Battalion and attachments, except for the Rifle Companies, who were posted to different FOBs all over Timor.

The day I got back was the day Tour de Force was there. It was a combination of the military band and some civilian singers and comedians, who would go to all the places in the world Australians were deployed and give them a bit of entertainment. It was a night out to take your mind off where you were and what you were doing. I had a different theory in regards to the Tour de Force, as it made people even more homesick and made them miss the simple luxuries. Luxuries such as the freedom to go to the shops or go to your local pub to have a beer and watch a game of football.

...

One morning after PT, we were told to pack our stuff and get ready to leave. As we were QRF, our stuff was always ready to go, though we made sure all our water bottles were full and we had the required rations.

We were told that an armed person had tried to breach the perimeter at the re-trans station on Everest and that shots had been fired. We were to go up there immediately to try and track down the armed person. Within 20 minutes we were up there. The Battalion Regimental Sergeant Major (RSM), recon Section and the military police, with their tracker dog, were already up there. For a while we sat around thinking, *Why would they send a whole PL up when recon was already there?* There was no way we could track the person quicker, but this was our role after all, not the role of the recon Section.

After about 500 metres the dog handler stated that he could not find a scent. We were told to patrol down to the bottom and that Alpha Company had set up a blocking position, so that if there was someone still coming down the hill either we or they would see them and be able to cut them off. The walk down Everest quickly turned into a semi-slide and a very, very dangerous decision. As it turned out, we got stuck halfway down the hill at night and were required to set up a harbor. There was no flat ground, so we were sleeping at what was pretty much a 45 degree angle.

It was early the next afternoon when we finally made it down to the point where we felt safe. We knew that we were not going to have to evacuate anyone with a broken back or leg due to the terrain. While in the area we did some patrolling through the villages there and spent another night out. This time it was on flat ground, thank Christ. By this time, Alpha Company had packed up their blocking position. If anyone wanted to get down off that mountain they would have done it much quicker than us, as we were patrolling and carrying huge amounts of weight.

...

Once we finished our month at FOB Moleana on QRF we were moved to FOB Gleno, about an hour's drive inland from Dili. When we arrived at Gleno it started to rain, and it seemed to come at the same time every day. It would last for about an hour or so, then stop. It was like a scene out of the movie *The Odd Angry Shot*, about Australian

SAS soldiers in Vietnam, where it rains at the same time every day and they say, 'You can set your watch by this fucking rain.'

Our task was to provide security for the FOB, conduct local patrols and longer patrols in the areas surrounding Gleno. It would be a bit easier this time because we would be able to utilise the 6Bs, six-wheeled Land Rovers with eight seats in the back facing outwards and a hole in the roof for the gunner. As the main gunner I would be the person standing in the hole, with my gun fixed to a swivel that would allow me to spin the gun 360 degrees. I was so happy to be doing these patrols from the vehicles now, as the terrain throughout Timor was the hardest place I had ever patrolled.

...

When we first moved into Gleno, we had tents that leaked regardless of how many tarps you put up. After a couple of weeks we were moved into an area that had been turned into accommodation. Originally, they were old bathrooms and laundries. We did not have much room though, just enough for our bed and what we could fit under it. There was a room that no-one wanted to go into because it was a little bit small, but I said I would take it and it ended up being the best decision. I had a mattress and a big mosquito net set up. I also had some shelves and made a door using an old blanket. This meant I had a bit of privacy when changing. I had a team poster of the Essendon Football Club and a poster of Matthew Lloyd, my favourite player. I also had a photo of my new car (that I had recently purchased, as my house in Colac had been sold while I was deployed) hanging on the wall. It was amazing how the simplest things like a shelf and a couple of posters after a while felt like luxuries.

...

One day at Gleno a CPL was driving the mog, which was the allocated rubbish truck, and required someone to go along with him to drop off the rubbish, so I volunteered. I thought that I was there to keep him company, but when we got about one kilometre short of the tip he gave me a big fat stick, and instructed me to get in the back of the mog and hit off anyone that jumped on while he was driving. Then when he backed up at the spot where the rubbish was to be dumped, I was to get the rubbish out as quickly as possible and let him know if we were safe to drive forward and get out of there.

About 200 metres short of the tip, a local started running after the mog. When we slowed down to turn off the main road and onto the dirt road that led to the tip, adults, both male and female, and children, started jumping up onto the mog. I started to hit them off, lightly, so they wouldn't be able to get a hold of it. When we arrived at the tip, regardless of how many times I tried to push people, I was fighting a losing battle. There were about 15 to 20 people ripping at the bags of rubbish. The driver came out and gave me a hand in throwing the bags off the back. We were parked on the edge of an embankment that went down about 30 to 40 metres.

At one stage, when throwing bags off the back of the mog, I noticed there were about 50 people down at the bottom. Three or four people would be tearing into the bags, trying to get the stuff from inside. That's when I realised exactly what they were doing. They were trying to get the food. They were all starving and they figured that the best source of food for them was to go through the Army rubbish.

We quickly threw the rest of the bags off and the CPL started driving. I made sure no-one else was left on the truck, then climbed around and got back into the cabin. On the way back to the main road along the dirt road, I noticed shanty huts made from pieces of material from the tip. It was sad to see that so many people relied on our rubbish to eat and that whole families were living at a tip. When I got back to the FOB I wished I hadn't volunteered, but I was happy that no-one else had to see what I had just seen.

...

As we were only about an hour's drive from Dili, one at a time the Sections were allowed to go and spend a couple of days there relaxing and getting away from everybody else. We were able to swim at the beautiful beaches that surrounded the capital. It was also good to spend a night in air-conditioning, and not have to worry about doing a picket or PT.

During vehicle patrols we would travel miles and miles of road cut into the side of the mountains, that had not had the full weight of a car on it for many years. At parts where the roads had slid away, the locals had placed fallen trees to bridge the gap. They were suitable for their requirements, though for us they were very unstable. At one stage, a 6B vehicle got stuck when a log fell away and we were very close to losing a car with a Section in it. After that, when we did crossings like that, all the blokes in the 6Bs would get out, apart from the poor driver.

Another time we were driving around the thin roads that were cut into the mountains where, if the driver made a mistake or the road gave way, we would almost certainly fall hundreds of metres to our deaths. The area we were driving through closed in a bit and we were on the edge of a cliff. Then a corner came up and the driver did not turn. My immediate reaction was to yell out, 'Turn, turn, turn!' But he was unable to hear me, and we went straight into a ditch about a metre deep. I was shot forward and my chest hit hard on the edge of the gun hole, though due to my body armour the impact was minimal. No more than 50 metres prior to this we would have driven off a cliff and fallen hundreds of metres to our deaths. When the driver got out of the car and I asked, 'What happened?' he replied, 'The steering arm broke.' When I got out and grabbed the steering wheel and spun it, it freely spun around without any resistance.

As we were doing patrols in the vehicles, we were able to visit a lot of villages. We would hand out lollies, chewing gum and biscuits from our ration pack to the kids. The CFAs would do what they could in regards to putting antiseptic and bandages on cuts. Sometimes the locals would put on cock fights, though they never attached razor blades to the ends of the roosters' claws as they usually did. It was more just a show for us.

The Fijian Army joined us for a lot of these patrols towards the end of our stint at Gleno, as they were taking over the FOB when we left. While we were at Gleno we would sometimes play AFL or soccer on the oval. Sometimes the locals would join in and we would teach them how to play AFL. I got the impression that the Timorese people just wanted to get on with their lives and be left alone to do that in peace. This was where we came in, to assist them in feeling safe in their own country.

My first deployment came to an end. I had spent two months in Maliana, mostly patrolling the hardest terrain I have ever walked in my life. I had spent one month in Moleana and three months in Gleno, where I had done some fantastic vehicle patrols and saw a lot of the countryside. Most importantly, perhaps, I realised that many people in the world are nowhere near as lucky as us. Just to have four walls is a luxury for some of them.

...

When we returned home to the Townsville Barracks, it was a Saturday night. We were all very keen to have a shower, get changed and get out on the town. However, I had a surprise waiting for me when I tried to open my door. I put the key in and unlocked the door, then went to slide it open. The door didn't open, so I tried again. This time it opened. *My mistake*, I thought. I walked in, placed my bags on the ground and went straight to the bathroom.

Once finished in the bathroom, I realised my room didn't feel the same as it had when I left. I stood there for about 30 seconds, thinking that something was off. That's when I realised all my electrical appliances, DVDs and anything that was worth money was gone. Someone in the Army had broken into my room while I was on deployment and stolen everything that was of value. I was devastated. How could this happen on an Army barracks? How could someone do this to someone who was overseas representing their country?

I went outside, looked at the door and noticed that someone had forced it open enough to lift the latch and get in. When I had tried to open the door originally I had actually locked the door instead of opening it.

I walked outside to call the military police and noticed my next-door neighbour's door had been smashed in completely. Being careful not to touch the door handle, I looked inside and noticed that his room was a mess and that his TV, and all his other electrical equipment, had been stolen as well. He was not due home for another week.

I rang the military police and they said that nothing could be done until Monday, so I went down to the 1 RAR guard room to report the incident. After waiting for at least an hour, I was told I would have to wait for the military police on Monday and to try not to touch anything in my room until then.

I returned to my room, had a quick shower, got changed and went out on the town. I got so drunk that I ended up waking in someone's bed, not at the Army barracks. I quickly got dressed and returned to base, where I had a shower and slept, before going out for another Sunday session.

FIVE

BETWEEN TIMOR AND IRAQ

In February 2004, after returning from the Christmas break, it was time to get back into a big year of training. As most of the Battalion had been away during September and October the previous year (which was when specialised courses were conducted to improve the capabilities of the individual soldier) the Battalion decided they would run the courses at the start of the year.

As I was the newbie I didn't have much of a chance to get a place on the course. However, two days after the Direct Fire Support Weapons Course (DFSW) had started, I was told to quickly grab my webbing and bush hat and run up to the DFSW headquarters, as I was to be participating in that course. The blokes were already two days ahead of me, but I did my best to catch up.

For the first few days we learnt the weapons of choice used by DFSW, which was the MAG58 machine gun, which fires 7.62-millimetre rounds, and the 84-millimetre shoulder-mounted rocket-launcher. We then went outfield for two weeks to conduct DFSW drills. DFSW is the main fire support for the Battalion, and it is their job to know what type of equipment the enemy uses and where their vulnerable points are in order to destroy or disable them. We were taught about foreign vehicles, and taught how to conduct the navigational requirements in regards to setting up a DFSW line (when a certain amount of weapons are pointed at a target in a line).

After two weeks of this, we did a cumulative exercise on everything we had been taught. Once we had finished and returned to base, we cleaned up all the equipment and handed it back, and waited for our results. I had passed everything, apart from the navigation. I was 12 millimetres out, when the allowed variant was 10 millimetres. I was told there and then that, because I did not know my navigation, I had failed the course. The officer that was on the course with us, and was taking over DFSW, saw this happen. He told me that next year when he took over, he would get me to come up to the headquarters of DFSW, I would redo the test and he would qualify me as DFSW-qualified. As I could not do anything about it at the time, I had to be happy with that result.

Going back to my Company and telling my boss what had happened was not easy. The way everyone looked at me for a period of time after that did not make me satisfied, as I felt the people who ran the course had not treated me fairly. It was noted in bold letters in my course report that I was unprepared when I arrived and that I should have done the homework that was provided. How I could have done the homework for the course when I was put on the course two days after it began is a question I will never be able to answer! As it turned out, I would be unable to finish the DFSW course due to my deployment to Iraq. Not completing the course was the only blemish at 1 RAR that I wish I could wipe from my record.

...

After the DFSW course had finished, I decided that I needed to have a bit of fun, as I was getting very down because I felt that I had been cheated somewhat. A friend suggested we go skydiving. Throughout our entire time in Timor, we had talked about doing the course. When we returned home, he again suggested it. I was a bit sceptical, as I thought it was just an idea we were tossing around to keep us occupied while we were overseas. But now that we were home there was no way of getting out of it, and I decided that maybe this could be the thing that would cheer me up and take my mind off the DFSW course.

The skydiving course was conducted about three hours' drive from Townsville and it was to be done over two weekends. We would conduct 10 jumps from approximately 10,000 feet, or just over 3000 metres. For the first part, we did drills for what would happen once we jumped out of the plane, what happened if we got into trouble while falling and what happened if we ended up heading towards power lines or trees. We were put in a hanging harness, where we conducted most of the drills. Next we went out to the aeroplane to practise the method of getting out, as the first couple of jumps we would have instructors hanging onto either side of us for stability while freefalling (I was soon to find out that it is very hard to stay in the correct position while falling when you are a beginner). I was to follow an instructor onto the wheel of the aeroplane and balance there, then another instructor would hang on to the door, and we would all jump at the same time.

I was nervous about the height due to that roofing incident I had while plumbing. However, once I stood out on the wheel at 10,000 feet, the height was not an issue. At that height everything looked unreal, like looking at the satellite view on Google Maps. You could not make out any definition. I soon found out that my problem with heights was when I was closer to the ground, not further away.

The first time I jumped out of the plane was an unbelievable feeling, something that I will never be able to describe fully. For the first millisecond I felt like I had blacked out. Then I regained consciousness and experienced the best rush I have ever felt in my entire life. Freefalling at up to 200 kilometres an hour is like travelling at 200 kilometres an hour in your car with your head out the window. Just before you open your parachute, the instructors let go and fall for a bit longer, to get out of the way. They then open their parachutes and are on the ground waiting for you to float down, as their parachutes allow them to fall quicker than the training parachutes. The instructors guide you down and, if you follow their instructions, landing is just like taking a normal step.

On my third jump, one of the instructors overcorrected when he jumped out and we did a 3000-foot tumble. I was unable to regain control and was forced to conduct the same jump again (this was all caught on film). After six jumps, the wind increased and we were unable to continue. Beginners can only jump in certain wind strengths, so the course was over for us for the day.

On the way back to Townsville, I as the passenger had my head out the window of the car the whole way, pretending to be freefalling. On our arrival the Battalion was put online, which included restricted leave, so we were unable to finish the course. It was disappointing, as I'd had so much fun and it had taken my mind completely off the DFSW course.

...

One of the favourite sayings of the SGTs and WOs was that 'you joined the Army, the Army didn't join you'. This was used a lot when it came to going outfield for extended periods of time, being placed on guard duty on a Saturday night or being on restricted leave. A Battalion is always online in case a crisis occurs overseas, particularly in Timor, Fiji or the Solomon Islands. Being online sucked, as you had to be within a couple hours drive of the base. You had to get special permission to go home and only on strict conditions, for example, illness or the death of an immediate family member.

For guard duty, every night 10 people were required to be in the guard room. During the night a roving picket was constantly run and the front entry of the base had to be manned. All personnel entering or leaving the Battalion had to have their details recorded, in regards to identity and car registration. Also, three times a week the Section on guard would perform formal drill on the parade ground wearing their ceremonial uniform. These uniforms would take hours to prepare to be at an acceptable level, and would be inspected by the Battalion's CO while on parade. There was incentive to be the best dressed, as the person deemed to have the best uniform, in terms of ironing, the sharpness of the lines in our pants and shirt, the cleanliness of our weapon and the condition of our brass and shoes, would not have to do guard duty for the night. The rest would have to stay and conduct roving and front gate pickets.

An exercise was coming up for the Battalion, where we would go on one of the Navy ships (the HMAS *Kanimbla*). It was a troop and cargo ship, perfect for moving a Battalion and all its equipment, including vehicles and attachments, from one place to another via sea. I went on a few of these exercises and hated every one of them. Conditions on the ships were always so cramped and there was never much for us to do. Smokers, during allocated times, were able to go to an area on the rear deck to have a cigarette. During mealtimes you were able to go up to the mess but otherwise, if you were not training, you were confined to your bunk space. The bunks were four tiers high, with just enough space in between them to roll over and lay on your side. You were allocated a little locker area where you could keep your pack, webbing and a spare bag with a change of clothes and PT gear. The Company of about 90 people would be crammed into a space around the size of a new family home's entertaining and dining area, and after a day or so the area would really start to stink. But we got used to the smell, as it was our own. There were showers on the boat, though these were very confined as well. A Company would have to share about four showers.

Sometimes we would go up on deck to do Section formations training, just to keep ourselves occupied and stop ourselves from going insane, instead of lying below in our sleeping quarters, located well below the waterline. The Navy would also conduct drills, such as coming under attack, firing on the boat and damage to the boat. During these times they would shut all the hatches and we would be locked well below the waterline for hours at a time with no power, which meant no air-conditioning. After a couple of hours blokes would literally be yelling out, 'There are fucking human beings down here!' due to the heat. I could understand that they had to do their drills, but I wished they could have done them when we were not on board. By the time it came to leave the boat to do land activities, we were all very happy.

During land activities we would secure an area, such as a clearing, that would act as an airport where we would evacuate 'Australian citizens' from a 'war-torn country'. After doing that for a couple of weeks we would return on the boat to Townsville. This I hated even more, as they would still conduct their drills and we would smell even worse.

I remember a time during this period, when we did a joint exercise with the Americans and were placed on an American ship. This ship was basically the same as the HMAS *Kanimbla*, but a lot larger. The Americans had brought out an entire fleet, which included submarines and aircraft carriers. Compared to their fleet, our Navy looked like a bunch of tugboats. The food on the American ships was not as good as on the Australian ships, though, because it was so fatty and felt like it sat in your guts for days.

One day, while waiting in a queue at the mess, an American walked past and saw the weapon slung over my shoulder. At the time, I was carrying an F88 with a grenade-launcher attachment. It was the same as the one Al Pacino used in the movie *Scarface*. The only difference was that in the movie the grenade-launcher was attached to an M16 rifle. At the end of the movie, a large number of people break into Al Pacino's house and try to kill him. Al Pacino shoots at them and then, just prior to firing his grenade-launcher, he says, 'Say hello to my little friend!' He then fires the grenade, killing several of the intruders.

The look on the American's face when he saw I was carrying the same grenade-launcher attachment that Al Pacino had was priceless. He was so excited that he asked if he could hold it, and I replied, 'Yes.' As soon as he took hold of the weapon he took up the stance Al Pacino had in the movie and said, 'Say hello to my little friend,' over and over again. The blokes around us were all laughing but he didn't care, as at that point in time he was the happiest person on the ship.

On average we would conduct an exercise once every two months, and each would go for around two to three weeks. We would mainly go to the High Range training area, which was about an hour and a half's drive from Townsville, and was a huge military area where we could conduct a number of different exercises. Regardless of the season, it was always hot up there. The types of exercises we would conduct would seem like old-fashioned Vietnam War-style training. We would go out as a Company, then break up into our individual PLs and conduct the required training — usually PL and Section patrolling, that included repeated attacks on an 'enemy'. Only on specific exercises, such as pre-deployment Mission Readiness Exercises (MREs), would we set up a firm base similar to what it was like in Timor, Iraq and Afghanistan and operate from that. The old-fashioned training methods would annoy us, as we felt like we were training for the past and not for the future.

In between these exercises, we would be in training for the particular exercise that was coming up. Also, we would do individual specialised courses like the CFA and the Drivers course with the 6B Land Rovers. I conducted a Basic Combat Communications Course, which qualified me to become a Company Signaller. For a period of approximately six months I was the Platoon Sig, which I did not like as much as being in the Sections. When the Sections were sent out on their individual tasks, my job was to stay and man the radio with the boss and the SGT, and to relay information back to Company headquarters. On some exercises, I would basically sit around for most of the day manning the radio and making brews. The time dragged and I hated being left out, even if it was just a training exercise.

A typical day started at around 0730. This was the time when everyone in the Company was to be accounted for, so the PL SGTs made sure that everyone was there at 0720. We had to clean up the working area prior to starting work for the day, so we had to be there

10 minutes earlier for that. Typically, when we arrived at work the 2ICs would let our Section Commander and the SGT know that we were accounted for. After that, we would do a Section or Platoon PT session, which would go for up to an hour. We would then return to work lines, have a shower and have breakfast at the mess. As I lived on base, I would go home for a shower and a cereal breakfast. At 0930 we would have Section or PL training. At around 1230 we would go to lunch, then return at 1330. From 1330 onwards we would continue with our training or conduct administration, if required, and then if we had time available, we would conduct another PT session. Sometimes we would go for a run in the morning and do push-ups and sit-ups, or could do our own thing, such as go to the gym or play touch football. On a normal day we would finish at about 1600, though this varied. For example, if we were required to take out weapons that day, no-one was able to finish until all the weapons were accounted for.

Thursdays were Brigade sports days. For PT, if you participated in a sport you would train for that. If you were not playing a sport you would have to go and support your Battalion. We were encouraged to watch the rugby, and then afterwards everyone would meet up at the boozer parade, where the results were read out. I usually participated in the mini triathlons and most times my team would win. I would always do the bike leg, which was about 15 kilometres. This started with a 500-metre swim and finished off with a five-kilometre run.

As we were often required to fly in by helicopter off a ship, we had to be qualified in Helicopter Underwater Escape Training, or HUET. A lot of people do this course, such as the Coast Guard, rig workers, helicopter pilots and anyone who is required to fly over the water. HUET involves a crane that holds up a boxlike structure containing a number of seats, doors and escape windows set up the same as in a helicopter. You are strapped into your seat and then the crane lowers you down into the water. Once it is in the water, you have to escape. First you have to decide which escape route you are going to take, then if someone is in front of you, you have to wait for them to open the escape hatch and then swim out to the surface. We did this a number of times until everybody was confident in all positions. After this, the helicopter would be placed in the water and turned upside down. We would then repeat the escape process. We would do this until everyone was confident in all positions. We then conducted the drills wearing goggles that were blacked out. The reason for this was that if it was at night and visibility was limited, you would be able to remember how to get out without being able to see. I used to enjoy these days, as it was a day spent at the pool and I had always been comfortable around water. However, most of the other blokes could think of other things they would rather be doing.

The Battalion birthday celebrations were coming up again and that meant the boxing was coming up as well. I had let my fitness slide a little bit. I was still able to pass a BFA and BFT, but I was not as fit as I used to be. I was out drinking every weekend that I was not outfield. Usually on Thursdays I would go to the university bar that was just down the road from base, as they would have cheap drinks there. I would also go out on Friday and Saturday night, then finish it off with a big Sunday session down on the waterfront.

This year I was to fight, once again at the end of the night, which I knew I wouldn't enjoy. Last time I was so nervous that I didn't enjoy any of the night. This was the case again. We were lucky enough to have a guest judge, a professional boxer from Townsville who had fought Anthony Mundine. He was the first person to go the distance with him, so he was a very good fighter.

By the third and last round it was about even, with me slightly ahead. However, the last 30 seconds I had nothing left, so I just blocked all the punches and did not fire one back at my opponent. He won and when I stepped out of the ring, feeling very disappointed, our celebrity judge came up to me and said that the only reason I had lost was that in the last 30 seconds I was not active enough. He also stated that if I was to come to the gym where he trained and begin a training regime, I could have a good future in amateur boxing, and maybe even be able to move on to professional boxing one day.

As I had enjoyed boxing so much before joining the Army, I thought this would be a good idea. I researched whether the Battalion would allow me to pursue boxing. Due to the nature of some sports, because of possible injuries, it was required that the CO approve the possible injury risk. The Battalion had to ensure someone could fill your position while you recovered. When I submitted an application, it was approved.

As I got back into fitness, I started seeing very good results. I realised that maybe I could achieve my long-held dream of joining the Commandos. The mental and physical strength needed was unbelievable. Until then I didn't think that I could do it, but as my fitness improved I started to believe I could. So I decided to put in an application to see if I could pass the Special Forces Entry Test (SFET). The test was not until February of the following year, so I had plenty of time to prepare.

If I passed I had a chance of leaving the Battalion, so I wasn't put on any support courses at the end of 2004. This really annoyed me, as nothing was confirmed yet and I still had a long way to go. But the Battalion wanted to give the courses to people who would be staying there indefinitely; they didn't want to put time and money into a person who was trying to further their career outside of the Battalion.

During this time I moved off base with a military friend and a civilian friend. My civilian housemate used to participate in a lot of triathlons in America, meaning he did a lot of running and riding. I would join him, which helped me out a lot with fitness.

...

I was in peak condition when the Battalion went on Christmas leave of 2004. After a couple of weeks on leave and not doing any PT, I lost everything I had worked for in regards to my physical strength. I decided to come back early from leave and start training again so I would be able to pass the test that was coming up.

As mentioned in the Introduction, I passed the SFET without any issues. However, due to the number of personnel who had completed the SFET that year, I was unable to participate in the Commando Course in March. I was put on the second course, which was being run in February 2006.

A furphy (another word for a rumour, pronounced 'firthy') had started that the Battalion was possibly in line for a trip to Iraq. The rumour mill went crazy for about three months. I was called into my boss' office and asked if I would like to go to Bravo Company, and be on the reserve list for deployment to Iraq later that year.

The furphy had actually come true. Straight away I said, 'Yes.' How could I knock back an opportunity like that? Boxing and SF would have to wait. Even though SF don't like it when you withdraw from a course, when there is an opportunity to deploy overseas, well, that is a different case. Even though I was only on the reserve list, I was confident that I would be going due to my excellent work ethic.

SIX

IRAQ: FIRST BLOOD

The Iran–Iraq War began when President Saddam Hussein invaded Iran in 1980. The war ended in 1988, with casualties of 1.5 million people in total. Iraq invaded Kuwait in 1990, with an estimated death toll of 100,000 people. In 1998, President Bill Clinton signed the Iraq Liberation Act. In 2003, the US invaded Iraq, stating that Iraq was creating nuclear and chemical weapons, which was in violation of UN Resolution 687.

Iraq has had a long history of war — it has rarely seen much peacetime. The issue was that as soon as the Coalition forces, mainly the US, started to secure themselves in Iraq every person that wanted to fight the infidels flooded into the country. They came from Saudi Arabia, Jordan, Syria and Kuwait. They wore no uniforms. It seemed as though the Coalition forces were just waiting to be picked off by IEDs and snipers.

...

I marched into Bravo Company with the slim possibility that I might be deployed to Iraq later that year. A PL was put together and we were to shadow everything the confirmed PL was doing. This was in case someone got injured, was not up to the required standard or just stuffed up in the Army or civilian world. I had to prove that if someone was required, I would be that person. There was only one LT, one SGT, three CPLs, three LCPLs and 24 PTEs in the other PL, meaning that as a PTE I had a better chance percentage-wise of getting a position.

Our task was to protect Australian VIPs at the Coalitions Operations Base (COB), as well as at the Australian Embassy. This meant that there was another possibility that I could get a position, as one PL could not be in two places at once. However, nothing was confirmed at this stage. What I learnt in the Army was that until you have your boots on the ground you are not there yet.

The deployment was to be called SECDET 8 (Security Detachment, eighth rotation), as part of Australia's Operation Catalyst. A number of units would be required for this deployment, such as cavalry to drive the ASLAVS (Australian Light Armoured Vehicles), military police and us, the infantry.

All the units came to Townsville, where the majority of the training was done. The blokes that had been confirmed to be going had been issued their desert cams, and other equipment they would need overseas. They were told that from now on they would be wearing their desert cams everywhere they went. There were only about 40 of them, compared to the almost 900 people in the 1st Battalion. The only thing we were given was an old set of body armour and a helmet. We had to get used to them in regard to the weight, and the fact that it held in body heat. I thought this was ridiculous, as it was bad morale for the rest of the Battalion. It was like they were showing off that they were going overseas and that they were better than the other blokes.

We began to do language training, culture and cultural awareness training, study the history of Iraq, PL and Section contact drills and first aid training. We also did Section drills over and over again. We did a lot of manning and running checkpoints. This would be done 24 hours a day for our entire tour at the Australian Embassy. This was very mundane work. Deployments are 98 percent boring and two percent adrenaline-pumping. We knew we would be located in the Green Zone, which was the 'safe' area for the Coalition forces. The majority of the vehicles that were searched entering the Australian Embassy or the American hospital, both of which shared the same checkpoint, were either going to be American or Australian vehicles, garbage trucks, or Iraqi civilian vehicles that would be coming to pick up their injured or deceased loved ones. The vehicles coming from the Red Zone would already be searched.

A lot of the stuff we were doing in Iraq was going to be very repetitive. However, chances were that the moment we didn't concentrate would be the time something would happen, or something dangerous would make it through, such as a Vehicle Borne Improvised Explosive Device (VBID), or a car bomb. Our Section came up with a saying that was known to everyone in the PL. If you ever said, 'That's how we roll,' the closest person to you would know that you had spotted something that was not right, such as wiring coming out from under a car's dashboard, the signs of a weapon, or even a bomb. Using this system meant the person you were searching wouldn't know that you had noticed the problem, which would allow us to deal with the situation prior to that person being able to act.

We did urban training at the Line Creek Junction. There we would break off into PLs and Sections to conduct urban contact drills and patrols in built-up areas. While we were at high range, we were also conducting patrols with the ASLAVs. This included embarking and disembarking from the vehicles to form a contact formation. We also conducted drills where a vehicle would run over an IED and we would practise our first aid and vehicle recovery drills.

...

After we had completed our MRE, only days prior to those who were deploying left for their pre-deployment leave, our PL assembled on the parade ground. We were told by the Major of Bravo Company that an extra two and a half Sections would be required. He read out the names of all the people who were going. Four PTEs missed out. I didn't hear my name and was devastated. I had worked so, so hard. What had I done wrong?

I asked my Section Commander and he said, 'Your name was called out, congratulations.'

I couldn't believe it. I wasn't convinced, so I asked the boys around me if they had heard my name. They said they had. It was at that time I was satisfied I was going. People were giving high fives to each other, hugging each other and congratulating each other. The only problem was that the Major had made the announcement on the parade ground and the four PTEs that had missed out were also assembled there. They were trying to confirm with us whether we had heard their names. They were asking the same question, but deep down they must have known they had missed out. As the blokes who had missed out had completed all the training, they were told that if something happened to anybody while on leave or overseas they would be joining us.

...

Once I got home I called my parents and told them that I was going to Iraq, and that I would be visiting them soon for a quick break prior to deploying. They were, I feel, pretty worried, as all parents, partners and loved ones would be about a soldier going to the Middle East, and not in a peacekeeping role as in Timor. I was too excited to worry.

My parents' last words to me before I left were, 'Be careful. Call when you can.' My last words to them were, 'Don't worry, I'll be okay.' Mum did cry a little, but that was to be expected. My parents knew this was why I had joined the Army and was what I wanted more than anything.

I had recently met a woman (I will call her Shelly). We had some long discussions and decided that we would not go any further with our relationship. We would wait and see how we felt about each other when I returned home. Shelly felt okay about me being deployed, as she was in the Army as well and knew how important this was. In this case, my career came first.

I couldn't wait. This is why I had joined the Army, especially the infantry. A couple of days later I was back in Victoria and having just over a week off, prior to deploying to Iraq.

...

When we returned to Townsville, the remainder of us were issued the necessary equipment. It was basically what we had been issued when joining the Army, though it was all in desert camouflage style — yellow, brown and a darker yellow/orange. We were also issued a lot of warm and wet weather gear, as we were going there over the winter period.

A couple of days later we flew to Kuwait by civilian airliner. When we arrived after a long flight, we were picked up by bus and taken to a large American base outside the city. The Australians had a small base within the American base. They utilised this base for logistics and for people coming in and out, such as us, as well as people going to and from ROCL.

We were required to stay in Kuwait for approximately five days. This was to get used to the heat, which at the time was approximately 55°C, and to conduct some final training over there. Training included zeroing (alignment of) our weapon sights and confirmation shoots. During this we noticed that the shoulder attachments of the body armour restricted us. We were unable to fully fit the butt of the weapon into our shoulders to get well-aimed shots away. We had only been issued the new style of body armour once we arrived in Kuwait, meaning that we did not have much time to get used to it. This was something that was talked about a lot, but fell on the deaf ears of our higher commanders. The armour also affected my movements as rear gunner in the ASLAVs.

We did live fire training at checkpoints. A car would be pulled towards us on rails by an electric winch and we would have to react to what the car was doing. Sometimes it would stop when we made the correct commands but sometimes, even if we gave the correct command, it would keep coming and we would have to shoot at the car to stop it.

We also did live fire urban drills. The problem was that we were required to have safety personnel following us (NCOs or officers). The only people who were not doing anything were the MPs, so they would come and follow us. Afterwards there were many smartarse comments, in regard to what we were doing, made by the MPs. I have total respect for everyone in the Army and the Defence Force, however you don't criticise people who are trained in something that you aren't specialised in.

...

When it was time to leave Kuwait for Bagdad, we were taken to the huge American Air Force Base, squeezed onto an Australian C-130 Hercules Air Force plane. It was very hot on the plane and, just prior to entering Iraqi airspace, we were told to don our body armour and helmets. That's when it got even hotter. However, as soon as we were told we had entered Iraqi airspace, the heat wasn't an issue anymore. I was so pumped up, as we were only a few hours away from landing in the capital city of Iraq.

It was night by the time we landed. We were taken from the Air Force Base to another base on the outskirts of Baghdad, where we would be picked up by Chinook helicopter and flown into the Green Zone.

There were two options when it came to getting to the Green Zone from where we were. One was to go along Route Irish, which was a highway in between the Green Zone and the main base, and was the main supply route (MSR). Our second option was to fly in by helicopter.

We loaded onto the Chinook and flew over the Red Zone. As we were flying over it, I was looking out the back and could see the city through the open door. There was a bloke manning the helicopter's tail gun. I was thinking how that would have been an awesome job, when all of a sudden red flares started pouring out the back of the helicopter.

I nearly shat myself, because I thought we were under attack by RPGs and that we were firing off flares to try to distract the rockets from hitting the helicopter. Nobody knew what was going on. The tail gunner seemed pretty calm, so I calmed down a little bit. There was not much I could do anyway.

After we landed in the Green Zone, I found out that firing flares was standard procedure. I wished they had told us that in the safety brief prior to leaving.

We were picked up by ASLAVS and taken to the Australian Embassy. We were given a safety brief and a bed for the night, and were told to get a few hours of sleep. Trying to get some shut-eye was next to impossible; I was so excited that we were there, that I had finally put my boots on the ground. I did, however, manage to get an hour or two of sleep.

After this we were given a tour of the embassy and were shown the DFAC, where we would eat. We were shown where the hospital was, which was next door, and then we were taken back to the embassy and were paired up with a person who had arrived a week earlier. We were required to shadow them for their shift so that we would know what to do. Each shift went for six hours.

Firstly, we would go into a room in the embassy where monitors controlled the cameras that were located around the exterior and interior walls. These we would monitor for an hour. Secondly, we would go on top of the embassy roof and do a two-hour shift of overwatch. Next, we would do a roving picket of the embassy grounds for another hour. We would then go to the Vehicle Checkpoint (VCP) overwatch, where we would cover the entrance to the checkpoint, as well as the person on the VCP searching cars, and people entering the hospital and the embassy. During the final hour would be down on the VCP conducting searches.

We would have eight hours off, then start the shift again. In between shifts we were required to maintain our equipment and do jobs around the embassy, such as making better overwatch positions and strengthening the stand-to positions (the areas we would go if the embassy came under attack). In that time we would also have to eat and maintain our hygiene and fitness. Every night our boss was required to go to the other base, called the Coalitions Operations Base (COB), where he would get regular updates in regard to security, what had gone on around Baghdad that day, attacks on Coalition forces and other basic admin issues. He required personnel to drive him. So with all the jobs in between our shifts, we had to be really careful how we used our time off, as well as making sure we got enough sleep. But I could live with that; there were plenty of people back at the Battalion who were more than willing to take anyone's position at a second's notice.

After a couple of days of me hounding the boss, I was finally given permission to work in the hospital helping out the Americans. I and another CFA, who I affectionately called 'The Old Man' and who I have the utmost respect for, went into the hospital. There I saw, for the first time, the real cost of war — the Iraqi civilian with his left leg blown off.

Trying to explain some of the things I saw is hard. Very hard. I have photos and videos that were taken while I was working in the hospital, but I struggle to look at them as they bring back a lot of memories. I have put myself on the line for this book. I must find a way of getting my experience into words, no matter how hard, so you can understand what soldiers do in the name of their country. War is not like a video game. When you die you can't just reset the game or be magically healed. These injuries, whether physical or mental, are with you forever.

...

A pattern started to emerge: I would do my shift at the embassy and once finished I would sleep for a few hours (if it was night), have a feed, go into the hospital, then back for another shift at the embassy. If I finished my guard shift during the day I would go to the hospital first and rest later.

During the period we were there I averaged around three to four hours a day in the emergency room at the hospital. There was a range of persons coming in, such as Iraqi civilians, private security contractors and Coalition forces from all countries. There was also the odd member of the enemy forces who had been injured in a gun battle and brought into the hospital, escorted by heavily armed personnel, to be treated prior to being sent to their next location. The injuries ranged from car crash victims to soldiers missing multiple limbs, as well as major injuries caused by the large range of IEDs that were out there.

An IED that the enemy was starting to use more of, and was causing a lot of injuries and deaths, was called an Explosively Formed Projectile (EFP). An EFP is a self-forging warhead or shaped charge designed to penetrate very thick armour. The charge is formed into a metal slug or rod shape and accelerated towards a target. The EFP had a lot of success penetrating armoured vehicles, which had been impenetrable before, such as the American Abrams tanks.

The other IEDs that we had to worry about were Person Borne Improvised Explosive Devices (PBIED), which is a person with a bomb strapped to their body, a Vehicle Borne Improvised Explosive Device (VBIED), which is car bomb, and the everyday IED. This can be something as simple as an unexploded bomb wired up with a detonation cord and detonator, with an arming device, such as a mobile phone. An even simpler IED is a pressure cooker (used at the finish line of the Boston marathon in the US). Filled with nails, glass, ball bearings and anything that can do damage to a person's body, it is propelled towards them at an extreme pace. Another arming device is a pressure plate, which is basically something simple, like two wood saws placed together with a gap between the metal of the two saws. When they are run over or walked on, the two metal saws touch, which creates a circuit that is connected to the bomb. This is, for the enemy, an effective device, as they don't have to set it off themselves. They can place it in a highly trafficked area and wait for someone to walk or drive over it.

An injury that came hand in hand with IEDs was burns. The heat generated within the vehicle and around the IED blast is very intense. Sometimes patients would come in with their limbs missing, however there was no need for tourniquets or bandages as the area where the limb had come off was cauterised. Other people would come in with burns to half their body. The wounds were terrible.

One of my jobs was to hold down the soldiers' or civilians' arms or legs while the medic cut around the base of their fingers or toes, and peel off the blistered and burnt skin. We would give them drugs to help control the pain, but nothing could stop it all. Sometimes patients would come in with their body so burnt the skin that would come off would be like a plaster mould in the shape of their hand or foot.

I remember one time there was an American soldier who came in and the wrist on his left arm had been cauterised. His hand had no damage, but his wrist had been burnt and his hand was just hanging on by some veins and skin. Nothing could be done other than amputate his hand, which was done in the surgery room after we had stabilised and prepared him.

Other times, soldiers and Iraqi civilians would come in and their faces, arms and legs would be cauterised from IEDs. The burns were one of the most horrific injuries I dealt with while working at the hospital.

...

Between patients, once they were stabilised and they were sent to surgery, we would practise the things we had learnt. This was combat first aid, with the American medics and doctors. It included placing intravenous (IV) drips into each other's arms. We also memorised where everything was kept in the emergency room, such as the needles, swabs, tourniquets and other things that would be needed at a second's notice. We had to know by heart where everything was kept. We would be a hindrance if we delayed patient care; there would be no point in us being there.

And for myself, I wanted to learn absolutely everything I could, as one day I might be called upon to save one of my brothers injured in battle. I also had to learn to be calm when I saw horrific injuries. Another important reason why I was so keen on working in the hospital was that I wanted to contribute something, to help our fellow Coalition soldiers as much as I could. The soldiers who were coming in with major injuries had put their lives on the line, so I wanted to do everything I could to help, even if it was just cutting off their clothes and passing equipment to the nurses and doctors. This was sometimes the only thing I could do.

It must have been hard for the American medics and doctors to put aside the fact that the soldiers coming in with these horrific injuries were wearing the same uniform as them. Every time I left the hospital I felt guilty, as I could come and go whenever I wanted. They were working 12 hours on and 12 hours off, for 12 to 14 months.

Being deployed overseas was about representing my country and doing what I loved doing as an infantry soldier. A bonus was that we received tax-free pay, along with danger money. If you did not spend too much money on your ROCL, you could come home at the end of your deployment with a very good amount of cash in the bank. Even though the money was good, when I compared the hours I did and the risks I took, it evened out.

The American soldiers, however, didn't get this. They got an extra allowance for serving overseas, but it was nothing compared to what we were receiving. They didn't complain about this at all. I was personally told by some of them that their families were relying on food stamps to survive. A few of them did say that it would be great to be on the sort of money we were, but for them it was all about representing their country. Whenever I asked the question, 'Why did you join up?' most of the time the answer was, '9/11.' They were so proud of their country and the fact that they could represent it overseas. I have the utmost respect for every single one of them. Working with these soldiers at the hospital was in the top five greatest things I have experienced in life.

One thing I can specifically remember is when an American soldier came in after an IED had gone off. He had been the gunner in the humvee and had received minor fragmentation wounds to his face. One of the cuts was about two inches long and I, with an American medic watching over me, stitched up the cut. Halfway through stitching up his face, the injured soldier said to me, 'Make the stitches a bit wider.' This was so it would scar. A war wound would always be there to remind him of how close he came to death, and I suspect maybe something he could use to impress the ladies back home.

After I had finished, a two-star general came into the hospital and presented the soldier with the Purple Heart, a medal the Americans receive if they are injured while serving overseas. It was such a great honour to have worked on him, then to have been there when he was presented with his well-earned medal.

A little Iraqi girl came in one day, approximately six to eight years of age. She had fragmentation wounds to her body, with the most serious wounds being in her buttocks. She was screaming and crying when she first came in, but after a while she stopped screaming and was just crying. A few of the medics and doctors asked if they could be excused from working on her, as they had children of similar ages back at home. Seeing the girl in that state would have been so hard for them, which was understood by all. A doctor, a couple of the medics and I stayed in the emergency room and treated her until she was picked up by an Iraqi ambulance and taken out of the Green Zone to an Iraqi hospital.

For the medical staff, sometimes facing the injuries during the long shifts got a bit too hard and they were able to step out when there were spare hands on deck. But sometimes, when the more seriously injured patients came in, or there were mass casualties (four or more injured personnel) it was all hands on deck. There were only four beds in the emergency room.

Once, three American soldiers came in with major injuries after their convoy had been hit by an IED. Three of their teammates — their friends — had been killed instantly. They were taken into the emergency room to be stabilised prior to surgery. There was one soldier who was about two metres tall and around 120 kilograms of muscle, lying on a stretcher covered in a blanket in the hallway. He was in a major state of shock; he was sick of being overseas, of seeing war every day, of seeing his mates get killed and injured, and his body basically could not function anymore. This was the first time I had seen a soldier, or anyone, mentally shutdown. For a long time we talked to him, trying to let him know that he was in a safe place and that his friends were in the right hands, but he wouldn't move. The only thing that did move was his chest when he breathed, and every now and then a tear ran down his cheek. He looked as though he had nothing left. He looked as if he was thinking, *I give in! You win!*

Years later, I would come to understand how he felt as he lay there in that hallway. His mind would not allow him to continue.

...

An Iraqi soldier came in one day because he had shot himself in the foot. The round had gone straight into his foot, hit the bone, run along the bone and come out three quarters the way along the bottom. As there were three other people in the emergency room at the time, myself and one other medic were assigned the soldier. The medic set up an IV drip for him and pain relief medication, while I was setting up a device to clean out the inside of the wound. This device was to ensure that we would get rid of any foreign matter within the wound.

The machine pumped fluid into a hose, which I would move around inside the wound, cleaning out the foreign matter. This was done for about 20 minutes, until we were satisfied that the wound was clean, and then it was dressed. We gave him some crutches and he was taken to the Iraqi hospital by his fellow soldiers, who had brought him in.

The reason the Iraqis would come into the Coalition hospital was because we had the facilities there and they would get the proper treatment straight away. Prior to my time, when Iraqi patients on life support were picked up by ambulance and taken out to the Red Zone hospitals, they were still attached to the life support devices. Once in the hospitals in the Red Zone, the devices would often be taken off the person and sold on the black market, leaving the person to die. During my time there, it was decided that to stop the loss of these machines the doctors would declare the patient deceased. We would then have to remove all the devices that were hooked up to the patient prior to them being picked up by their family or friends.

The worst part for me, other than having a person declared deceased in front of me, was the next step. They were taken to another room, where all the needles and tubes that had been placed into their body would have to be removed. A cannula (what the IV plugs into) is usually placed into the inside of each leg, where the main vein runs, and in each arm. A catheter was inserted into the penis and pushed down into the bladder. Once it was inside the bladder, air would be pumped into the tube using a small hand pump, causing a ballooning effect on the end of the tube in the bladder. This would ensure the tube would not come out. The other end was connected to a colostomy bag, which would allow the patient to urinate while unconscious, in a coma or under surgery. This would have to be taken out by doing the reverse when putting it in.

The worst part of removing the medical equipment from the bodies was the tube that went down their throat into their lungs. This would allow the patient to breathe if they were sick, and would be utilised if staff were required to do Cardiopulmonary Resuscitation (CPR) or Expired Air Resuscitation (EAR). When this was removed the deceased made a gurgling sound. The first time I heard this I said to the medic, who was explaining the process, that the patient was still alive (although it was evident by every other sign, and his injuries, that the patient was in fact deceased). I hated this job the most. But it was something I could do without any supervision, which allowed people to rest or to work in the emergency room. After that, a person of the same nationality would come in and clean the body prior to it being picked up.

...

The worst injury I saw is one I will never, ever forget. It was when a young American officer was brought in one afternoon. He had his left leg missing from below the knee and his right arm missing from just below the shoulder. He also had major injuries to the rest of his body, face and other limbs from an IED incident. The soldiers who had worked on him on the battlefield, and in the medical evacuation helicopter, had done a fantastic job of keeping him alive, so that we could do our job. Almost immediately it was found that he could not breathe unassisted, so he was hooked up to a breathing machine. I was cutting off his clothes and removing the tourniquet from his leg, as the blood on the exposed veins had clotted and the tourniquet was no longer required. We had to quickly get him into the MRI room to scan his body and see where the shrapnel was, so the surgeons could remove it. However, unless it was near any vital organs, for now it was most likely staying inside his body. In this case it was probably going to stay in there for a while, as he had other, more life-threatening injuries.

While he was having the scans done, my job was to keep the oxygen going into his lungs. I was required to stand with him and squeeze the oxygen bag every three seconds. In that time, I felt like I had a special bond with this soldier. All of the patients I worked on after that would never compare to this one. Possibly because for a long period of time it was just he and I in the room, and I was breathing for him. As long as I live, I will never forget that experience.

After the scans were finished and it was deemed that he was stabilised enough to go to surgery, we handed him over and that was the last time I ever heard about him. I can only assume he was flown to Germany, to the American hospital, then flown back home to the United States.

SEVEN

IRAQ: THE EMBASSY AND THE COB

After approximately a month, we did a changeover with the other PL and were stationed at the COB for a month. This was so that we would not relax too much and let our guard down. It was also a change of pace and scenery. The COB was where the hierarchy of SECDET 8 was located, along with other units such as the cavalry and military police. While we were here we would conduct overwatch security on the roof of a six-storey building, located in the middle of the base. The building was the old international Ba'ath Party headquarters, which we shared with the Americans. We would also be the QRF and a security group when other Australian units and visitors were moving around in the Red Zone, as well as provide security for the Australian VIPs located at the embassy.

On top of the roof, where the overwatch security was conducted, were two positions opposite each other where we would sit for anywhere from four to six hours during the day and three to four hours during the night, keeping an eye out for possible threats and bomb blasts. When an IED went off you would be able to hear it and see the black smoke. We would radio in to the command centre the direction it was from our location, the time it went off, approximate distance and the area we thought it was in. Then the command centre would ensure that the reaction forces would know that an IED had gone off in that area.

As we had arrived in Iraq at the end of summer, we would experience the full brunt of winter before it started to warm up again. Baghdad was such a beautiful place prior to the occupation of the Coalition forces. The buildings were unbelievable. There was a mosque named the Al-Rahman mosque that was three-quarters finished, with cranes around it. Saddam Hussein began building it as he wanted Baghdad to have the largest mosque in the world, but he never lived to see it completed.

A lot of the buildings had been damaged due to the occupation, however they were still very beautiful. The building where we conducted our overwatch from had a huge hole in the centre, going from the roof all the way down into the basement. It had been targeted during the bombing of Baghdad prior to the occupation, but the bomb had failed to detonate, which was lucky for us and the Americans as it was in a fantastic position. Other landmarks that surrounded us were: the Tomb of the Unknown Soldier, dedicated to the soldiers who were killed during the Iran–Iraq War; Al Sijood Presidential Palace; a number of other mosques; and The Crossed Swords. This is a parade ground with two hands at each end, holding up large swords that cross at the top. This is where Iraq's defence forces would once have conducted its presentations to their president and to the world. At the base of the hands are hundreds of Iranian helmets in large bags that were collected from the Iran–Iraq War. We would sit up in the viewing stands, where Saddam Hussein had stood to observe the parades, while we were on QRF.

When the Australian Ambassador or other personnel working at the embassy were required to visit areas outside the Green Zone, we would act as their security. Sometimes we were required to pick up and drop off personnel at the other Coalition base, next to the airport where all the hierarchy (officers) were posted. This was where Saddam Hussein's palace once was. We were also required to pick up equipment and mail. To get to the other base we had to travel along Route Irish, a highway where a lot of IED and machine-gun ambushes happen. When travelling along routes like this, it was important to vary our travel time to avoid developing a pattern for the enemy to follow. Prior to leaving we would make sure there had been no attacks where a traffic jam might be, as this was one of the worst places to be stationary in Iraq. I have watched a video of a private security convoy getting ambushed by machine-gun fire. They were caught in a traffic jam on Route Irish. In the background you could hear one of the contractors, who had been shot, slowly die.

Some Iraqis would celebrate their team winning a game of sport in a different way to how we did: with celebratory fire. One night the Iraqi international soccer team drew against their opponent, so the people celebrated half the night by firing their weapons into the air. Some would fill their magazines full of tracer rounds, which when fired you would see a red flash go through the air, causing a light show effect. At first we did not know what was going on, and thought that possibly the Green Zone was under attack. When we found out they were celebrating because of the football match, we still had to remain undercover because when the rounds were fired into the air they had to come down again. Over at the embassy, rounds were landing on the roof. The next day during briefings we found out that over 20 people had been killed, and many more injured, due to the celebratory fire.

When we were required to provide protection for the VIPs around the Green Zone, they would travel to buildings such as the Ministry of Interior. We would be in a group of two people. One person would stay with the VIP at all times and the other would stay with the vehicle. We were in constant contact with each other, so that if something happened we would be able to communicate and say things such as, 'We are coming out now, so have the car parked at the front door.' When the VIPs were picked up, they would be given a safety brief, such as what we would do if we got hit by an IED and what would happen if we were attacked inside the buildings. It was important that they were very clear about what to do because the last thing we wanted was to have to explain this while under attack. After long enough, VIPs had heard the safety instructions hundreds of times, however it was still important that we briefed them so we were all on the same page.

When we got out of the car at buildings such as the Ministry of Interior, we would walk in with the VIP either just behind us, or just off to our side. The Iraqi bodyguards would look at us with such intensity. Inside, everyone seemed to have a gun. The VIP would go into his office, and we would stand outside the office door and wait until he finished. Sometimes it was for half an hour and sometimes it was for up to six hours. During the longer shifts, it was best to be out in the car.

I remember one time there when I was given a break, I was very relieved because I had to go to the toilet. I opened a door that I thought led to a toilet, however it opened to the outside. I had walked straight out into the Red Zone. I was yelled at by an Iraqi soldier and although it was in his language I knew that he was telling me off. I quickly realised I should not have been out there and hastily went back inside, as there was a large threat from snipers.

While conducting overwatch from the Ba'ath Party headquarters, we would watch the new American Embassy being built. It was huge, with many levels underground. It would take a fair bit to get into that place, especially with the amount of concrete and reinforcement that they were putting into it. The construction went on 24/7, and from where we were it looked as though hundreds of people were working on it. While it was under construction, the Americans used their old embassy and sometimes we were required to take the VIPs there.

One day we were doing some filming around the Green Zone while driving around, when we approached the area of the American Embassy. We were stopped and told by a very angry American to delete the footage, which we did in front of her. The Americans did not want anybody seeing how their checkpoints worked at the embassy, as someone might possibly find a weak spot. This was fair enough; we did not allow personnel to film the entrance to the Australian Embassy, either.

Another time, a random checkpoint was set up within the Green Zone. I only noticed it at the last minute, and an American marine put his weapon to his shoulder and aimed it in my direction. The marines were normally outside working in the Red Zone and rarely came into the Green Zone, so the fact that they were on edge was perfectly understandable. Prior to leaving for Iraq, I had been watching a lot of VCP videos on YouTube. There was one in particular that I can remember. In fact, I will never forget it. An American soldier walked up to a car at one of the entrances to the Green Zone. The driver had complied with all of his instructions. When the soldier reached the vehicle, the car, along with the driver and the soldier, were vaporised by a large IED. I could understand how easy it was for them to be on edge, especially after I saw the injuries to the patients who came into the hospital. I would hate to have seen the condition of the soldiers who didn't make it to the hospital.

The Green Zone was a reasonably safe place for us, however you never, ever let your guard down, as someone could always bring weaponry into the area. Some of the government officials in the buildings, such as the Ministry of Interior, were fairly corrupt, and would sometimes bring weaponry into the Green Zone. There were many times when government officials were to be arrested, but had been tipped off early by other government personnel prior to their arrest and had been able to escape.

The main threat to us while in the Green Zone was from snipers and from mortars or rocket attacks (indirect fire). The enemy would let off rockets and mortars in the Red Zone, firing randomly into the Green Zone. At one stage there was a truck driving around without a roof, with a mortar set up inside it. They would drive around the streets, park the vehicle, fire off a number of mortars and drive off again, then repeat the process in a completely different position.

At one stage, at the entrance to the COB, there were three mortar rounds that landed in quick succession right at the front gate. They were either the luckiest shots fired or somehow the entrance had been zeroed in on by a specialist in indirect fire.

While posted to the COB, when I had time I would grab one of the vehicles and head over and help out at the hospital. Even though I was only gone for a month, I wanted to maintain the friendships that I made as well as the skills I had learnt. The vehicles that we utilised were all big oversized American Chevys. They were great to drive, however to drive around on normal streets and try to park in a car park at a shopping complex would be a nightmare. Also the fuel they consumed made the Australian V8 look like an electric car. Nevertheless, they were what we needed.

While posted to the COB, opportunities came up to be a gunner in one of the ASLAVs when doing pick-ups or drop-offs of personnel or supplies to the main base next to the airport. This meant we were required to travel along Route Irish. A gunner would provide side and rear protection for the vehicle. Another job for the gunner was to relay information about the surroundings to the driver and commander of the vehicle. If we were stationary it was the job of the gunner to check the area for things such as wires and other objects that looked out of place, which may possibly be an IED.

I used to love this job and volunteer every time it came up. It was such a rush to be out in the Red Zone, as we didn't get too many opportunities to do this. Out there, you had to be on the ball 100 percent of the time. On the back of the Coalition vehicles there is a sign saying 'Stay back 100 metres or you will be shot' in both English and Arabic. These signs didn't work a lot of the time, as the drivers over there, even though the Coalition had been in Iraq for many years by then, didn't pay attention and often got too close. This caused a lot of vehicle engines to be shot, and even civilian drivers and their passengers were shot. I did not have this happen to me, however it happened to other convoys on a regular basis.

Another task I loved at the COB was when we were required to escort the Australian Ambassador or VIPs into the Red Zone. This was the main reason I wanted to be there; it was where it all happened.

Being in the Red Zone really pumped us up! Anything could happen at any time. Anything! There was rubbish everywhere. No-one cared about the road rules. The smell was overwhelming, as there was poor sewerage infrastructure due to the lack of maintenance since the war began. I wondered how people could live in that environment, not excluding the fact that an IED could go off at any time, sometimes in the busiest places, such as markets. But it was their home, after all.

…

After a month at the COB, we returned to the embassy and began another stint there. While in the overwatch box on top of the embassy you would be staring directly at the Sheraton Hotel, which was about one kilometre away. The hotel was popular with foreign journalists and contractors after the 2003 invasion of Iraq, but due to its size and position it was a very inviting target. It was hit with a lot of indirect fire during the early years of the occupation and, while we were there, it was seriously damaged during a bomb attack in October 2005. The hotel was hit by a coordinated VBIED attack, which caused a hole for a second VBIED, a cement truck, to drive through and get very close prior to exploding. The hotel was closed for more than a year due to the damage.

One night while I was on duty monitoring the cameras around the embassy, I heard over the radio that shots had been fired. I was wondering what was going on, when I was told that a round had whizzed past the heads of the guys who were in the overwatch box. They got down as low as they could, while scanning for the possible location of the sniper. At the same time, the COB was notified and our snipers came over with their telescopic equipment to see whether they could locate the sniper. After about 40 minutes they stood down, as they were unable to find him.

I then went to sit in the box for the next three hours. ROCL had started, and with four people at a time gone we were even more undermanned. This required us to spend more time on picket, as we had to cover their shifts. It was obvious that, in the planning and process of SECDET 8, the numbers required for infantry had not been taken into consideration, especially when blokes went on ROCL. Our breaks in between shifts got shorter and the shifts got longer.

Another thing about the overwatch box on the embassy roof was that it was just downwind from the ventilation pipe coming from the roof of the hospital. During the day they would burn the rubbish used in the hospital, such as the bandages, the plastic IV bags, swabs and everything else from the emergency room and the surgery room, which included body parts. The smell was horrific. It was thick black smoke and there was no way we could avoid it. After a while we started wearing ventilation masks. When it was bad, it was the worst thing I had ever smelt. I started looking forward to when my shift was at night time. I could put up with the cold more than I could put up with the smell.

Bagdad in winter was cold. Really cold. We wore three layers at night time, especially when we were required to be in the overwatch boxes. It would get down to well below zero degrees Celsius and sometimes the shifts were a minimum of four hours long.

Daily updates would include reports of things such as how many IEDs had detonated, what new strategies the enemy was using, any big operations that were coming up and the number of deceased Iraqis. There were always deceased Iraqis. The Sunni and Shi'a factions were fighting and it was turning into a civil war. Every morning the Iraqi civilians would wake up to find hundreds of dead civilians, who had often been tortured and decapitated.

As the entrance to the embassy was shared with the hospital, we would have Americans assisting us with the vehicle searches at the VCP. We had to be careful with the American soldiers, as they were not specifically trained as infantry soldiers but were administration personnel who would join us for a few hours. They would also take care of cars if a convoy came in that had been hit by an IED and was carrying someone injured. We also had, at the end of the tour, Iraqi security contractors helping us out. We had to be very careful with the Iraqi contractors, as they were prone to becoming distracted while on the job, especially at night when they preferred to be asleep.

There was an American Sergeant there who was in the Rangers (one of many types of Special Forces within the US Army) who was in charge of security at the hospital. He would often join us at the checkpoint. After a while I got to know him pretty well and, after a few conversations, I found out that he had been one of the soldiers in Somalia during the firefight chronicled in the book, and later the movie, *Black Hawk Down*. He told me stories of what he had experienced, and it was interesting talking and learning from him.

...

One afternoon while I was sitting in the camera room of the embassy, a woman who was working there told me there had been some riots in Cronulla, a suburb of Sydney. I didn't think too much of it and thought maybe the media was overreacting, as they often do. However, when I returned home to Australia I watched the replays and realised it was not just some story the media was using to try to ramp up ratings.

The woman who told me about the riots was certainly attractive, and after five months I thought she was prettiest woman in the world. There were women military police on SECDET 8, however I didn't get along with them at all due to things that had happened during our training. I did work with a lot of women who were medics in the hospital, though I was always under too much pressure to look at them closely. I saw them as very brave, and I have the utmost respect for them and what they do.

This deployment was a lot easier for me compared to the blokes with partners back at home, because it was over the Christmas and New Year period. The hierarchy did their best to try and make Christmas a bit more enjoyable in Iraq. On Christmas day we had a big lunch and were able to have two beers each, which made me feel almost drunk to the point where I had to go to bed in the early afternoon. The hierarchy also ran the security for us, which meant we had a period of about 36 hours to relax and do whatever we wanted, which I used to catch up on sleep.

...

In early January, I and another bloke received mail that stated we had been selected to participate in the February 2006 Commando Selection and Training Course. In a way I was disappointed, as we were not due home until March, so I would miss the opportunity. This would be the first of two occasions I gave up the chance to conduct the CSTC due to overseas deployment.

Mine was the last group to go on leave. I spent 14 days in Bangkok, then two weeks later I returned to Australia. In a way it felt a little pointless, though I did receive a free flight overseas. If you didn't want to return to Australia you were able to fly anywhere in the world that was approved by the ADF, to equal or lesser value of the flight to Australia. Some blokes went to the US, which cost a little more, however all that was required was for them to pay the balance.

The day before leaving I received an email from Shelly, asking me if I remembered her and if I would like to catch up when I returned home. I replied straight away and said that of course I remembered her and would love to catch up.

On the day we flew to Kuwait, I volunteered to stay with the Quartermaster store (Q-store) Sergeant to help escort the weapons. When the plane that I was flying out on landed, our replacements were getting off the plane, which included my friend Jacob Kovco. I yelled out to him as he walked past me, but due to the sound of the planes on the tarmac he didn't hear me. After I got on the plane I wished that I had just moved over a few metres as we were walking past each other, and given him a tap on the shoulder and a quick, 'Hi, good luck!' A few months later, I would regret that I didn't do this.

As it was just me, the Q-store Sergeant and the flight crew on the Australian C-130 Hercules, I was able to sit in the cockpit behind the pilots for the entire flight. It was a great experience. I wore headphones and listened to the checks they had to do. We left Bagdad in daylight and I was able to see Iraq from the air and then, as it became dark, all of a sudden the lights appeared in Kuwait. It was exciting watching the pilots do their thing and being in the front of the plane when we landed. If I was able to talk to them I would have been saying, 'Aren't you taking this a bit close?' But they had landed these large planes hundreds, maybe thousands, of times.

...

We spent a few days in Kuwait, cleaning our gear and doing a psychological screening, where we were asked so many questions about how we were feeling. We handed most of our gear back, ready for the next lot of blokes to use. We were cleared by Australian Customs, who had been flown over especially, and relaxed until we flew home on our month's leave.

Overall, I spent four months at the Australian Embassy and two months at the COB. I was happy with this because I was able to spend more time at the hospital. It was very, very hard to say goodbye to all the people I worked with over there. I felt excited to go home, but also guilty leaving them behind because I didn't think I had done enough.

EIGHT

BETWEEN IRAQ AND AFGHANISTAN

During my break I went home for a few weeks and visited my parents in Victoria. I had a great time relaxing and not worrying about much, though I would wake up at regular intervals and reach down beside my bed to try to grab my weapon, which wasn't there. This was because I had carried it everywhere and made sure it was within arm's reach for the previous six months.

When I returned to Townsville, I contacted Shelly and we began a relationship. This was significant for me, as I had not been in many relationships prior and it was a massive commitment. But I knew she was 'the one'. For me to be in a relationship, it must have been serious. While I was in Iraq I had seen what it was like for the boys who were in relationships. Although it was hard on them, they had someone special waiting for them back at home, and I wanted that. I had my parents sending me packages, but it was just not the same. I wanted to have someone who I could go home to.

When I saw Shelly again, I was so comfortable with her. Everything seemed perfect. We would go out some nights, and other nights we would just get some takeaway and have a few quiet drinks at home while watching the footy. I had never had this before and I loved it. I was so happy.

...

On 21 April 2006, just a few days prior to Anzac day, I saw on the news a headline that we all feared. The first soldier had been killed in the Middle East Area of Operations (MEAO). Not long after, I found out it was my friend Jacob Kovco. I was so upset. It felt like yesterday that we had walked past each other on the tarmac in Iraq.

For weeks after, I had nightmares about us walking past each other, and I was trying to run towards him, yelling out his name and saying, 'Don't go!' But it didn't matter how hard I tried to run towards him, I just couldn't move. It didn't matter how loud I yelled, he still didn't hear me.

When his body was being brought home, a mistake was made and a different body was sent. When this happened, I thought they may have made a mistake and Jacob was still alive. But it wasn't the case. I would have hated to be his wife and family when that happened.

...

As my relationship with Shelly developed, Timor started to spark up again, and she was on call. Her unit was on four hours notice for about a week to go to Timor. It was a stressful week, as we didn't know if the call for her to go would come. Were we going to go to sleep, only to be woken up by a phone call saying Shelly was to be deployed?

After the week finished, her unit went back to 24 hours notice, which meant we could go out and have a few drinks. A couple of days later, Shelly was informed she would be deploying the next day. I was disappointed at the fact I wouldn't see her for a long time, but I was excited for her, as this was her first overseas deployment and this was the reason we had joined the Army.

I said goodbye to her at my room, as I didn't want to go over to the parade ground to say goodbye. I thought Shelly might get upset and I definitely knew that I was going to be upset.

As the majority of the Defence Force had left Timor a couple of years prior, they didn't have secure compounds there, so she was flown up to Darwin and then put on a Navy ship and motored over. For the first week or so we had no communication at all, but after a while she was able to call me every couple of nights.

Meanwhile, I had volunteered for the sniper pre-selection course.

On the first day we did a BFA, two BFTs and a long pack march from the base, up and over Commanders Hill towards Mount Stuart, then over to an area where we stayed for the week. During the day we conducted exercises, such as observation, judging distances and stalking, which involved approaching a target without being seen and firing a blank round in the direction of the target, while an instructor determined if you could be seen in the location you had taken the shot from. This is because when firing a round from the F88, a flash can be seen at the end of the weapon.

Prior to going to bed we would be given grids, which we would have to locate and mark on our maps. These grids would be places to go to if the camp came under attack. Within an hour of being asleep we were 'attacked'.

On the second-last day we did an individual navigational exercise, which went all day and night. We were carrying our marching order, plus radio, and when we arrived at a checkpoint we would be given another grid to go to. This process continued until the instructors were happy we had covered enough distance. I travelled, from memory, a minimum of 40 kilometres.

The last afternoon we did a fighting withdrawal from our camp. We then did a stretcher carry, a stores carry (carrying large ammunition boxes full of rocks and jerry cans full of water) for a distance and then we walked back the remaining distance to base in marching order. When we arrived back at base we went through the obstacle course, which finishes you off physically. Once we had cleaned up the equipment, I was told I would be on the sniper course, starting in two weeks time.

When I arrived back at my PL area, my boss said that the Company Sergeant Major (CSM) needed to speak to me, and to go over to his office straight away. I walked into the CSM's office and he told me to sit down. He asked me what the last week had been like. I told him the basic rundown of the course, then he asked me if I was interested in doing the promotion course, Subject 1 for CPL, which started in three weeks time. I was worried that maybe the last week had been for nothing. I told the CSM how I was feeling and he told me to take the weekend to think about it, but he needed to know my answer by Monday.

I thought about it a lot and I decided that I loved being part of a Section. Although snipers were infantry and did everything we did, they would usually only work in pairs. Also, sometimes the snipers would be in an overwatch position, whereas the Sections would be right up in the fight. I preferred to be at the front.

On Monday I told the CSM that I had made the decision to do Subject 1. I didn't regret the sniper pre-selection week. Although it had been physically and mentally very hard, I had pushed through it without any problems. The selection course for the snipers was a mini version of the CSTC, as I would soon find out.

I missed Shelly a lot. We would only be able to talk for a short time when she rang. I told her I would wait for as long as it took and that I would be here when she got back.

For a couple of weeks prior to the promotion course, I went out to my favourite place — a venue called The Mad Cow. As soon as Subject 1 started, however, I had no time to go out and by the end of the week I was too tired to go out anyway.

The course was almost exactly like recruit training at Kapooka. In some Corps in the Army there is no rank of LCPL. This meant that some people, after they have completed Subject 1, would be promoted to full CPL and could be posted to Kapooka as an instructor. You needed to be able to instruct recruits on all of the things we were taught there. The course taught me how to become a 2IC and Section Commander, even though I had been an acting 2IC for the past year, along with the majority of the infantry soldiers who were on the course.

The worst part about it was that we were divided up into Sections and those in the Section who were not acting as the instructor would pretend to be the recruits. We would have to do everything as though we were in recruit training, as well as learning how to instruct. We also did military law. There was a huge amount to learn about this. At the start we were given about 10 thick books, which we had to read and understand in case we had to charge or defend someone. We were each allocated a room in the old lines, which was like going back to when I first arrived at the Battalion. We were required to keep our rooms exactly like they were at Kapooka and were given the white glove test on these rooms at least once a week. This test is when a white glove or a piece of white material is rubbed over a surface, such as the top of a cupboard. If there is any dust on the cupboard it shows up very obviously on the white material. If your room was not up to scratch you would be given extra duties or your room would be up for inspection all the time, sometimes at no notice. This meant they could find us at any time throughout the day, take us up to our living area and do an inspection on our room, without us having time to clean it.

The course was full-on. Often when we were required to give a lesson, we were given the lesson brief at the last minute, prior to knock-off, so we had to write the lesson up in our own time. When this was the case I was focused more on the course, and the fact that Shelly was away during this time made it a lot easier.

Shelly's posting to Townsville was finishing at the end of the year and she had the option of being posted back to Townsville, Brisbane or Sydney if she requested it. We had discussed it a lot. A month after Subject 1 finished I was going to do the SFET. If I passed I would be conducting the CSTC in February 2007 which, if successful, would mean a posting to Sydney. So we decided that Shelly would put in her application to be posted to Sydney. If everything worked out we would be posted to the same location again.

In the second week of my promotion course, Shelly received confirmation that she was going to be posted to Sydney, which was great news. Now it was just up to me. Shelly was due home in a few weeks. However, the week she was to arrive I was going to be outfield. We seemed to have the worst luck!

The field exercise went off without any problems and I passed Subject 1 for CPL with very good results. And Shelly was back, so I was happy. It was so great to see her. The moment I gave her a hug I knew that it was worth the wait a thousand times over and that, once again, she was the one for me.

While Shelly was away I had planned a week away for us in Cairns, which is just north of Townsville, on her arrival home. We had a great time there, relaxing and enjoying being together. Nothing could spoil what we had.

When Shelly returned to work she was told she was going to be on the next Subject 1 course, which started in two weeks.

...

On my first day back at work I was walking up to the mess for breakfast, when my old CO from Bravo Company in Iraq was walking back to command headquarters. He said that I had done a very good job while on the promotion course, and that if I was to withdraw my Special Forces application I would be promoted to Lance Corporal and deploy with Delta Company to Afghanistan next year, in 2007.

I was gobsmacked. The blokes in the Battalion hadn't been told this and he said I was the first of only a few who knew out of the NCOs and PTEs like me. He said that he needed to know asap and I told him that I had to talk it over with my partner. A spanner was thrown into the works once again. It was time for Shelly and I to have a talk.

I wanted to say yes right there and then, but I also wanted to say no. Every time I had applied for SF, something had happened. I had no-one to blame. It was my choice, but if I pulled my application again I was worried that the staff at SF would think my heart wasn't in it and wouldn't allow me to apply for a third time.

The experience I would gain in going to Afghanistan as a Section 2IC would be fantastic, with a good chance of being able to test myself in battle. I thought they would be crazy not to accept me on the SF course if I did reapply. However, I also had to think about my relationship with Shelly, about her being posted to Sydney and whether we could be separated for at least another year. And I still had to pass all the SF tests.

After serious discussion, the decision was made that I would go to Afghanistan and, while deployed, I would put in my application for SF again. I would complete the tests when I got home at the end of the year, and if I was accepted I would do the CSTC in February 2008. I promised myself that I would not delay it again.

NINE

AFGHANISTAN: THE BATTLE BEGINS

The difficult decision was made that I would stay in 1 RAR and go to Delta Company as LCPL, and be deployed to Afghanistan on Operation Reconstruction Task Force 2 (RTF 2). This was effectively putting off my chances of doing the CSTC until early 2008, and delaying the chance of Shelly and I being posted to the same town again for at least another year. I was excited that I would be deploying to Afghanistan and that I would once again be able to perform my job as an infantry soldier. I thought this was my best chance to perform the role I so desperately wanted to.

I packed up my equipment and moved to Delta Company. I was assigned to the Section called 'call sign 41C', which meant 4th Company (Delta), 1st Platoon, Charlie (the 3rd Section). My Section Commander, who I had known for a while, was a great bloke and I thought we would make a really good team, which we did. The one thing that did annoy me was the fact that I had not been promoted to LCPL yet. I felt I should have been promoted straight away, as I was going into a position of authority. For the first three months of our training together, although I was in the position of 2IC, I was still a PTE. It was not until the CO came out to visit us during one of the exercises outfield that I was promoted, but I thought it was too late by then. The blokes in the Section had seen me as one of them for so long that I felt it was hard for them to adjust to the fact that I had now been promoted, even though I was always going to be, and that I was now officially higher in rank than them. This may have not been the case for the boys in the Section, but this was how I felt. It was an extremely unprofessional way to go about it.

...

On 11 September 2001, Al Qaeda, led by Osama Bin Laden, was reported to have attacked the US by flying aircraft into the World Trade Center and the Pentagon in New York City and Washington DC. It is estimated that nearly 3000 people were killed.

Not long after the attacks, it was announced that Australia would be assisting the Americans, and many other countries, in the fight against terror. This was how I became involved in Afghanistan.

We were going to be deployed to the Uruzgan Province in south-central Afghanistan. It is a mountainous area, lacking in vegetation, which makes it prone to landslides and avalanches. The area contains the six administrative districts of Deh Rahwood, Cahar Chineh, Khas Uruzgan, Chora, Ghizab and Tarin Kowt, the capital city where our base was located. The Tiri and Dorefshan Rivers, or *rud*, were central to the Green Zone, which was surrounded by the *dasht*, or desert.

The local people are mainly of the Pashtun tribe. They cultivate wheat, barley, sorghum, corn, orchard trees and opium poppies. Many live on less than US$1 a day and most children aren't able to go to school, though this number has been increasing since the Taliban was removed from power in 2001.

...

Just prior to the 2006 Christmas break, 44 units from around Australia, which included infantry, cavalry, engineers, military police and many more, gathered in Townsville for the first time to begin training for RTF 2. Townsville was always hot and had extremely high humidity, especially at this time of year. This weather would condition us for the temperatures we would encounter in Afghanistan, as we were being deployed during the summer period. Over there, summer is also called the 'fighting season', as this is when the snow has melted and the temperature is not freezing, so the locals are more active and not confined to their compounds.

Altogether, 393 personnel were to be deployed on RTF 2. There were many others helping with preparation, such as the Combat Training Centre (which conducts MREs), administrative units in Canberra, the staff at the main Q-store of 1 RAR.

The equipment we were issued was the same as what we had in Iraq. This camouflage didn't work as well as had been thought when designed, however. In the desert we were easily seen due to the brighter colours, and in the Green Zone we stood out. Not long after being there we would wear our initially issued camouflage uniform, which were green cams. Eventually, after a few years, the Army changed its uniform colours to blend in better with both the desert and Green Zone.

Fitness was something we focused on, due to the high altitude of Afghanistan. We did two PT sessions most days in Townsville and the hills around the base were utilised. As I was an NCO I also did a lot of my PT after work.

We also began language training, culture training, cultural awareness training, PL and Section contact drills, first aid training and studied the history of Afghanistan. We did Section drills over and over again. It was the first time since Vietnam that the 1st Battalion was deploying to a major war zone, where there was a 99 percent chance we would be involved in heavy contact with the enemy while conducting our job as infantry soldiers. As it turned out, the Section break contact drills we had practised came in handy in Afghanistan.

In November of 2006, all units involved in RTF 2 conducted the first training exercise at the High Range Training area near Townsville. We'd conducted similar drills there while preparing for Iraq in 2005. The only difference was this time we had Bushmaster vehicles, and the contact drills and recovery drills had changed somewhat since then. We also did a lot of IED drills, such as securing an area where an IED had been found. This would enable the engineers to disable the IED. This training took us up to the Christmas break of 2006. Over the break, the NCOs were given books to read about the Russian tactics that had been used against the mujahedin during the Soviet war in Afghanistan, in the 10 long years from 1979 to 1989.

Shelly and I had a great Christmas break, spending time visiting my parents in Lorne and her parents in Perth in Western Australia. I fell in love with Perth and decided that I would like to live there one day.

...

In January 2007 when we returned to work, the contingent of RTF 2 gathered and conducted a major training activity at Shoalwater Bay in central Queensland. Here we practised more of what we had previously trained in prior to the Christmas break.

The personnel of RTF 2 were finally assessed at the MRE, which was conducted at the Wide Bay Military Training Area, located inland from the Sunshine Coast. We had to wear laser equipment that would tell us if we had been 'shot' by the enemy. We also had a laser device on our weapons, which would register a kill, or an injury to the enemy. This mission, called 'Afghan Dusk', was a culmination of all that we had learnt since we started training for Afghanistan, and was an assessment to see whether we were ready for war.

After we successfully completed the MRE in Brisbane, we moved back to Townsville to organise our pre-deployment leave. We would have two weeks off and then return to work to be deployed.

As Shelly was posted to Sydney at this time, I went down and spent my time off with her prior to leaving. It was hard knowing that as every day came to an end I would be leaving sooner, and we didn't know when we would see each other next. Shelly and I worked out how, when overseas, I could let her know how long I was going to be on a mission. I would say to her that I would be depositing $600 in the bank. This would mean I would be away for six days, as $100 equalled one day.

We said our goodbyes at the Sydney airport and I flew back to Townsville, ready to deploy. It was so hard saying goodbye to Shelly at the airport.

We flew to Kuwait to conduct some final training. We spent around four days there, zeroing our weapons and conducting urban warfare drills with ex-American Rangers who were posted to Kuwait. Their knowledge was invaluable, as they'd had a lot of experience fighting in close quarters in both Iraq and Afghanistan on multiple tours. The four days we spent in Kuwait was also to adjust to the heat, which throughout the day was close to 40°C. It was just coming to the end of winter, and while in Afghanistan we would have to get used to temperatures well over the 50°C mark.

After a few setbacks from the Air Force due to the landing conditions on the runway at Camp Holland, our home for the next six months, we finally loaded into a C-130 Hercules and left for our final destination of Afghanistan.

TEN

DIARY ENTRY: THE SANDBOX

The following are extracts from the journal I kept while in Afghanistan. Notes in bold have been added to provide clarity.

14 April 07

Arrived in TK **(Tarin Kowt)** three days late due to the Air Force. Landed in TK at 1300 hours after a five-hour flight. As we got off the plane, two Apache helicopters took off and came past us. 50 metres away and 15 metres off the ground. Wow! Picked up by mogs and taken 500 metres over to Camp Russell. Camp Russell was named after SAS solider Andy Russell, who was the first Australian soldier killed in Afghanistan. We had a quick lunch and then moved into the briefing room for the regular briefs. These briefs included what you do for incoming rounds, the sounds over the microphone that indicate our rounds going out and rounds coming in, what happens if the base comes under attack, about the area we are located, e.g. where the mess hall is, phone, laundry etc. After that we were taken to Camp Holland. There we were moved into our sleeping areas. Five metres x three metres, with two bunks. The same size as a jail cell, but for four people. No aircon at the moment so it is hot in the rooms. 36 degrees in the day at the moment, but compared to two months down the track it is not too bad. Set up bed, so to speak. It's good to have a proper pillow and doona. Had a shower and shave. We have four toilets, four showers and four sinks for 96 people. Went to bed at about 2330 hours in the Ghan. Wow, we have actually made it.

OUT!

<u>15 April 07</u>

Up at 0600 and over to Camp Russell for brekkie. Had toast and rice bubbles, not too bad compared to the Dining Facility **(DFAC)** at Kuwait. 0730 started briefings and tour of camp. Section commander **(seco)** and 2ICs got on mogs and did a tour of the base with the RSM. The base is huge, with soldiers from countries such as Australia, Holland, America and many more small contingents occupying it. What is surprising is there is a green belt running north-west, which is of thick green vegetation running along the base of the mountains. Another amazing thing was the mountains 360 degrees around us. They were huge. We were at 1300 feet above sea level. Now I understand why they call the area the TK bowl. The boss gave us a quick overview of the up-and-coming operation **(OP)** which was a 22-kilometre patrol with no vehicles, eight litres of water, two day rats **(rations)** and a shitload of ammo. NO VEHICLES. We were told that we would not leave the Forward Operating Base **(FOB)** without armoured vehicles, but the op was on foot all the way. Had more briefs then tea, not too bad: fish and salad. Had a shower and hit the hay at 2300. As I got settled, seco came in at 2305 and we were given a brief on our upcoming op. It was to go from the 21st to the 24th and we were due back the day before the Diggers' birthday, Anzac day. We are to leave on foot and secure a d-fold **(a vulnerable point on a road, track, creek line, etc.)** in this case a dried-up creek six kilometres from Camp Holland for a convoy of Australian armoured vehicles to move through. After they move through we are to walk along the green belt **(the enemy's safe haven)** inspecting villages along the way to another d-fold **(a river crossing)** and secure that for two days, then move back to Camp Holland in vehicles after the engineers conduct their tasks. All up, a 12 to 13 kilometre, as the crow flies, walk carrying a bullshit amount of weight at around 35 to 40 degrees, and that without thinking about the enemy on our first time out of the wire **(Camp Holland)**. Seriously, I cannot wait, all this time spent to get over here and our first operation is not far off. I doubt I will get much sleep tonight, might have to watch a movie.

OUT!

16 April 07

Slept in today. Got up at 0730, got dressed and went up to Camp Russell for brekkie because we missed the mess at Holland. Ham and cheese toasted sandwiches and rice bubbles again. Moved to the Q-store in Camp Holland to be issued with grab bags with half the stuff missing **(a grab bag is a backpack containing food, water, thermal blanket, extra ammo etc. that would be stored under the seats in the vehicles. If we got into trouble, such as if an IED went off, and the vehicle and/or packs that were clipped to the outside of the vehicle were damaged, we would have supplies for at least 24 hours)**. Infantry always seems to be issued the essential equipment last. Go figure. Spent two and a half hours sitting around because the whole Company arrived to be issued equipment when it was supposed to be just our PL. After we finished at the Q-store, we went over to the mess for lunch. Waited in line for over an hour. Good feed, though. Had spring rolls, fresh bread and fresh salad. It tasted fresh anyway. After lunch we went back to the cells and worked on our gear. At 1530 we walked to the range, which is about two kilometres from our accommodation and test fired our weapons. We fired two mags **(60 rounds)** through the F88s, 2 x 40-millimetres from the GLAs, 200 rounds through the F89s, 2 x 7-millimetres rockets, two rounds through the 84-millimetres and also balanced and zeroed the MAG58s. We then moved back to the cells at 1800, had tea and points from the SGT. Did some 2IC stuff, watched *Odd Angry Shot* and bed. Ready to see what's next in TK.

OUT!

17 April 07

Up at 0700, had brekkie then moved to the RAP **(Regimental Aid Post)** to get IV bags for the PL. All the Diggers were on work parties so I took some time to laminate the maps **(making them waterproof)**. My portable DVD player broke last night. I spent about an hour trying to fix it but in the end it was more stuffed. I need a new one anyway. I will get one in Phuket, Thailand on ROCL. Had CFA training. I will make a medical kit up tomorrow, including drugs such as morphine and methoxyflurane. Did some more 2IC stuff for a while and found out we are not going to get our packs until after SFTG **(Special Force Task Group)** get their equipment shipped from Kuwait, which may take up to a month. What are we going to use now? Fucked if I know.

Got our ROCL dates today. We are going on 27 May, which is a month and a half earlier than we were told. But it will be good to see Shelly. We get two weeks in Phuket, but that is when Shelly is on Subject 4 **(promotions course in her field)**. I said we don't have to go but she insisted. Got to love her. BBQ for tea, best meal since we have been here.

OUT!

18 April 07

Woken up at 0627 saying I had to be at the stables **(where all the vehicles are stored)** at 0630. Got there at 0650, waited for an hour and after no-one rocked up the other 2ICs and I went for brekkie, then went back to the cells. Went over to the RAP and made up a med kit. Had lessons in All Arms Call For Fire **(AACFF)** then went over to the Dutch compound for brief of ammo and the capabilities of the Apaches. They are unbelievable. Weaponry includes a 30-millimetre chain gun, rockets and 4 x hellfire missiles. Got orders, which took over two hours. This is going to be an awesome mission. Had tea, got bullshit points from the SGT about a BBQ in two weeks. That was the last thing on our mind prior to a mission. Watched the movie *300* and went to bed at about 0000 hours.

OUT!

19 April 07

Up at 0700, went over to the stables to pick up some binoculars then down to the Q-store to get more equipment, which included our Soldiers Personal Radios **(SPRs are radios that allow the Section, PL or Company to talk to each other using different channels, and can also be also hooked up to the encrypted radios)**. Got drugs 2 x morphine, 2 x adrenaline, 3 x methoxyflurane, then went to lunch. Had a culture brief by the interpreter. Got more ammo and stores. Had a speech by the Australian Defence Minister Brendon Nelson, then went to tea. Had my first shisha since Iraq. It was the CSM's and it was great, so relaxing. Found some packs for my Section, as ours hasn't arrived yet. Packed our gear for a kit check tomorrow evening so we will be able to store our gear at the stables for our first op, leaving at 0330 on 21 April 2007.

OUT!

20 April 07

Woke up this morning with points saying a T-54/55 Main Battle Tank was seen at the place we have to secure for two days. A suspected IED was spotted by Tiger Shark **(a remote-controlled aircraft with a video camera that feeds footage back to the base)** being placed at a road junction, so we have to clear that as well, which will be very interesting. Got more ammo today. I will carry 10 x mags, 12 x 40-millimetre High Explosive (HE) grenades, 6 x 40-millimetre illume, 1 x red smoke, 1 x green smoke, 1 x red para flare, 1 x green para flare, 2 x grenades, 8 x pen flares, not to mention 10 litres of water, sleeping gear, first-aid kit, ET **(Entrenching Tool, a small fold-up spade/pick)**, body armour, 24 hours rations and more gear, adding up to a shitload of weight. We leave at 0200 hours, in the morning. I can't wait. This is going to be a FUCKING RIPPER. Fingers crossed this is not my last entry.

OUT!

25 April 07

Happy Anzac day. Back from OP Brisbane around 24 April 1200. Had a good few days.

We left at 0330 on 21 April in full marching gear, helmet and flak jacket under darkness, using NVG. We marched until daylight, when we stopped and took off our NVG. We then cleared the road/track junction using the engineers' metal detectors and the explosives dog named Sarbie. It was deemed clear, so we moved to the first d-fold — the creek/river crossing — and cleared and secured it. The convoy moved through, then we moved to a village named Talani. The first thing I noticed was the poppy fields everywhere. We were walking past millions of dollars worth of opium. The village had high walls all the way through it. It was like walking through a maze. If you lost sight of the bloke in front of you, you would be in a lot of trouble. We then rested for most of the afternoon, because there were a few blokes in the hurt locker due to the heat and the amount of equipment we were carrying. Also, we hadn't acclimatised to the area as yet. There were no trees or shade anywhere. The only shade was man-made, so we sat in the sun using umbrellas to keep ourselves as cool as possible. We watched as locals loaded soil onto trucks and also noted that a lot of people were carrying weapons. We moved into an admin harbor and prepared our NFE. This involved setting up the NVGs, NAD and the NWS for the F89s and the MAG58s. Once it was dark, we moved about two kilometres to our night harbor. This was so the enemy would think we were at the previous spot.

Up at 0330 on 22 April. We moved to a village called Spenchker. Once the engineers cleared the final d-fold, the PL moved across, leaving my brick of four to secure the western side by ourselves. A bit scary I must say, as backup was across the river/creek, approximately 150 metres away. After about four hours separated from the PL, we moved across to join up with them, which was good as my brick's job was to block the road so the engineers could do their thing. There were a lot of unhappy locals we had to control. We were then resupplied with rations and water, 24 hours late. Went to bed for the night, did a two-hour picket. Had a bad sleep. Was awake shivering most of the night, as our warm weather gear was with our packs in Kuwait.

Awake at 0430 on 23 April. At first light, my Section moved across to the standing patrol **(usually in a forward position from the main force)**. We talked to an old mujahedin fighter with an AK-47 rifle, and he told us that the tank our Intel told us about was an old Russian tank from when they invaded Afghanistan during the Soviet war between 1979 and 1989, and that he and his fellow fighters had RPGed **(Rocket Propelled Grenade)** the tank. Thanks Australian Intel for another great job. Got photos in front of the tank, the mujahedin fighter and the poppies.

Moved back to the PL just before last light, had tea, did picket, had a bit of a sleep, still cold and up again at 0430 on 24 April. At first light we packed up our gear and moved four kilometres to the Bushmasters for a lift back to base. Arrived back at around 1300, had debriefs, cleaned our gear, showered, shaved and bed.

Up at 0400 on 25 April for the dawn service. Had three beers, played two-up and called Shelly. It was great to hear her voice. Love her. Had a nap, had another shisha, watched the movie *Casino*. Finished reading a book about a personal security contractor and started to read a book called *Hell Fire Pass*. Wrote a letter to Shelly and basically relaxed. Ready for Section training tomorrow. I love Shelly.

OUT!

26 April 07

Not a bad day. Up at 0730 and did PT. Ran up to the range and up and down the range hill twice. The altitude is 1300 feet above sea leave and we are on the low ground. Back in Townsville some of the bigger hills are around 300 to 400 feet above sea level, so there is less oxygen in the air, making it harder to catch your breath. I did very well compared to some of the other boys, so I was happy with myself. We then ran back to the cells and did heaves. We filled out our leave for ROCL. Great, I get to see Shelly! We then unloaded a mog full of water and rations. Had lunch. Called Shelly. Love her. I looked on the internet at the hotel she booked in Phuket and it looked great, right on the beach. Got a package from Mum and Shelly. Mum's package had some great photos of me and Shelly when we visited them before I left. We then did AACFF, first aid lessons, emergency casualty evacuation and rules of engagement (ROE). The 2ICs (me) and the SGT moved up to the stables to do checks on all our gear. We were there for about two hours, did nothing and then went to tea. After tea I went to the gym and did cardio and push-ups. Got an idea of our next mission. Won't say too much now, but it has something to do with the gateway to the badlands **(they call it the gateway to the badlands because on the other side is where a majority of the TICs, or Troops in Contact, happens)**.

OUT!

27 April 07

Up at 0700, did picket at Camp Russell front gate. Uneventful. Came back and watched some Vietnam documentaries. Had a chicken burger from Echo's. It was fantastic, I will go there again for sure **(Echo's was a place where you could buy food if you missed the mess or wanted a change of diet, run by the Dutch)**. Rang Shelly again, it was great to hear her voice. Love her. Posted a package to her. Went to the gym and did cardio and heaves. Had tea and went to night picket. Uneventful. Got a warning order about our next mission **(so if you need to replace faulty equipment you have a chance to prior to orders, which are usually given a day or two prior to an op)**. The mission is to secure the One Hour Bridge from 30 April to 5 May **(called the One Hour Bridge because it's said to only last one hour before it's blown up, it takes one hour to clear it and the** way you pronounce the name of the bridge – Wanow – sounds like 'one hour'). Hopefully it will be fun.

OUT!

28 April 07

Up at 0700, chilled out for a while and had toasties at the Australian recreation room **(this room had a kitchen, internet access, TV, DVD player, chairs, couches, tables and phones)**. Went up to the range and fired five mags. My zero was off so I spent a bit of time adjusting my sight. Then we did some firing from different positions that the US ex-Rangers taught us in Kuwait. They were cool blokes and the biggest war dogs I have ever met.

Went back to the cells area, cleaned our weapons and had a BBQ for tea. Great feed. Then me and a few of the boys had a shisha. It was the best one I have ever had. Got rations for the next op. Were given some American 'Meals Ready to Eat' (MREs), which was a good change as they have more food in them. They take up too much room if you are on foot, but this mission was in vehicles. Had a shower and went to bed, ready for the next day and whatever it will bring.

OUT!

29 April 07

Up at 0630, sorted out ammo at the stables. Went to the Q-store and was issued with cold weather gear, one op too late. Went back to the cells and watched the movie *Shooter*. Not too bad a movie. Went down and confirmed leave app was all good. Called Shelly. She is sending me her portable DVD player tomorrow, so that will be good when it arrives. Talked to her for ages, which was good. Can't wait to see her. Found out op has been pushed back a day, so tomorrow is battle prep and rehearsals. Watched the movie *300* again and went to bed at about 2245 hours.

OUT!

<u>30 April 07</u>

Leaving tomorrow at 0730 for the gateway to the badlands, which leads to the Choir Valley. We are to relieve the Dutch QRF at the bridge, and secure and hold it for a minimum of five days. Because we are securing the bridge, it will allow freedom of movement of the Australians and the Dutch. Basically, we will be sitting targets for a long time. The poppy eradication team **(personal security contactors and personnel with whipper snippers)** was ambushed by up to 200 people at the same place we secured the d-fold for three days **(our first op)**. So the way it must look to the locals is that we were the reconnaissance team for them, which is not a good look for the Australians. It should be interesting to see how this turns out. I will miss not talking to Shelly for five days.

OUT!

<u>5 May 07</u>

Well, it's happened. We got hit, in particular our gunner. On 3 May, a Person Borne Improvised Explosive Device (PBIED) went off next to the Bushmaster, obviously killing himself, and injuring my gunner's left arm and two civilians.

It all started on 1 May. It was all going well, until at night our call sign **(41)** fired an illume round using the 84s. When the illume was fired, the Afghan National Police (ANP) contacted call sign 42 with small arms and then withdrew. We were told the enemy was going to attack us with a large force, so the Panzer **(a tank used at Camp Holland for illume and artillery missions)** and the Apaches were put on five minutes notice to move, as well as Tiger Shark being launched, which circled our area all night. We were put on 50 percent watch **(meaning half the blocks could sleep and the other half had to stay awake)** all night. Illume rounds were fired throughout the night from our call sign. Nothing came of the attack and we were all up at 0430 on 2 May.

The previous day we had built a sandbag fighting bay in a local's crop and we had to move them all back because he flooded the crop **(the farmers have irrigation channels running through their fields)**. We were all fucked because there were a shitload of sandbags and it was a fucking hot day. Normal pickets throughout the day. Took over VCP at night. The other Section fired illume rounds most of the night. Fucking loud, especially when you are nearly asleep and they are fired.

On 3 May up at 0215. We were into normal pickets until the afternoon, then *BOOM*. **(Myself and another 10 people were in a pit under a hutchie. I was supposed to be on picket in the Bushmaster, overwatching the western side of the area we had secured. Instead the SGT had me doing 2IC stuff, so I asked the gunner to go on picket until I was finished. At first, I thought it was an 84-millimetre being fired, until there was silence and then I knew something had gone wrong. I ran to the Bushmaster in the middle, then looked over to our Bushmaster. I couldn't see my gunner. I also noticed two civilians lying on the road. I called out to my gunner via the SPR and there was no answer. I yelled out to him. Still no answer. The medic and I ran over to the vehicle and opened the door to see the driver of the Bushmaster placing a bandage over the gunner's arm. I left the medic with him, as I still had one person unaccounted for. As I ran to the last Bushmaster in line, I noticed body parts everywhere and I thought that this was my missing member. I got to the last Bushmaster and opened the door to see the missing member asleep in there. He hadn't even heard the blast. Earlier, he'd had bad allergies so the medic gave him some pills and advised me that it may cause him drowsiness. I briefly told him what had happened and to gear-up, but to wait there as he was still very groggy.**

By the time I got back to my Section area, everyone had stood-to. I notified the SGT that everyone was accounted for. He was doing the medivac for the gunner. The medic had strapped him up and given him a big dose of methoxyflurane and was moving him to the middle

Bushmaster. He was high as a kite and didn't know where he was. He was pretending to drive the Bushmaster, without it running of course. It was kind of funny. Sometimes, you have to see the funny side of things to be able to keep going. This was the case in my stand-to position seconds later. I was sitting down and felt something warm on my behind. When I looked down it was what seemed to be the suicide bomber's arse cheek. I told the boys this and they all started laughing. It was good to lighten the mood after such a tragedy.)

I and another member of my Section treated the two civilians for minor fragmentation (frag) wounds and told them to go to the hospital in TK. The Dutch medivac convoy arrived and my gunner was evacuated to Camp Holland. **(Then there was the job of putting our gloves on, getting in an extended line and picking up the body parts so that the suicide bomber could be identified later on. At the time I thought nothing of it. It was just another job.)** We were then informed that a Vehicle Borne Improvised Explosive Device (VBIED) was going to come to our position on 4 May at 0100. A car did come at that precise time, but stayed back. When the driver noticed that we were all awake with a lot of weapons pointed at the car, it pissed off.

Fuck-all sleep, up at 0400 after stand-down and normal picket started. Later we were informed that the car was coming back at 1000 hours, so we stopped letting cars through. After a while, there were about 50 cars either side of the bridge with some pretty pissed off drivers in them. But one was supposed to be a VBIED. The boss decided that all personnel should either get in the Bushmasters or get on the opposite side of the thick mud wall either side of the road, and let one side of cars come through and then the other side, while we all hoped for the best. That five minutes sitting on the other side of the wall was a fucking long five minutes **(I was waiting to hear the biggest bang I had ever heard in my life)**.

Later that afternoon we started to move back to base, handing the bridge over to the ANP. I forgot to say, we arrested two males who we thought were possible spotters for the enemy, which was a good feeling. I am a gunner now, which means I'm not cramped into the vehicle and it gives the other boys a rest when in transit **(I stand up when in the Bushmaster/ ASLAVs, overseeing what is going on. I relay this information to my Section Commander, so if need be we can have a plan before exiting the vehicle)**. The amount of poppy fields over here is amazing. Got back to base, cleaned gear, had a shower and a shave. Our gunner met us in the stables with a big smile on his face, which was so good to see. He'll be okay but will miss out on one or two missions. Had tea at Echo's and went to bed for a good night's sleep.

Up at 1000 on 5 May, watched movies all day, had a BBQ for tea and then watched Tour de Force, which was really good. Then bed.

(After the BPIED went off, I decided that on ROCL I would to ask Shelly to marry me.)
OUT!

14 May 07

Not much going on to write about for the last six days. Went to the 100-metre range the other day. Was there for three hours and only fired one mag. The day after, we went to the High Explosive (HE) range. I fired 5 x 40-millimetre HE rounds. Another waste of time, as we could have utilised the range a lot more. Got orders today for the next op. Phase one will be going out for two days to secure a school and a mosque for the engineers to do their thing. Then back for two days, then out for three days on phase two. Then our Section will come back to base, ready for ROCL while the rest of the Company does phase three. We have been doing Section lessons and training, and I do CFA training with the Regimental Medical Officer (RMO) twice a week when we have time. I do cardio every day when we are on base, and the Section does heaves and push-ups on alternate days. Looking forward to ROCL and seeing Shelly, but I don't want to miss out on too much here. Hopefully, when we get back from ROCL we will do a few more METROs **(patrols around the city of TK)** and other missions.

OUT!

19 May 07

Back at 1600 on 17 May, loaded up with rations and water for three days. Had a shower, chilled out and went to bed at about 1930. Up at 0300 on 18 May. Moved to the Talani school, secured it by 1100. The engineers had installed a water tank, sea saw, monkey bars and a swing. They also made up outdoor tables and put in chairs and desks, seats inside, fixed up the windows and put locks on the doors. We are doing this mission for the hearts and minds stuff **(showing the locals we are here to help)**. Stayed at the school while we were there. We had two IED threats but nothing come of it. Up at 0200 on 19 May. After stand-down we moved over to the mosque and secured it while the engineers installed carpet and speakers. Moved back to the school, packed up and then moved back to Camp Holland. Tomorrow we are on Quick Reaction Force (QRF) for the SF, so that might be interesting.

OUT!

20 May 07

Uneventful day. Was on QRF for the day for SF but nothing happened. 41 call sign took over at 2100. Got orders for tomorrow. Our Section is to provide security for the LAVS and engineers while they secure the Talani d-fold, then we are to provide security for the LAVS while they overwatch the Spenchker d-fold while the rest of our PL go through to the 42 and 40 position to resupply them. After 43 returned, we went back to the FOB and got orders to go out on the 22nd for two to three days on phase two.

OUT!

<u>21 May 07</u>

Up at 0500, did the task. Uneventful. Dutch in major contact and one of their convoys was involved in an IED incident. My seco is in getting orders now (2000 hours) for phase two. He will probably give us orders at all hours, so I will try and get some shut-eye now.

OUT!

<u>23 May 07</u>

Back again. The mission went okay. Our Section was overwatch for the rest of the PL. Then we had to go to a school that the ANP had taken over after they moved into it. The Taliban had taken their headquarters. When the Americans found out, they dropped a bomb on it, destroying it. The problem with the ANP is they swing both ways **(the Afghan National Police and the Afghan National Army have been involved in the wounding and even the killing of Australian soldiers in the past)**. ANP one day, Taliban the next. They had a 4 x 4 twin cab ute that they had 'confiscated', parked at the back of the school. In the back of the ute was an RPG-launcher and three RPG rockets that they had kept. We couldn't do anything about it. When we got to the school, the 'ANP' were all drugged-up and on edge.

After we finished there, we went for a patrol in the village. The area was dodgy as hell, but a beautiful place right next to a flowing river **(I said to a few of the boys that if it was a different country I could have lived there)**. We then went back to our overwatch position. At 1600 the ASLAVS picked us up and we moved to the top of the hill, had tea and conducted night routine. When we looked back at the school we noticed that the ute had another RPG-launcher and two more RPG rockets in it, but still we couldn't do anything about it until we were engaged or in imminent danger. We did night routine, got a few hours sleep and were up at 0400 on 23 May. After stand-down we moved back to the FOB, cleaned gear, repacked everything and watched the first origin game. Queensland won, stuff them. Went back to the cells and chilled out. Might have to go out on the 25 May to resupply 42 call sign on the other side of the Tiri Rud. Should be fun.

OUT!

24 May 07

Got orders for tomorrow. We have to go and resupply 40 to 42 call signs with one days rations and water. It should only take three hours, but we are crossing the Tiri Rud at a spot that no Australian has crossed yet. So we are hatches battened down across the river, which is supposed to be only 600 millimetres deep, but who knows, not us. We have to be at the vehicles at 0500 tomorrow.

Got mail today: three packages from Shelly and one letter, a letter from my sister, one package from Mum and Dad, and two containers of homemade cookies from my aunty, which are awesome. Shelly sent me two DVDs of her talking into the camera, which was unreal **(I watched these DVDs over 100 times, at least)**.

OUT!

26 May 07

Mission went okay, but we were at the resupply place for three hours instead of 25 minutes because the LAVs had to be refuelled, which we didn't know about. Back at FOB we were put on radio picket until Sunday afternoon. Today I packed my bags for ROCL. Tomorrow we hand some gear in at the Q-store, ready to go to Kuwait Monday morning.

OUT!

28 May 07

Sitting in the cells again. Supposed to be in Dubai by now but we've had problems with our plane and have to spend another night in the Ghan. By rights we fly out at 0915 tomorrow straight to Kuwait, so we get there on the same day we were supposed to.

OUT!

ELEVEN

ROCL

Shelly was already in Phuket, Thailand when I arrived and it was great to see her. The hotel was fantastic, right on the main beach. Every day we would get up and have a full buffet breakfast, which included the freshest fruit I have ever tasted, and then go down to the beach and sit on the banana lounges. As it was not the peak period, we had no trouble getting a seat. You would pay around five US dollars and a local would set up an umbrella for you, moving it throughout the day as the sun would move. We would lay there half the day reading books, having the occasional swim and nap. We would also buy items from the locals, such as ice-creams and drinks. Every night at our hotel we would go to happy hour and drink vodka at half price, then go to one of our two favourite restaurants.

On maybe the fifth day, I sort of asked Shelly to marry me while we were walking along the beach, though it didn't come out right. She sort of said yes.

The next day we went on the hunt for a ring. Shelly found one that she loved, so I bought it and put it in the safe in our room. We agreed that I would have to surprise her when I asked her and do it properly this time.

The next day after happy hour at the hotel, we went to the room to get changed. While Shelly was doing her hair, I got the ring out of the safe without her knowing. We went to one of our favourite restaurants and had a few drinks. While Shelly was in the bathroom I asked the waiter to hold our table, as we were going for a short walk. When Shelly got back I said I needed to get some air and we went to the beach across the road. I got down on one knee and proposed to Shelly properly. She said yes and cried. We were officially engaged.

We went back to the restaurant, had a great meal, got tipsy and danced until the wee hours of the morning. We even ran out of money and Shelly had to stay at the table while I went back to the hotel room in the pouring rain on the back of a scooter to get money from the safe to pay the table bill.

The next day, we called our loved ones to tell them the news. We did a boat tour of the islands and went to the spot where some of the scenes from *The Beach* were filmed. The next night we saw a show about pirates and there were lots of loud banging noises, which scared the shit out of me and made me feel really uncomfortable for most of the night.

On the last night Shelly had to leave, so we checked out of our hotel and I checked into a hotel that didn't have the luxuries we'd had at the other, and cost less than a quarter of the price.

Saying goodbye to Shelly at the airport was one of the hardest things I have ever had to do. After she went through the gates, I went to the toilets, locked myself in a cubical and cried for almost 10 minutes. I then went straight back to my hotel.

That night I couldn't sleep, so I watched movies and Thai TV all night until it was time to go to the airport at 0700 the next morning to fly back to Kuwait.

TWELVE

DIARY ENTRY: CONTACT

<u>20 June 07</u>

Back from a very good ROCL in Thailand. I am now engaged, which is the best thing ever. Got back to Afghanistan on Saturday after a 24-hour delay, as the Air Force planes had some issues. Have aircon now, so it's nice and cool in the cells **(the aircon had been turned off for long periods during the day, as fuel supplies were running low at Camp Holland)**.

I went out on Sunday afternoon to do a medical evacuation from 41 call sign for a bloke that hurt his back. On Monday morning our Section went with the engineers to the hospital so the engineers could do a recon. It was crazy searching everyone who came in, especially after a VBIED in TK killed two Dutch soldiers and 13 civilians. This included seven kids. This VBIED was probably aimed at us, however the Dutch patrol was most likely an opportune target **(meaning the VBIED had a specific target, but as a better target presented itself, it attacked that)**. After we finished at the hospital, we walked over to the boys' school to join 42 call sign to assist them with security while the engineers were building a soccer ground. We did a recon in TK the next day, which was Sunday, for a future task that the engineers would possibly be doing. We then walked back to the school to continue our security with 42. When we got back to the school we met an ANP bloke named Asterix, who was in our minds crazy. He would stand in the middle of the road without a care in the world. The people there said the cars moved around him. He had a huge banana magazine on his AK-47 and it was decorated with different colours.

The task was completed at the school, so we walked to the roundabout and secured it for trucks to come from the base to pick up all the engineers' equipment. This was not the ideal place for us to be standing around for too long, and we were only supposed to be there for five minutes. However, we stood there for approximately 50 minutes, until the trucks came from Camp Holland. When they came through we moved to a harbor away from the roundabout and waited for the trucks to load up the equipment. We were told the Taliban was in the area and that they had approximately three IEDs and were looking for opportune targets **(such as slow-moving trucks)**. Once the trucks had been loaded up, we got a call to move back to the roundabout and secure it while the trucks moved to the FOB. After the trucks moved through without incident, we walked back to base, which was approximately three kilometres away. It was a very hard walk. We were lucky not to get hit on the way back to base, as we were a vulnerable target. Very lucky.

Go out on a METRO on Friday, planning is tomorrow. We found out today that 40 ANPs marched out of training yesterday. They were given their posting orders and loaded onto a bus. Once on the bus one of their classmates had set off a PBIED, killing all 40 people, along with himself. This is a fucked up place and a fucked up enemy we're fighting.

OUT!

21 June 07

Got orders for tomorrow's METRO. Our Section is to move to eight spots in and around TK in order to allow the recon group for RTF 3 to see the area, the jobs we're doing and the future tasks. Found out today that the Commando Selection Course doesn't start until June 2008. I'm shattered beyond words and I don't know how I will tell Shelly. I think I will wait until I get back. It just means our plans are pushed back six more months, but I love her and nothing will stop me from being with her.

OUT!

24 June 07

All went well on 22 June. Cleared all the spots for recon group to do their thing. A very hot day, about 48°C. Aircon has stuffed me around a bit, I think. We had a chloroform bomb thrown at us today from over a wall. Nobody was affected. We tried to find the person who threw it, however there was no chance. We tried very hard to find him. Got back at about 1630. When I took my body armour off I noticed that I had chafed all around my waist, about three inches thick. It's very bad.

Chilled out on Saturday and today we are preparing to go out in the next few days. It is going to be a very busy few weeks.

OUT!

26 June 07

On 25 June we went out on a METRO to the east and west checkpoints in TK as security for the engineers. All went well. Today we went to the Yaclankar medical centre and hospital, doing the same as we did the day prior. All went well, though bloody hot, 45°C plus. Today we only had five hours of power from 1700 to 2200, as there is no fuel because the Taliban 'owns' the road from Kandahar to TK. If we don't get diesel in the next day or two, the whole base is in a lot of trouble. Cannot sleep at night because it's too hot. It has gone on now for the last three nights.

OUT!

27 June 07

Got orders today for tomorrow. Up at 0230. We are going east of the One Hour Bridge to do a recon for crossing points north of the Tiri Rud. Should be okay, with about a five-kilometre walk along the river in the badlands. We also have to do a recon for an ANP checkpoint five kilometres east of the One Hour Bridge ANP checkpoint.

OUT!

<u>30 June 07</u>

28 June went okay. It rained most of the day. H hour **(the stepping-off point)** was at 0300 and spent three hours in the Bushmasters. Arrived at the ANP checkpoint to find out they had been attacked the other day by the Taliban. The Taliban had got as close to the checkpoint as the wire that surrounds it before the ANP were able to fight them back. Eight Taliban were KIA and three ANP were in a serious condition.

We walked along the Tiri Rud west, looking for crossing points, then walked through a cemetery to be picked up by the vehicles. A shot rang out and we all took cover. No-one knew what was going on. Two minutes later we found out that one of the blokes took a shot at a dog that was committed to attack him, but he missed and the dog left. Picked up and moved back to the FOB.

On 29 June we were QRF for the SAS out doing a mission for four hours and then we were QRF for a visitor, Alexander Downer. We met him and talked for about 10 minutes. On 30 June we non-teched our controlled stores, played cards and chilled out. Still only have power for about two hours of the day. We will be bone-dry of fuel if it doesn't arrive in two days. Because of the fuel shortage, the up-and-coming mission has been postponed until probably 4 July, possibly later.

OUT!

<u>5 July 07</u>

Not much happening in the last two days. Did some Section and PL training. Yesterday we were QRF for 41's METRO. Today an IED was found by the ANP at Sar Regin. We went out and secured the site while the engineers recovered the IED, then moved back to the FOB. Found out from Tiger Shark that we had been shot at. We were returning to base, but due to the noise of the vehicles and our hearing protection and radios, we didn't hear the shot.

Heading out to the range tomorrow to check our weapons are operating correctly. On 8 to 11 July we go up to the Choir Valley and will apparently do a bit of hunting. Should be really good.

OUT!

14 July 07

After orders we went out to the One Hour Bridge. We secured the bridge for 40 and 42 call signs. Once they pushed through, we moved forward and secured the crossroads for the V33 (ASLAVs) and 41 call sign to push forward up to Ponijak. After that we moved to our vehicle hide, to send our patrols from there.

On 8 July at approximately 1200, just before we were going out on patrol, we heard explosions and rocket fire approximately one kilometre to our north-east. V33 had been engaged with RPG and machine-gun fire. They returned fire at enemy positions as the enemy withdrew. We set up blocking positions to the south, but nothing came of it.

The following day 41 call sign assaulted where the enemy was, but they fled after the enemy had engaged 41 with rifle and RPG fire. 41 did not fire, as they could not see any of the enemy. However, V33 did see the enemy and got some confirmed kills.

The next day we conducted patrols around the Green Zone for the engineers' recces. That evening, we had two rockets fire over our heads. They were fucking loud. We thought we were in a bit of trouble, until we realised the rockets were aimed towards TK.

We conducted recces again the next day, and V33 and a Section from 42 were attacked by the enemy. Once again, enemy kills were confirmed. That afternoon, we had another rocket go over our heads. The Dutch fired 10 mortars at the position, which we watched from one kilometre away.

Back to the FOB on 11 July. On 13 July we had orders and preparation for METRO 44 **(44 stood for the number of METROs we had conducted).** It was cancelled the night before, as the president of Afghanistan was coming to TK to visit the government compound. We got orders to clear the village from where the rockets had been fired, and just before we left I asked the boss if there was any chance of contact with the enemy. He said that if it turns out the way everyone thought, every person in the PL would be able to write a book about the contact.

We left at 1300 on 13 July to the village and a possible imminent contact. We were all pumped up to the max. At 1800 we arrived at the village in advance to contact and swept through the village, finding that the village was deserted and there was no enemy present. We found a few old rocket casings and areas where the rockets had been fired from, but other than that there was nothing found. We then moved back to the vehicles **(disappointed, as the enemy had left)** for the night. The Taliban fired at the LAVs that night, but missed.

On 14 July at approximately 0430, we were told that the visit from the president had been canned due to the threat of IEDs. There were approximately 1500 Coalition personnel in the area, but it was still too dangerous for the visit. We had two other tasks of clearing two more villages, however these were cancelled, as they were no longer needed.

At around 0700 on 14 July, we were about to move back to base when a pressure plate IED prematurely went off approximately 400 metres from our position. It was fucking huge and it was on the track that we would have used to go back. We then moved back to the base without any more incidents.

We have a METRO on 17 July and an eight-day task in TK coming up. Should be interesting, as there are plenty of VBIEDs and PBIEDs in the area. **(The**

village we cleared was where eight rockets had been fired from. The mortars were zeroed-in on the vicinity of the governor's compound, as that was where the president would visit.)

OUT!

22 Jul 07

Went out on 20 July at 0200 to patrol base Jumbo, then did patrols all day. Yesterday at 0200 we secured a cordon around the AHDS compound. The pickets were two hours on and two hours off until 2300. We then moved back to patrol base Jumbo. Up at 0500 today. We did patrols all day and at 1700 found an IED-maker. We had orders to clear it, but were then told to come back to base to plan the raid better. Started planning, then the Dutch took it off us. Those bastards! If it was in IED place, it would have put RTF 2 on the map. We are leaving at 0300 in the morning to continue tasks at the AHDS building for five days. Just waiting for an IED to fuck us! What a great job! **(Being in one position for a long period of time greatly increases the chances of being attacked by an IED.)**

OUT!

27 July 07

Back on 26 July at 0400 from a long operation. It was only for six days in total, but a lot of night ops were conducted. On 23 July we went back to Jumbo. At 1300 we had orders to go in and clear a suspected IED compound. We were all pumped up, ready to go. My brick was the third to enter the compound and by the time we got in there everything had been cleared. We then set up a perimeter around the compound and secured it while the engineers searched for IEDs and IED-making material. My brick nearly shot a bloke driving his car, as he was not paying attention to the road and what was in front of him. What he didn't realise was that all four of us were on instant and had our triggers partially squeezed. He stopped at my final call. But I think he understood after I yelled at him.

After two hours the engineers didn't find anything, so we moved back and secured the AHDS compound. Later that day, shots were heard near 42's location. We found out later that they shot a bloke dead because he didn't stop when ordered to. **(As it turned out, he was no threat to us but wasn't paying attention. Our boys acted according to the rules of engagement.)**

The next day, after doing constant pickets around the compound while the engineers were flattening out the ground, at approximately 1600 the LAVs shot at a car because it didn't stop. They hit two kids. The locals were pissed off, so we came to the base early. Two of the local employed civilians **(LECs)** at the base protested about the shootings, but if the locals didn't listen to our commands then that was what would happen. **(We had so many threats in regards to VBIEDs that we had to treat every car as though it was a VBIED.)** The LECs were back at base today.

Been trying to relax as much as I can. Cannot sleep. There is still no power throughout the day and it's bloody hot. Looking forward to getting home. I miss Shelly something chronic.

OUT!

2 Aug 07

Starting to get on in the trip. Returning to Australia on 28 October, looking forward to seeing Shelly. Not much else worth writing about. Yesterday we did a METRO and will do one today, but the Dutch shot and killed some civilians yesterday, so we came back in early and all operations in TK have been stopped for at least 48 hours. Operation Sydney 3 is on from 6 to 15 July at Sari Gin. Our Section is attached to the LAVs, which should be good. If anything should happen out there we should get there first. I just want to use my weapon for once. I would be extremely satisfied with this trip if I got to fire back at someone firing at me. Fingers crossed.

OUT!

3 Aug 07

I am over this place. I am ready to go home. I miss Shelly like I never thought I could miss someone. It's driving me nuts. I hope to make it up to her somehow, she is so strong and so supportive. To top it off I have the shits. But I should be over it by the time we go out on Monday.

OUT!

5 Aug 07

Aircon back on from 1700 till 1200 the next day, which is good. Operation Sydney postponed until tomorrow at least. Sara Gin 1 and Sara Gin 2 checkpoints are fighting each other. The ANP in TK have arrested the commander of the Afghanistan version of the Highway Patrol. It is a fuck-fight, to say the least. One of the boys from my brick has been admitted to the base hospital with a possible liver infection.

OUT!

12 Aug 07

Back four days early, as the engineers finished ahead of schedule. Our job was to disrupt the Taliban freedom of movement at a village called Sinha Masaza. On August 8 the PL patrolled in to the village, minus my brick, which was overwatch with the Bushmasters. At around 0830 the PL was in contact for the next two hours. We were watching from the overwatch position and I had my radio over my ears, and when I took them off I could hear the rounds whizzing past the Bushmaster. There were no friendly casualties and they withdrew under the cover of the Apaches and the LAVs. We picked them up and went back to our harbor position. My brick was devastated. We had missed out on a chance at being in the action. The PL should not have been split up.

The next day we went back to the same area as the previous day, and as the bloke from my brick with the possible liver infection was not with us

I was lead scout. We caught a local in the area and questioned him for a while and then released him. We then withdrew to our harbor.

On 10 August we went back to the same area. **(We knew something was likely to happen, as just prior to us moving into the village the women and children were seen to be leaving from the opposite side to where we were located.)** With our Section leading, at around 1215 we were walking up an alleyway when we were contacted by RPGs and a fuck-load of small arms fire. The RPGs flew just above our heads, and the walls and the ground in the alleyway were exploding from small arms fire. We returned fire and broke contact. My boss had decided that the other two people in my brick would stay out of the alleyway, meaning I was the last person to withdraw from the area. When my Section Commander in front of me broke contact, I fired a 40-millimetre grenade and approximately 25 rounds of rapid fire from my rifle. I then withdrew from the alleyway, which was only about 10 to 15 metres, but felt like 100 metres. When I was clear of the alleyway the boss fired an M72 shoulder supported rocket down the alleyway approximately half a foot away from me, deafening my left ear for nearly 30 hours. Once I cleared the alleyway, the two personnel the boss had held back from my brick fired a number of rounds towards the enemy. **(I was told later that they could see the rounds chasing me back up the alleyway, hitting the walls and the ground.)** My brick was then told to move to the left-hand side and secure it so the other Section that was in the village could meet up with us and we would have all-round protection while calling in fire from the LAVs, the artillery back at Camp Holland and the Apaches. **(The order to secure the left side was given to me by hand signals from my Section Commander, as all I could hear was ringing in my ears.)**

Once my brick arrived on the left-hand side of the area to secure it, I noticed a Taliban fighter with his AK-47 across his chest advancing up an irrigation drain towards my position approximately 30 metres away.

I told my brick that once my 40-millimetre grenade landed for them to fire at the same position. I also fired approximately 15 rounds into the same direction, and the enemy was not to be seen again. **(We could not confirm the kill, as we were unable to advance and the irrigation drain was running back towards the enemy.)**

Myself and other members in the Section were then instructed to fire 40-millimetre grenades in the vicinity of where the enemy could have withdrawn to. The artillery from Camp Holland began firing at possible enemy locations, and the LAVs were also firing at enemy and possible enemy locations.

Once the Apaches arrived, they located our position and started looking for enemy positions. The Apaches engaged the compound containing a number of enemies with a hellfire missile, and also engaged enemies within the vicinity with their 30-millimetre chain guns. We then started to advance towards the compound that was hit with the hellfire missile. At that time, the Apaches were called to another contact in another area. Due to us being so deep in the Green Zone and with the number of enemies present, the Apaches would not leave us alone there, so we had to withdraw quickly back into the desert to be picked up by the Bushmasters prior to the Apaches leaving. **(Apparently the pilots got into some trouble over that, but I thank them for their decision to stay. We found out later that one of the pilots was an Australian woman, who had become a member of the Dutch Defence Force.)**

We were picked up by the Bushmasters and quickly moved back to our harbor. That night the Panzer, the artillery from Camp Holland, fired a number of illume rounds above the village, keeping the enemy on their toes the entire night. The next day we moved closer to the village with the Bushmasters and fired illume rounds from the 84s over the village to see if we could get a response from the enemy.

One night, it was observed by Tiger Shark that two people were setting up an IED in the area where the LAVs had been firing from. This area was the hill just across from our harbor. A sniper was set up to fire at the personnel setting up the IED. The sniper was to fire when an 84-millimetre illume round was fired in their direction, however the back blast from the 84-millimetre lifted up all the dust in the area and it obscured the sniper from a clear shot, allowing the personnel planting the IED to escape. Chatter was picked up and it was heard that the Taliban were saying, 'We can't sleep, we can't eat, we don't know who these people are but this is no jihad. We are leaving, these Australians are too good.' **(When we returned to base, we found out that the ANP had been ringing up the Taliban and saying, 'The Aussies are going to fuck you up, you are fucked,' and then hanging up on them. We also found out that a lot of important people had been either killed or badly injured.)**

We returned to base early, as the engineers had worked day and night to finish the job as quickly as possible. They did a great job.

I feel really sorry for the lead scout who missed out on all of the excitement due to being in hospital with a liver infection. Hopefully he will get another chance to get a contact under his belt.

The 8th was the worst day, as I missed out on the contact. The 10th was one of the best. I really love my job right now. I finally got to use my weapon.

OUT!

16 Aug 07

Been relaxing the last few days, which has been great. I have done a fair bit of PT, watched movies and slept. We watched the Apaches' footage from the contacts on the 8th and the 10th. I saw myself, my brick and how close the enemy was. It was good to see what we actually looked like from a bird's-eye view, especially during contact **(I wish I could get a hold of that footage for my personal collection)**. We watched the Apaches kill some enemies using the 30-millimetre chain gun and watched the footage of the hellfire missile being fired into the compound. Today we found out that we killed a minimum of 10 people total and a shitload more were in hospital. We also killed the enemy's doctor, meaning more will probably die shortly. It was heard from certain sources that the Taliban won't attack Aussies anymore because they feel like they're too good **(this we found out later to be incorrect)**. Also, the ANP and the civilians want the magic pills the Aussies take to keep them awake 24 hours a day. I have no idea what they are talking about! I can barely keep my eyes open now.

OUT!

20 Aug 07

Relaxing the last few days. Since the last operation the hierarchy have left us alone, which has been great. I have been going to the gym twice a day, but not much else. I read the book *The Real Bravo Two Zero*, which was 250 pages in 18 hours. It was a great book. We have a METRO tomorrow and another the next day. Not much chance of a firefight, but a high chance of a big bomb. We will see what happens.

OUT!

24 Aug 07

METROS went well, no dramas on 23 August. The other boys went out and hit a pressure plate IED. No-one was injured. Some damage to the Bushmaster. Today we were QRF for SF, then at 1600 had to go out north of the One Hour Bridge to drop off the piece of equipment that some people left behind and didn't take out this morning. They risked 40 blokes' lives because they didn't check their kit before they left. 41 got shot at from 900 metres away with small arms. Nothing came of it. Not much planned the next few days, possibly a METRO on 30 August.

OUT!

<u>25 Aug 07</u>

41 and 42 had RPGs fired at them this morning. We have to go out tomorrow morning and take a new tail shaft to them for the Mack Truck at their position. Should be an interesting ride out, as there is a high threat of IEDs and RPG attacks on the routes we are taking.

OUT!

<u>27 Aug 07</u>

Took stores to 41 and 42 yesterday. Cleared the road about five kilometres past One Hour Bridge, then came back later that day. 42 engaged the enemy, killing one and capturing two weapons. At 1300 today we go back out and set up OPs and blocking positions, and clear the same road we did yesterday in order for the withdrawal on the morning of the 28th.

OUT!

<u>29 Aug 07</u>

Yesterday we cleared up to the cemetery in the north past One Hour Bridge, and walked two kilometres back to the intersection to set up an overwatch on the road. I set up a Claymore, which was pretty cool. At 2300 that night, we got woken up because ScanEagle had crashed **(America's version of Tiger Shark)**. Our Section was about to set off when the boss decided to send 43A to find it, as they were closer to the area of the crash. Stood-to until about 0130 while they were out looking, however they didn't find anything. We then stood-down and I did a two-hour picket and went to bed.

Up at 0400 and at about 0600 did protection for the engineers while they cleared 500 metres north up the road. The Section in front of us, on the eastern flank, fired shots. We initially had no idea what was happening until the word came down to us to send a CFA up, which was me. **(Everywhere I went, I carried my 15-kilogram CFA bag. However, on this**

short mission I had decided I wouldn't need it. How wrong I was.) I sent a person back to get my bag and rushed forward to where the incident had happened. When I arrived, I found out that a van had not stopped when instructed and the boys were forced to use the rules of engagement. As in previous situations, the driver was not paying attention and was shot through the upper left shoulder. The round had gone through his shoulder bone, shattering it and exiting at the back of the arm. I cut his clothing off around the area of the wound, applied a first-aid dressing, gave him a bag of fluids and methoxyflurane for his pain.

While I was doing this, the other boys had secured the area and were inspecting the vehicle that was shot, taking photos for evidence for when we got back to base. Once the evidence was all collected and I was happy that the patient had been stabilised, we put him in the car and directed his friends to take him to the hospital at Camp Holland. We then moved back to the intersection and secured it while all the other call signs went through. We tagged on to the back of the convoy and returned to base.

When we got back to base we had two visitors: Minister of Defence, Brendan Nelson, and the Commander of the Defence Force, Angus Houston. They made some speeches and told us how good a job we were doing. The Minister of Defence was very funny. After that we had some tea and then got orders for a METRO on 30 August.

I then went to the hospital at Camp Holland and talked to the doctor in charge and he showed me the X-ray of the person I administered first aid to. That's when I saw how the round had shattered the injured man's shoulder. I was told by the doctor that I had done a great job, which felt pretty good. All the jobs in the hospital in Iraq had paid off. I did my SF application and relaxed.

OUT!

<u>30 Aug 07</u>

METROS went okay. We went to the eastern causeway and the hospital in the morning, and then to the Yaclankar medical centre in the afternoon.

OUT!

<u>3 Sep 07</u>

Home next month. Not far to go. Nothing on at the moment. SF briefing tomorrow. We don't go out until 14 and 16 September on Operation Villa, which is at the hospital. Been doing a fair bit of PT lately. Went for a 10-kilometre pack march last night with heavy weights, but I have a sore back today. Might have to lighten the load next time.

OUT!

<u>19 Sep 07</u>

Haven't written for a while. Not much going on. Still doing a lot of PT, results improving and training at 1300 feet above sea level. Should have good results when we return to Australia. Operation Villa went okay, nothing happened. Read the book *Bravo Two Zero*. 41 are going home in two days. We leave TK in one month and four days. Going out on an interesting operation on 23 September. Have planning in the morning.

OUT!

<u>26 Sep 07</u>

Well, where do I start? What an operation, with everything in it. Our mission was to disrupt enemy movement in order to allow 42 to recon checkpoints with the new engineers from RTF 3. The first place we went to was the sharkies defol **(dry riverbed)** to clear that. We were rear security until chatter came across that the enemy was going to attack us from the east side, so we moved over to that side to reinforce the other Section. At the end of the clearing we set up a defensive position while

42, 40 and the engineers came through. The enemy realised there were too many cars and withdrew. We then moved to the outskirts of Dew Jawz Barakzai, where we patrolled north through the Green Zone. Chatter indicated that there were enemy spotters in the area.

Something I forgot to mention was that north, past the 20 northing in the Green Zone, an ANP bloke assured us not to go there as it was a Taliban safe haven and that Coalition forces had not been there for a long time, if at all, and that no ANP or ANA personnel were willing to go into the area. So, naturally, we decided to go and have a squiz. Just short of the 20 northing we stopped for a 10-minute break, as it was so hot. We were told that if we wanted to we could remove our helmets and air our heads for a little. Then we were told contact was imminent **(from chatter)** so we put our helmets back on and started looking for possible targets. Also, due to the atmosphere in the village we were pretty sure, even without word from the chatter, that something was about to happen. The Section Commanders were given orders in regards to how we could initiate a contact. We were then instructed over the radio to move to our Section Commanders to receive orders.

As my lead scout stood up, all hell broke loose. **(When I think back on it now, this may have been how the boss thought we could initiate contact, by all of us standing up and giving away our position. Due to the position that my brick was in — a small irrigation ditch barely deep enough to get complete cover in — I felt that it was a bad idea for us to move, because if we did move we would give up the only cover in the area that was available to us. As one of the blokes in my brick stood up to move to the Section Commander, I told him to stop and stay down. But it was too late, and that was when it all began.)** We were engaged by a shitload of small arms and RPG fire from the north, from exactly the area on the map marked as 20 northing. We returned fire with small arms and the 40-millimetre. At this time, the lead scout indicated to me that he had been shot in the back **(he had been the bloke who had missed out**

on the previous contacts due to a liver infection). I told him to stay calm and keep firing. After a couple of minutes, when the firing had slowed down, I crawled over to him. Rounds were flying just over our heads and hitting the ground in front of us, kicking up little dust particles. Initially I didn't understand what these dust particles were, until I realised they were rounds hitting the ground.

I cut the strap on the lead scout's backpack, as I couldn't get it undone. I unclipped his webbing, then undid the side of his body armour. I then placed my hand under his shirt, placing pressure on his back. With my other hand, I grabbed my knife and began cutting his shirt away. He indicated to me that he had been shot where my hand was, and as I didn't feel any blood I was very relieved. I slowly moved my hand and noticed there was bruising and a small lump. I was so relieved. However, this feeling only lasted a second. That was when he told me he had been shot in the upper back as well. I repeated the same process and found the same result. I then instructed him to put his armour and webbing back on and to keep firing, and that we would sort the rest out when we got back to base, which he did without complaint **(even though he explained later that it was like being hit in the back with a sledgehammer)**.

I crawled back to my position and continued firing on enemy positions. It was at this stage that an RPG was fired in my direction and hit a small tree directly above me **(how I wasn't covered in shrapnel from the RPG still makes me wonder today)**. We were continually being engaged by a compound to the north-east. My brick was at the front north-west position of the PL. At this time, the brick that was in the position facing to the east was engaged by heavy fire, the rounds of which were landing at our feet and heads. Grenades were being thrown from the compound to the north-east as well. We were also being engaged from the north-east and west. Over the radio, we heard that at the compound to the north-east the enemy fighters were holding their rifles over the wall and shooting randomly in our general vicinity. It was just a matter of time before one of us was going to be shot in a place that was not protected by body armour or a helmet.

This was when we started engaging with our M72 rocket-launchers. Two were fired at the compound wall to the north-east, both hitting the exact same spot. However, no damage was done due to the thickness of the wall. Enemies were falling down after being shot. We kept copping a lot of rounds from the compound, approximately 100 metres to the north-east of us. Fast air **(Air Force jets)** were called in and the 500-pounder bomb was dropped, and landed approximately 160 metres away from us. **(This is what we call 'danger close', as for a 500-pounder bomb the minimum safety distance is 365 metres.)** It landed slightly west of the target, but it still made a huge impact. The firing slowed down in that area for a while. **(There was a lull in the battle for about 15 minutes. During this time, women and children were seen to be leaving the compound. I was wondering why we were just waiting there in the same position, being shot at instead of engaging the enemy. We were told, either during the battle or later, that a tier 2 leader was picked up talking on the radio, and that our command wanted us to stay in the area so that hopefully they could pinpoint his location and drop a bomb on him.)**

Over our personal radios, we had just heard that a member from the brick facing east had also been shot. Luckily, it hit his body armour and, other than a bit shaken up, he was okay. **(At one stage, one of the blokes in my brick stated that he could see an enemy popping his head up in the same position. I told him that the next time the enemy put his head up, he should shoot to ensure that he would not put his head up again. My bloke tightened the grip on his weapon and got into a good stable platform, for that perfect shot. I watched him breathe, while the weapon went up and down slowly with his breaths. About 10 seconds later, he fired and then paused. I yelled out to him, 'Did you get him?' to which I got the calm reply of, 'Yep.')**

The Apaches arrived in the area, located us and started firing at the enemy locations. We were in that position for approximately four hours, until it was decided that it was too dangerous for us to stay stationary. Under the cover of the Apaches we withdrew from the Green Zone, back out into the desert to meet up with the vehicles. It was decided that my brick would be the last to withdraw, so we provided covering fire using our small arms and smoke grenades. There was a shitload of firing from both us and the enemy. We withdrew to the south. We ran straight past a dead Taliban fighter.

When we got to a point where 42 had been sent to assist us with the withdrawal, we withdrew through their position and then patrolled back to the vehicles. However, once we got out into the desert, we were again engaged by the enemy in the Green Zone, with RPGs. I fired two 40-millimetre grenades into the area where I had seen the enemy fire from, and they landed within a few metres. The vehicles saw where my grenades exploded, which gave them a target. The Australian and American vehicles fired and we broke contact again for approximately 200 metres. **(I later found out from one of the Bushmaster gun operators that when they saw the explosions from my grenades, they also noticed the enemy. I was told that they were 'turned into pink mist'.)** We then patrolled up to the LAVs on the hill, about one kilometre away. We quickly reloaded our magazines, 40-millimetres and M72 rockets, and were told we were going back in.

As we were walking out, a 2000-pound bomb was dropped on the position that we had been in for the last four hours. 42 call sign went back into the Green Zone to engage the enemy and to see if the tier 2 leader was still in the area. However, after 20 minutes, they withdrew under the cover of the LAVs.

We walked back to the Bushmasters and set up all-round protection, approximately two kilometres away from the Green Zone, and watched as the vehicles did a fire mission on the village. It was the most amazing thing I've ever seen. Watching the rounds flying through the air, seeing the trace and then watching the secondary explosions. It went on for at least an hour or so, then we all loaded up and moved to a night harbor. It was approximately six hours since the first shot had rung out.

We had a feed, hydrated, pickets were conducted and we tried to get a few hours' sleep. Our sleep was interrupted by illume rounds from the artillery at Camp Holland and from the LAVs.

The next morning we secured the d-fold called Rabbit, which was near where contact had happened the previous day. 42 and 40 call signs went through the d-fold, then we went in and set up position overwatching the contact site. During the day we ran pickets, watching the village and the contact site and also getting a bit of rest. That night, the ANA fired at the village with a 50 cal.

The next day we went to an overwatch position at Mirabad. We were there for a while, until a huge bang went off when a herd of goats walked over a pressure plate IED, approximately 50 metres from the route we had driven. 42 call sign then moved forward for recon. They found some caves and with the assistance of the engineers these were blown up. We then moved back to base.

Just before we got back, one of the Bushmasters broke down and we had to tow it back. While removing the grenades from our webbing **(they were required to be placed in a secure area when we were not on a mission)** my Section Commander couldn't remove the grenade from his. We all noticed that he was having trouble and the Section converged on him. That's when we noticed that there was a round lodged in the grenade. This was why he couldn't move the grenade from the pouch. I tried to force it out, but then we decided to cut the grenade pouch open and take it to the engineers/bomb specialists. It was an amazing sight to see, a stripped round lodged in the grenade. The positioning of his grenade pouch and the fact that the round had hit the grenade saved his life. The grenade pouch was positioned on the right side of his hip. If it hadn't been there, the bullet would have gone straight into him. It is my belief, especially from what I've seen working in the hospital in Iraq, that he would have had no chance in the world, especially in the position we were in, deep in the Green Zone and under heavy fire.

Unsure of how many Taliban were killed. Reports at this stage say at least 20. Reports say that the amount of people that attacked us was up to 200. Who knows, but they got their arses handed to them. They realised the hard way once again not to fight with the Aussies.

OUT!

(Back at base I, and the scout who had been shot twice in the back, were video interviewed by the Army media. This footage was shown around Australia, and was also in the papers and on the internet.)

4 October 07

Back home to Australia this month. Can't wait. The other day we went out on a METRO to show RTF 3 members where the Talani school was, as well as the medical centre. On 2 October we went out there so they could build a veranda at the Talani school. We did our own thing, patrolled a little and did a few operations on suspected IED facilitators. Stayed two nights and came back today. We only have one major operation left, which is a recon in the Choir Valley. Apparently it is going to be either huge or massive. What a great way to end our deployment. I suspect I will be writing a few pages in this journal when we get back.

OUT!

9 October 07

Back from the Choir Valley on 8 October. It was an amazing place, huge mountains everywhere. We drove through the Green Zone and it was such a beautiful place, however it was full of enemy fighters. We did a vehicle checkpoint — two days searching a total of three cars. On the evening of the 6th, Tiger Shark crashed and we spent three hours looking for it, without success. The next day, 43B found it in two minutes.

On the way back to base, I heard over the radio that there was an IED incident at the cemetery. I heard 1 x KIA and 1 x PRI 2. **(As soon as I heard this over the radio, I passed it on to the rest of the Section. The only reason I could hear it was the fact that I was a gunner and was using the LAV's radios to communicate to the driver and the gunner/ commander. We were all in a state of shock and were told to hold position. We couldn't go down into the area and help out, as there was a strong possibility that there were more IEDs. We could see the black smoke approximately 200 metres away, however we couldn't move. It was so frustrating. The commander of RTF 2, who was back at base, was insisting that he be told the identification number of the member who had been KIA. But due to the severity of the explosion, his dog tags were nowhere to be found. The commander didn't understand, even after he was told why the identification number couldn't be found. This went on for what seemed like an eternity, until one of the blokes on the ground that was, understandably, frustrated said his nickname. It was the driver of the LAV from RTF 3. I passed it on to the rest of the Section. As our driver and commander were both from RTF 3, it was their friend who had been killed.)**

As soon as the engineers had cleared the area, we went down and helped secure the site. It was really great to see that all of the boys from 43B were okay. However, David Pearce had been killed instantly when an IED went off directly underneath his seat. **(I had chatted to him for about an hour, 20 minutes prior to the explosion while we were burning rubbish. When I returned home, I found out that the civilian roommate I had lived with**

before deploying to Iraq had been good friends with him. It's a small world.) It blew the hatch of the driver's compartment clean off and turned it into an oval instead of a circular shape. Just before we had arrived, the OC and the CSM had placed David's body in a body bag and laid it out in the back of the LAV.

We set up security with 43B while the damaged LAV was being hooked up to another LAV, ready to be towed back to base. Then we were told by chatter that we were about to be attacked. We quickly loaded up into the vehicles and the ANP led us back to Camp Holland. **(When we got back, we dropped our gear off in our rooms and then moved to the back of our accommodation and waited for the LAV to be towed back to the stables. It was like watching a hearse go past at a funeral. Seeing the damage done to the LAV, we knew David hadn't suffered at all. He wouldn't have even realised it had happened.)**

We had a ceremony today for David, which is the fourth we have been to on our tour. However, this is the first Australian ceremony we have been to. Tomorrow we will be on the airstrip to see David's body loaded onto a plane, ready for his trip back to Australia. I love this job so much, but sometimes it's just fucked.

OUT!

...

That was my last journal entry. After that, I didn't really care anymore. My main thoughts were getting home to Shelly, as well as seeing everyone else from RTF 2 get home safely.

We did some smaller missions after this. About a week later, we did METRO and went out to the Talani school and medical centre again. When we got back to base, after our last mission, it was such a relief that we had all made it.

We moved to Camp Russell, as most of the RTF 3 members had

arrived and taken over our accommodation. Our jobs there included cleaning and handing back all our stores and equipment, and cleaning our gear to the point where it would be satisfactory for Customs in Kuwait to clear it. This meant that all the grass, dirt and other organic material would need to be out of our equipment.

When sitting around one evening at Camp Russell, talking about what we were going to do when we got home, out of nowhere the Panzer fired three rounds in quick succession. The Panzer was only about 50 metres away from us, compared to the 200 metres it was to the cells. We had let our guard down slightly, as we had no more missions on and were not expecting any more loud noises.

When the Panzer fired, most of us who were sitting and talking jumped out of our seats, and at least five people ran for cover into the accommodation. I was one of the people running. But I was the last person to reach the accommodation door and when I got there only one person had gotten through. The other three were jammed in the doorway, fighting with each other to get through. They literally couldn't move.

By the time I arrived at the door, which would only have been a few seconds, most of us had realised that it was only the Panzer firing and that there was no threat to any of us. I pulled and pushed the blokes who were stuck in the doorway, to free them and let them know that it was just the Panzer. I let the bloke who had managed to get through the door know that it was just the Panzer and it was safe for him to come out.

We all sat down again and had a big laugh for a while, especially at the fact that the three blokes had been stuck in the doorway.

It was something I never really thought about until a lot later, years later in fact. This would not be the first time I would be jumping at loud and unexpected noises.

...

A couple of days later, we flew out of Afghanistan. I was 100 percent sure that this would not be the last time I would see this place. I was so, so sure that I would be back again. How wrong I was.

We spent about three to four days in Kuwait, handing back all our equipment so that it could be issued to the next lot of people coming through. We finished cleaning off the equipment that we would take back home and had it inspected by Customs. We had physiological briefs, then relaxed while waiting for our flight back home.

We eventually arrived in Townsville after a couple of stops, including three hours at the Darwin airport for refuelling, which dragged out a bit. I was so anxious to see Shelly that I must have gone to the toilet about 10 times, and as I was walking off the plane I had to stop and go in again, as my nerves were getting the better of me. I was quite surprised by this, as I figured that after six months in Afghanistan, after all the things I had been through, my nerves would be like steel.

The other blokes and I collected our bags, then there was a long wait to go through Australian Customs. Most of our equipment had been checked in Afghanistan, however it was required that it be checked again in Australia. There was no real order in regards to who went first, so there were a lot of people pushing in and trying to get through, as once they cleared Customs at the airport, they were free to go and wouldn't be required at work for a few days. It was a bit annoying that those who didn't have anyone waiting for them were going through first, especially when I knew Shelly was just on the other side of the doors.

After about an hour, I eventually got through Customs and came to the door I had been waiting to go through for six months. As soon as I walked into the airport terminal, there she was. Shelly was wearing a white dress that came down to her knees. She looked beautiful. I had never felt so happy in my life. To have her in my arms again was the best feeling, a feeling I can't explain.

We went to a motel that Shelly had booked on The Strand in Townsville, which is on the main road beside the beach. We spent a week there, before Shelly had to return to Sydney. It was so good to have her there with me. We went out to dinner most nights, had a few drinks and basically spent quality time with each other. As she could only stay one week, I spent all the time I could with her in between work hours. We were only required to be at work for a few hours a day and it was mostly administration, such as putting in our leave for the Christmas break. However, I wasn't able to have a break because I had a Special Forces Entry Test coming up in three weeks time.

I look at my mother and father these days and see that, during their 39 years of marriage, the longest time they have been apart has been about two weeks. When I think about relationships like theirs, it makes so much sense that the number of broken marriages and relationships within the Defence Force is so high.

...

While in Afghanistan everyone put some money towards having a book made up, detailing our deployment. It was titled *Rebuilding Afghanistan: the story of Australia's 2nd Reconstruction Task Force*. Some of the facts and figures that are included in the book are:

- Units involved: 44
- Personnel deployed as part of RTF: 393
- Dollars spent on construction projects: about US$4 million
- Afghan students trained by the engineers: about 120
- ANA soldiers trained: 180
- Contacts: six sustained attacks, plus numerous fleeting events with the enemy
- One suicide bomber attack
- One IED strike and another during the handover period with RTF 3

- Amount of mail processed: over 30 tonnes
- WIA/KIA: one WIA and three very lucky soldiers who were hit by Taliban rounds, but saved by protective equipment. David Trevor Pearce, who was killed in action on 8 October 2007, was part of RTF 3
- Combat rations consumed: 16,720 ration packs, or the equivalent of 50,160 meals
- Fuel consumed: 126,000 L of diesel
- Visitors: over 300
- Honours and awards given out included a commendation for gallantry, a Distinguished Service Cross, two Distinguished Service Medals, three Commendations for Distinguished Service, along with gold and silver soldiers' medallions.

THIRTEEN

SPECIAL FORCES: THE TEST

I began training for what would be my second and final attempt at the Special Forces Entry Test (SFET). This time I *was* going to pass with excellent results, and I *was* going to be accepted for the February 2008 Commando Selection and Training Course (CSTC). So, while the other blokes enjoyed their freedom, I used the fact that we had been in high altitudes for the previous six months to my advantage, and began training specifically for the test. I went to the hardest course on the base, a mostly uphill track, and began my training there. I practised sprints, interval training, pack marches, push-ups and pull-ups. For three weeks I absolutely smashed myself, to ensure that I would have no excuse at all when it came to the test.

I flew down to Sydney for the SFET. Over a six-hour period I did 71 push-ups, 100 sit-ups, 11 pull-ups, a 2.4-kilometre run in 10 minutes and 35 seconds, a 400-metre swim test in 12 minutes and 11 seconds, a 15-kilometre endurance march in one hour and 50 minutes, and a small obstacle course in 37 seconds. The results of the test were not to the extent of my ability, however while conducting the tests the directive staff (an SAS Warrant Officer who I had meet in Iraq) told us that all we had to do was pass. Then we would be on the CSTC in February. He had said to me, 'Don't go trying to excel yourselves at one component within the testing and wear yourself out for the next activity.'

So I did what I had to do to pass, and at the end I was given the joining instructions for the CSTC in February. The intention was that we would stay on barracks overnight, but if we had family there, or someone who could pick us up, we were able to go. I rang Shelly, who was not expecting my phone call until the morning, and told her that she was able to come and pick me up. My first challenge of getting to Sydney had been faced. Now I had to pass the second-hardest course within the Defence Force.

The SFET had involved a 2.4-kilometre run and a 15-kilometre pack march. The first part of the CSTC was an individual phase, which included a 3.2-kilometre run and a 20-kilometre pack march, along with a navigational phase and testing of basic infantry skills. After the individual phase, we went on to a six-day Special Forces Weapons Course, which went straight into the CSTC. This went for another 22 days so, in other words, I had a lot of training to do over the next couple of months. I figured I would be able to get through the course mentally because regardless of what you did physically, the mental part was what mattered and was going to get me through. I figured if I stayed in the same mindset I had been in for the past six months while in Afghanistan, I would be okay. Even though I was on holidays, I would always keep my mind on everything that I had done while overseas. If I had to go for a drive to the supermarket I would pretend that I was preparing myself to do a local patrol in Afghanistan. My mind would be focused on everything that happened, right down to the smallest detail, even to the point where I would be saying to myself, 'I should be at this roundabout by this time,' or 'I should be at the supermarket at a certain time,' and the same on the way home.

In terms of my fitness, as I was living with Shelly in Sydney I trained at Randwick Army Barracks. I had marked out the distance of the 3.2-kilometre run. When running I knew I had to be at a certain place at a certain time, and the next time I had to be even quicker. I was not going to give myself any excuses, mentally or physically, why I could not pass this course.

A week before the course was due to start I felt I could do anything in the world. Nothing could stop me, not even myself, even if I had wanted to. I had so much pressure on me to pass. I had promised Shelly the year before that I was going to do this course after she had made the commitment to move to Sydney. I had decided to go overseas and not move to Sydney. However, to pass a course like this you had to want to do it for the right reasons. If you wanted to pass the selection course just to tell the ladies that you were Special Forces, you wouldn't last two days. These courses were designed to break you, both mentally and physically, but if you had prepared yourself adequately you would come out on the other side, as long as you didn't injure yourself.

Unfortunately for anyone who had to spend time with me, between getting back from Afghanistan in late November and the beginning of the Commando Courses in late February, it was not an enjoyable time. I had to focus on what was coming up. To everyone who spent time with me then, I apologise. However, I believed that was what I had to do to complete the courses.

...

After what seemed a very short leave, I returned to Townsville in February 2008. I was posted to Alpha Company and put in a Section Commander's role. I talked to the boss, who had just been posted to the Battalion from the Australian Defence Force Academy (the officers' version of recruit and IET training, but goes for a lot longer) and explained to him my situation. I explained that in two weeks time I would be doing the CSTC, and that a few days after I had returned from Afghanistan in November 2007 I had started training daily. However, because he was new to this position, he expected me to do all the administration for the new blokes who had marched in the Battalion, as well as take over as a Section Commander. He was very keen to prove his position in the PL and in the Company. I just wanted to be left alone to do my training.

I went to the CSM, who is usually the only person the Diggers and the NCOs can talk to if they are having issues with the officers, and I requested that I be able to train. He said that he would have a talk to the boss for me, which I appreciated. Within half an hour of being

TOP: In position on an Armoured Personnel Carrier in Timor.
MIDDLE: Patrolling in the Timor bush.
BOTTOM: Waiting for extraction by UN helicopter.

TOP: The 6B Land Rover with the broken steering cable. The round hole in the roof was my position.

MIDDLE: Vehicle patrol around Gleno.

BOTTOM: Patrolling around Maliana.

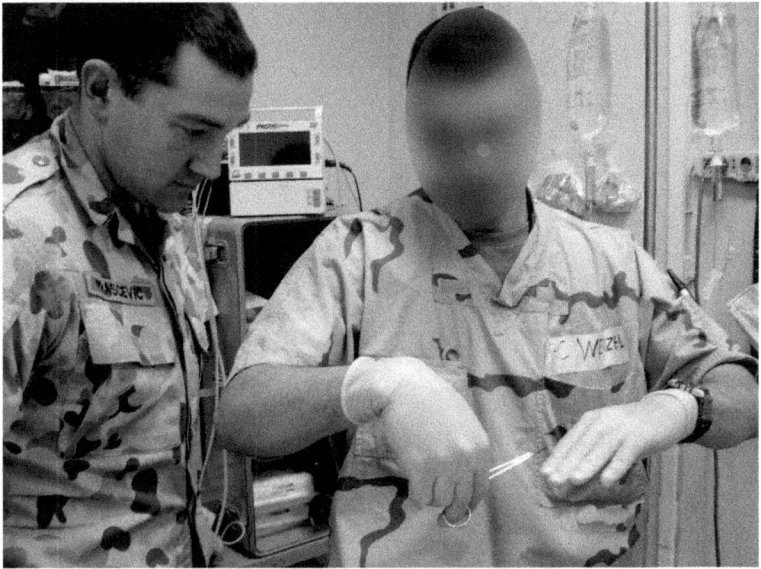

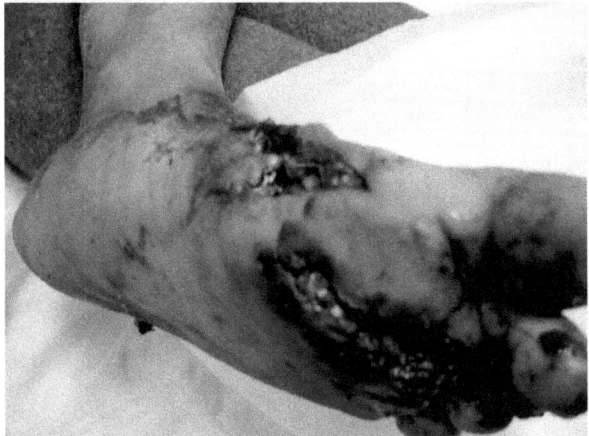

TOP: Demonstrating the heat generated when IEDs explode.

MIDDLE: Learning to 'stick' at the American hospital in Iraq.

BOTTOM: The Iraqi's foot I worked on with a fellow medic. The round went in the top of the foot and out the bottom.

'The Old Man' and I on the roof of the COB, with The Crossed Swords in the background.

TOP: Overwatch at the COB by day.
BOTTOM: The COB at night.

TOP: Looking at the Green Zone from the *dasht*.
BOTTOM: Preparing for a long march.

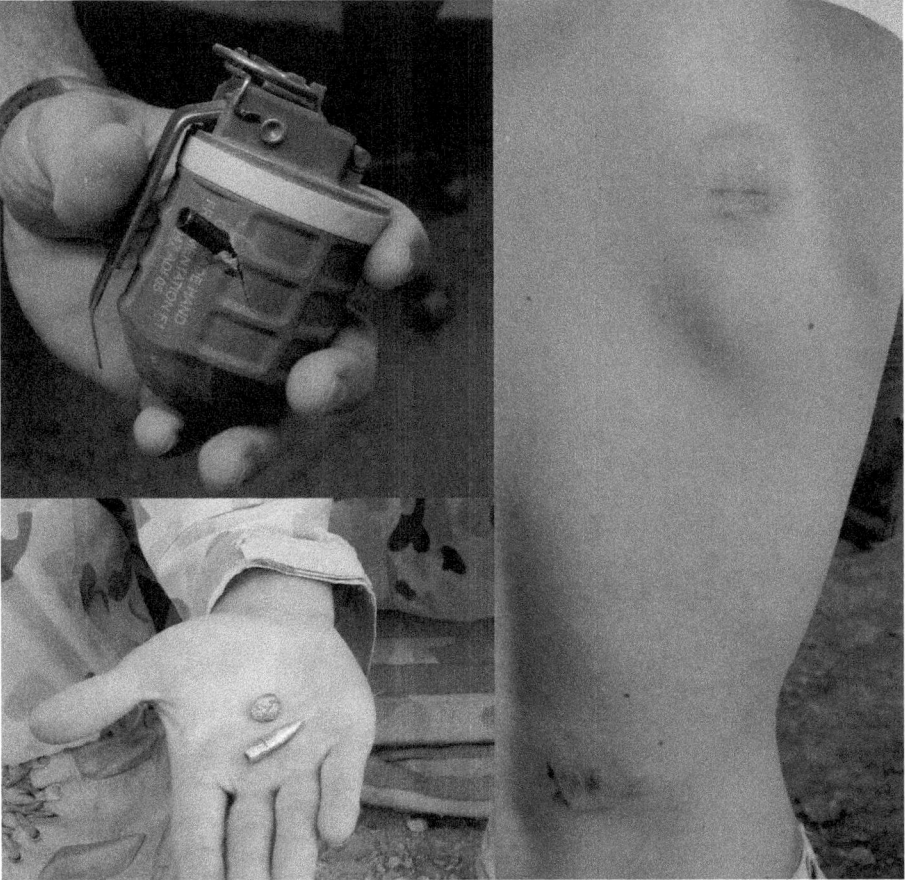

The round in my Section Commander's grenade. The bruises on my scout's back the next day and the rounds pulled from his armour.

Medals I received. At the top, the Infantry Combat Badge. From the left, the Australian Active Service medal with Clasps from Timor, Iraq and Afghanistan, Afghanistan Campaign medal, Iraq Campaign medal, Australian Defence medal, UN medal and the NATO ISAF medal.

back at the PL, I was called into the boss's office and told that he'd had a conversation with the CSM. I was to train the blokes as ordered. I tried to get across to the boss how important this was for me, and eventually he relented and I was able to do my own PT. This was a slight win for me.

Two days prior to going to Sydney to start the CSTC, I was told that due to the fact the Battalion might be going to Fiji, I would be unable to attend the CSTC. For the next 24 hours, I could have killed anyone who looked at me the wrong way.

The next day at the Battalion boozer parade, I approached the CO and the RSM of the Battalion and told them that I was disappointed at not being allowed to attend the CSTC, as I had trained for this for so long and had even gained experience overseas. I was told to stand aside for a couple of minutes, then I was called back and told that I was able to attend the CSTC. What annoyed me was the fact that when I had put in my application the year before while in Afghanistan, the CO had given his highest recommendation for me to become a member of the Commandos. However, when he told me that I was allowed to go at the boozer parade, he looked at me as though I owed him something. This moment fired me up, and during the tough times on the CSTC I thought about that moment and it inspired me. I never wanted to return to the Battalion.

The next day, I boarded a plane to Sydney. I met up with some other blokes who were also waiting for the bus to Singleton. We ended up waiting there until well after dark, until the bus came to pick us up. The bus driver told us that he didn't realise he'd had to pick up people from the airport and that he'd already been halfway to Singleton. He had turned around after receiving a phone call stating that we were at the airport waiting for him.

By the time we arrived at Singleton it was about 0100 hours. We were shown where to set up our stretchers. We slept until about 0700, when we were woken, had a shower and shave, had breakfast and then were told to line up in three files. We were then asked by one of the staff, in a very nice manner, to stand at the front one at a time and tell everyone why we had come here and why we wanted to become a Commando. After about three of four people had spoken and stated the basic response, that they wanted to further their careers and that what they wanted couldn't be offered in the Battalion, the staff began yelling at us, as though someone had flicked on a switch. The course had officially started!

We were told to pick up our gear and were marched down to the front of the gym. We had to lay out all our equipment, which was inspected. Anything that was not on the equipment list was thrown into a garbage bag with our name on it, and would be picked up at the end of the course. We were then given numbers to wear on our shoulders. They would be our names for the next 32 days. I was number 25.

As I was a big sweater and it was summer, I was sweating to the point that you could see the sweat marks through my shirt. One of the staff looked at me. I can remember the look on his face. He was probably thinking, *This bloke is going to collapse soon of dehydration.* He yelled out, at the top of his voice, 'From now on, everywhere you go you will have a water bottle on you at all times!'

We were given a 'withdrawal at own request' form. If we weren't injured, but we didn't want to continue with the course, we had to fill out and sign the form. We were told to have it on our person at all times, no matter what. However, I had gone through so much to get to this point that at the first chance I got I threw the form away. If I was going to get into trouble because I didn't want to carry around a piece of paper that said I was weak, I would accept the punishment. I didn't want to have that negativity in my pocket. If we were injured while doing the course, we would be able to come back and try again. But if we filled out the form, we would never be able to attempt the CSTC again.

After our gear inspections, we moved to a room and were told about the history and current setup of the Commandos. After that, we were quickly taken over to the beginning of our 3.2-kilometre run. The warm-up shocked me. There were some really fit blokes on this course. Had I trained enough?

After the run was completed, we were given a feed and told that in half an hour we were to know the names of every single person there. If not, we would be punished. At that time there were 76 blokes on the course. As I was still a bit buggered from the run, which I passed, and I didn't want to waste too much energy, I turned to the bloke on my left and said, 'Hi, I'm James,' to which he replied, 'G'day, my name is Merv.' We got talking and we both agreed that they would punish us regardless of how many people's names we knew. After a while, we realised that we had been in 1 RAR together.

After the meal, we were loaded into mogs and taken to the 100-metre range, where we were required to set up sleeping tents, a tent for the staff and a medical tent. We were then loaded back into the mogs and driven 20 kilometres away and dropped off for the start of our pack march. We had three hours and 15 minutes to complete it.

I came in just under three hours. It was now approximately 0200 and we were allowed to sleep until 0700, when we were woken up and given lessons on the radio we were to carry during our navigational exercise. The old radios were used in Vietnam and felt like they weighed a tonne, along with the heaviest spare batteries you could get. Throughout the day we were issued our equipment and then tested on basic soldiering abilities. This included judging distances and All Arms Call For Fire (calling in fire support). Later that evening when we were tired, we were given another lesson on a different radio that we would use later on. This was to see whether we would be able to remember what we had been taught days prior.

We were allowed to sleep for a few hours, then woken up early. We were loaded into the mogs to begin the individual navigational exercise. We were dropped off at different locations and given instructions, such as to not talk to anyone or walk on any marked tracks or roads. We weren't sure how many checkpoints we had to go to, but we knew there was a minimum we would be required to reach throughout the day and night. This meant that every time you got to a checkpoint you would continue on to the next one asap, remembering that you had to conserve your energy because you would be walking all day, for most of the night and into the next day.

After God knows how many kilometres, I decided that I had to sleep for a couple of hours, as I was unable to walk anymore. The weight of my pack, rations, water, radio, spare batteries and other equipment was starting to take its toll on my feet. I ended up sleeping on top of a prickly bush that was sticking into my arse the whole time, but I didn't care, as long as I was off my feet. After a couple hours of sleep, I woke and went to the next checkpoint. I was told to move to a road junction and wait for a vehicle. Did I do something wrong? When I arrived at the road junction I radioed in to notify that I was there, then the vehicle picked me up. When I was in the vehicle I asked the staff member why I was being picked up. He told me to shut up. I thought that was it for me!

When I arrived back at the tents, there were three people sitting around in the sun on the stretchers. The staff member told me to drop off my gear and wait. I asked the other blokes what was going on, and I was told that I had enough checkpoints and had finished the navigational exercise. Was I relieved!

Over the next couple of hours, three others arrived back via the vehicles. Then a radio call came through: we were to load into the mogs. Somebody had lost their pack and radio. We were taken out to an area where that member had been and he said that he had placed his pack in the area of the checkpoint while he boxed around to its exact location (walked around in a square-shaped pattern). We found the pack and radio and returned to the tents, where by now everyone else had returned.

We were given the rest of the day off after being divided into teams. I was given the job as Section 2IC and my Section Commander was a guy called Tim Aplin. I was happy to be working with him, as I had known him when he was the Pioneer Sergeant in 2 RAR when I was in Charlie Company.

The next day we began the Special Forces Weapons Course, which qualified us in the basic weapons that we would use during the course. Every morning we would be packed into buses and sent onto the base, where we would conduct the hardest PT sessions you could think of, which felt like they went forever. The PTI Sergeant (who was Commando-qualified) was the PTI from the SBS documentary *SAS: The Search for Warriors*. This was about the selection course for the SAS and, after watching it, I can say it is a somewhat accurate depiction of the CSTC. After these brutal PT sessions were conducted, we would return to our tents, then learn how to use the weapons before firing them at the range.

Throughout the day we would be punished, for small and insignificant things, with push-ups. We would be punished by the number we had on our shoulder, for example, because I was number 25, if I stuffed up it would be 3 x 25 = 75 push-ups. Although, if number 76 stuffed up it would usually only be times one, thank Christ. No individual was punished alone. If someone stuffed up, everyone was punished. If we didn't have time to be punished throughout the day, the punishments would accumulate and, prior to going to bed for a few vital hours of rest, the push-ups had to be done first.

For the first couple of nights during the weapons course, the blokes who had failed the 3.2-kilometre run and the 20-kilometre pack march had a chance to attempt them again. On the first night they conducted the 3.2-kilometre run and in the morning a few blokes were packing up their equipment, as they had failed and were going home. The blokes who had passed were joining us for another brutal PT session. The next night was the 20-kilometre pack march re-test, and once again the next morning there were people packing up their equipment and leaving. But there were also people there who were joining us for a PT session after finishing their second 20-kilometre pack march just hours before. The lesson was 'pass the first time', as there were so many other things to worry about. This nearly became the case for me, as my weapon continued to have stoppages when conducting one of the shoots to pass the qualification. Every round we fired was worth points, and the fact that I continued to hand back a minimum of five rounds every time a shoot was finished meant I was in trouble. I swapped my weapon after being warned about my shooting ability and the next time I fired a good score.

One day during the weapons course we had a legionnaires' day. We were required to run everywhere we went, including to the toilet, at a very fast pace.

Late one night, we cleaned weapons for hours. The staff were reading out instructions, which were given to us only to waste our time and to cut into our sleeping and relaxing time, which they often did to see if we would crack under pressure. One of my mates literally fell asleep while standing and fell over onto the ground. That's how tired we were and we had only just started.

After finishing the weapons course we began the CSTC. This was it. All the other crap that I had done before meant nothing. This was the only thing that mattered in my life now, and I was 100 percent mentally and physically focused. Nothing could break me! I was ready!

I knew it was about to get serious because I could see the PTI's car arriving. I could tell by the way the staff were acting that the game was about to step up.

Approximately half an hour after going to bed, we were woken up by the staff yelling out, 'Get into your marching order and line up in front of your tents!' They were yelling, 'Hurry up, hurry up!' Regardless of how fast we went, it wasn't fast enough for them. On these courses, regardless of what you did, it was never fast enough or good enough. Even if you were Superman, they would expect more out of you. That's just the way it was and we knew that.

Over the next three weeks we were taught Commando tactics, techniques and procedures. We also did live firing and were subjected to days without food or sleep to see whether we had the mental and physical capability to be part of the Special Forces. I won't give away too much about the details of the course, as it is designed so that the people who do it don't know what to expect. However, I will tell you about one part of the course that was exciting for us all.

Midway through the course, the Black Hawks were conducting training within the area and they became available to us. The staff took this opportunity to qualify us in fast-roping. Fast-roping is when a rope about 30 metres long is dropped out of the helicopter. From inside the helicopter you reach out, grab the rope and slide down to the ground without the helicopter landing. This technique is used on buildings, ships and uneven ground, and if there are trees or man-made structures that may get in the way of the helicopter landing.

Initially, I thought this was going to be a joke and we would get a large rope, throw it over our shoulders and start running with the staff yelling out, 'Now you are fast-roping, run faster!'

We went over to the ropes where we conducted our BFTs and there was a scissor lift, which we went up in and then practised grabbing onto the rope and sliding down to the ground. We did this until the staff were happy that we would be able to do this from a helicopter. We then went out to a cleared area and I was still thinking they weren't serious. That was, until the refuelling truck and three Black Hawk helicopters arrived.

We were given some briefs by the helicopter pilots and then did some dry runs, meaning the helicopter would be on the ground and we would practise kicking out the rope and getting out in order. We then did it for real. We went up in the helicopter with the rope coiled up at the open door and with me sitting on top of the rope. I was the first person out. When we got to the target position I stood up slightly and the person behind me kicked the rope out. Once the rope hit the ground, I grabbed onto it and slid down to the ground. We did this for most of the afternoon at different heights and also cruised around in the helicopters, which was a great break from the intensity of the CSTC. It was more of an instructional course, so they couldn't yell at us as much. We were being taught something that, if we stuffed up, could cause serious injury or death.

Another thing I can tell you about the course was the damage it did to our feet, as we were always on them. One bloke, later killed in Afghanistan, couldn't put any pressure on his feet at all and I had to carry him around once we finished the CSTC.

When the CSTC was finally over, only 26 of the original 76 had completed the course. Some had been injured, some had been kicked out and some had used their 'withdrawal at own request' form.

Once we cleaned all our equipment and handed it back, we had to wait outside the office to be called in by the CO to find out whether we had passed. This was the hardest part of the course for me. Twenty-three people passed, which included myself. I was told that I had completed the course extremely well, I was extremely well-prepared and that the staff didn't have any worries with me at all during the course, apart from the stoppage incident while conducting the live fire shooting on the weapons course. I was recommended to continue on with the reinforcement cycle to become a fully qualified Commando. At that stage, I was Commando-qualified 079-1. All I had to do was to get 079-2, which meant completing the reinforcement cycle. This moment was the proudest moment of my military career, and was at that stage the proudest achievement of my life.

The next day we loaded onto the bus and were taken back to Sydney, where we were given a week's leave to recuperate before starting the Special Forces Roping Course. I spent the week with Shelly. We went to a bush area, where we spent a few days relaxing in a cabin. And I needed it. My friend (the one who had fallen asleep while standing up) and I figured out that over the four-week test we'd only had on average three hours of sleep per night.

...

Once we returned, after a well-earned break, we conducted the roping course. We were taught how to ascend and descend ropes in different ways. We were taken to a five-storey building used by the fire brigade, where we ascended and descended ropes. The course went for five days. The first four days I hated it more than anything in the world because when I was a plumber working for myself, I'd had a bad fall while on a roof, luckily while using a harness. I had jumped out of planes at 10,000 feet without any issues, but being close to the ground gave me the shakes big time. Only on the last day of the course did I start to understand that I could trust my equipment, so I enjoyed it thoroughly.

Then we did a combination of everything we were taught over the week. We abseiled off a cliff face in the bush then, utilising the knots we had been taught, we pulled up an injured patient (a dummy filled with sand) and then ascended the cliff face using a climbing ladder. I was so pumped up that I was wishing I had just trusted my equipment from the start, as I would have enjoyed the week a hell of a lot more.

After that was completed we went back to Singleton, where we conducted a week-long shooting exercise. We were taught better shooting techniques by a sniper. I learnt more in this week about shooting than I had in all my years in the Defence Force.

Then we conducted the Special Forces Heavy Weapons Course, which would qualify us to use the 50-calibre heavy machine gun and the MK 19 grenade machine gun, which fired the same 40-millimetre grenades I used in Afghanistan, but were on a belt and fired in quick succession. We were also trained in the 84-millimetre rocket-launcher, which I was already qualified to use. Firing these weapons on the range and seeing the destruction they caused was unbelievable, especially being able to fire 40-millimetre grenades as a machine gun. It was a rush!

Next we went to Nowra to conduct the Basic Parachute Course (BPC) and I was soon to experience a rush of a different kind. I was to find that there was a huge difference between jumping out of an aeroplane at 10,000 feet with a square parachute, and jumping out of an aeroplane at 1000 feet using a round parachute, in marching order. There were two parts to the BPC. Part one was landing on land and part two was landing in water. Part two was normally only conducted by Special Forces, as it was one of their insertion methods, meaning they would jump into the ocean (inflatable boats with engines would also be deployed from the aeroplane) and insert onto the land to conduct a mission. However, prior to doing the water part it was required that we be qualified in jumping on land. This method is the same as the one used in World War II. It is designed so you fall quickly, so the enemy has less chance of firing at you. Due to this old method, many people injure themselves during the BPC. Unfortunately, I was to be one of those people. The BPC course was usually run over three weeks, but it was condensed into a two-week course for us. I felt as though we were rushed through the course.

For the first week we repeatedly conducted drills for when we were in the aeroplane preparing to jump out, what to do as we were falling to the ground, what to do if we were falling towards trees or powerlines and how to land. The parachutes used were not the easiest to steer, especially as we were falling so fast and only jumping out at 300 metres.

The Army parachutes are on a static line, with one end hooked up to the plane and the other end attached to the parachute. This means that when you jump out your parachute deploys immediately, so there is no freefall. When you jump out of the plane, it feels like you are on a big slide. If you have that feeling, you know that your parachute has opened.

The drills were done over and over again, until it was certain that we were confident and competent in what we were doing, before we were to actually jump out of the plane. During the drills, we had been strapped into harnesses hanging off a metal bar that would swing back and forth. We would fall off the bar, landing on mats in different positions, practising our landings. We would also go to a mock-up plane, where we would practise our drills. These drills were conducted all day, as well as at least two sessions per day, with an hour on each activity. After that was completed we went to an area that had a mock-up plane with lines that looked like a giant flying fox running from it, and we were to jump out of this plane. We would practise our falling drills while going along the flying fox. Once we got to the end we would practise what to do if we got caught in powerlines or trees. Then we would go back to the start and do it all again.

Just prior to jumping out of the plane we had to do one final test which, if we passed, meant we could continue on with the course. If the staff were not satisfied, we would be pulled off the course. In the tests we would be hooked into a harness and lifted up off the ground, about 30 metres, where we would conduct all our drills. We would then be released and come down at the approximate speed we would come down at when parachuting out of the plane. I was told that the impact of an average landing is equivalent to hanging off a second-storey building and then letting go. It was not like when I was a civilian parachuting where, if you landed correctly, it would be just like taking a step. I was just under 100 kilograms at the time of jumping, not including my parachute and reserve parachute, so I felt that I didn't classify as an 'average' person when it came to weight.

For some reason, I volunteered to be the first person to jump out of the plane in my stick (what they call a group of people who are jumping). As I had previous experience with jumping out of planes, I was very confident that I would be able to complete this course without any dramas. The first three jumps went okay for me, even though every time I hit the ground, I was surprised that I was able to get back up again after the impact. The round parachutes were definitely different compared to the square parachutes that I'd used in civilian parachuting. I knew that all I had to do was three more jumps and I would be qualified. Then I would rarely have to do land jumps again, because once qualified you were required to jump only once every year to keep your qualification. SF did water jumps to avoid the land jumps and the high risk of injury. It would be all water from then on in.

On the fourth jump we were given a parachute that we were not required to be tested on. This parachute gave us better capability to steer. As I had jumped out first every time, I asked my friend Tim Aplin if he wanted to go first this time and he replied, 'Yes.' So we swapped around, and he jumped first and I was second out of the plane. I didn't feel any different jumping out second, however when I hit the ground I knew something was wrong. I had dislocated my left ankle, and broken my tibia and fibula bones.

I didn't feel any pain at all, as I was in shock. However, after yelling out to the medics and personnel to come to my assistance, I started to cry my eyes out. I knew that my career in the military, or at least the infantry, was over. My Special Forces campaign had finished.

I was given methoxyflurane and, as I was CFA-qualified, I knew exactly how to get the most out of it. I sucked in as much of the drug as I could. The medics were placing a bag filled with air around my ankle and leg, which was off-centre, to try and hold it in place. I couldn't stop myself from crying because I knew how much effort I had put into getting to this point, and I knew that it was all over. A close friend, who was with me the whole time, later notified Shelly. I will never forget him saying, 'Stop crying you bastard, or you will make me cry!'

But I couldn't stop. How was I going to come back from this? All my friends who I had gone through this with would move on and forget about me, and I would be sent back to 1 RAR where I would wait for a medical discharge. I would never be able to recover to the point I was at no more than two minutes prior.

I was put in the back of the Army ambulance and taken to the Navy hospital, where my ankle was put back into place. Then I was taken to the Nowra Private Hospital, where I had pins and plates inserted into my leg.

I had passed the second-hardest course in the Army. I was stronger than this. This was not over for me, not by a long shot.

FOURTEEN

REHAB AND MARRIAGE

When I woke from the operation, Shelly was there waiting for me. The next day I was discharged from the Nowra Private Hospital and Shelly drove me to the 1st Health Support Battalion (1 HSB), which was the hospital at the Holsworthy Army Barracks. I was taken into the care of the doctor there and eventually discharged. I was able to go home to Shelly's house and try to figure out what I would do next. Was I going to go back to Townsville, or could I stay here in Sydney? Breaking my leg had not been part of our plan, and there was a very real possibility that I would be sent back to Townsville asap.

A week later, the doctor removed the staples from my surgery wounds and my leg was put into plaster. It was decided that it would be best for me to stay with Shelly. I didn't want to go back to Townsville. Because I lived on base, and due to the duty of care rules that the Army abides by, I would have had to stay in the hospital until I was able to return to work. For me, this was not an option. There was no way I could live in the Townsville hospital for eight weeks. I would go crazy!

During those eight weeks I was in plaster, I put in request forms to be posted to 2nd Commando, Special Forces Training Centre Detachment East (SFTC), and the reserve Commando unit in Sydney. After a time it was decided that I would be posted to SFTC, where I would complete rehab. Once fit again, I would finish off the reinforcement cycle. I could also do the non-physical courses while recovering. This took a lot of pressure off me, as I hadn't known what was going to happen to me for a long time. At least for now Shelly and I were posted to the same location. I would be able to focus on my rehab and come home to her every night.

...

While everything started to fall into place at work, as I was now posted to Sydney, my personal life was in trouble, big time. Every time I closed my eyes, I would re-experience the last two seconds of the parachute incident. It would replay in my mind over and over. This went on for weeks, until the only way I could shut it out was with alcohol. After a while, every time I closed my eyes I would re-experience events that happened while working in the hospital in Iraq. I remembered breathing for the young American Lieutenant who had lost his arm and leg and had major shrapnel wounds all over his body. I remembered pulling the tubes out of the bodies of the deceased personnel.

Shelly, who'd had her mother living with her for support while I was away, also had her old dog living with her. This dog was a black poodle named Kia. She was a beautiful old dog and Shelly wanted to get another one to keep Kia company. I agreed, as I thought it would give me something to focus on and it would also make Shelly happy. We bought a little black pup, another poodle, who we named Lily.

The people who sold her to us told us that she was eight weeks old. When we took her to the vet that evening to get her checked over, we were told that she was lucky to be three weeks old and that the paperwork they had given us was fake. She was smaller than my hand and could barely stand up. When she did stand she could only walk a couple of steps backward. We regularly had to take her to the vet for fluid injections under her skin, as she wouldn't eat or drink for the first few weeks. If we hadn't done this she would have almost certainly died. After Lily had eventually settled in, Kia took her under her wing and taught her how to drink, eat and where to go to the toilet.

As I have mentioned before, those people who exploit dogs make me sick.

...

Once I got my plaster off, I started to focus on being able to walk again. I would do two physiotherapy sessions a day, a session in the hydro pool, and also spend an hour swimming laps at the regular pool. My plan was to get off crutches asap, as Shelly was planning our wedding and I wanted to be able to walk on the day, or at least be able to stand without crutches for the photos. Shelly and her mum were planning the wedding. All I had to do was make sure I could at least stand up. Also, I had to make sure I didn't put on too much weight, as I was going to wear the suit I had tailored for me in Thailand, where I proposed to Shelly. For me the idea of a perfect wedding was one where I had the people who are closest to me there. That was all that mattered.

Shelly and I were married at the Chinese Gardens in Sydney. We then went on a boat tour of Sydney Harbour and finished with dinner at Quay Restaurant, situated between the Sydney Harbour Bridge and the Opera House. It was perfect, with 20 of our closest family and friends to share it with. Unfortunately for me, I was still on crutches, though on the day I forgot all about the discomfort and was at least able to wear matching wedding shoes instead of a CAM moon boot. It was still the best day of my life.

...

After a couple of months, when I was able to walk again without assistance, I was put back on the SF course. Firstly, I did the Special Forces Amphibious Insertion and Extraction Course, which enabled me to be qualified to perform as a crew member on a boat. This included setting up the boat, ready for insertion and extraction by sea/water. Next was the Special Forces Demolitions User Course, which enabled me to assist other members in setting up demolitions, and also carrying them in a safe manner. And then I conducted the Commando Signaller Course. By this time my fitness was improving and my ankle was healing so well that I was put on the Basic Mortar

Course. The course was available at 2nd Commando. In the Battalion, courses like this were run only once a year. This was what separated 2nd Commando from the Battalions: there was always a chance for you to improve your capabilities as an individual soldier.

Once I had finished the mortar course, I had surgery on my ankle to have the pins and plates removed. I then had six weeks to wait before I could begin to run and pack march again. The holes in the bone, from the pins, had to heal.

...

Although things at work were going along okay for me, I had a lot of problems going on inside my head that I was not dealing well with. The memories from working in the hospital in Iraq were constantly there. I would get angry at the smallest things, especially while driving, to the point where I was almost scared to drive. I was afraid of what I would do if I was involved in a road rage incident. Sometimes when I was driving, I would get so angry that I would just look for someone who I could yell abuse at, and sometimes I was even hoping for someone to get out of their car. I needed an excuse to unleash the rage that was building up inside me. If someone had gotten out of their car, I would have had no hesitation getting into a physical fight. I just needed to get rid of the pressure that was building up inside me, but I didn't know how.

On the outside things were going as well as expected, considering that I hadn't planned on breaking my leg in two places and dislocating my ankle. But on the inside, my head was going crazy. I was having nightmares about Iraq and Afghanistan. Everything that I did and everywhere I went, something reminded me of the hospital there. Everything seemed to be a trigger. When I was at work I was able to focus on rehab, but I could only do that for a certain number of hours each day.

I started to feel excessively guilty, as well as being very depressed, and I developed very low self-esteem. I began drinking nearly two and a half litres of wine a night.

With all this going on, my relationship with Shelly started to develop difficulties. Although I didn't want it to be that way, it was as though it was all about me and not at all about Shelly.

...

After six weeks, my X-rays showed that the holes in my ankle bones had healed. I started to push myself very hard so I could get back to the level of SF fitness. One of the Companies from 2nd Commando unit was doing an annual fitness test (which was the same as a SFET, without the navigational part) and I decided to prove my fitness by doing this test. There was a course coming up and, if I passed, I would be able to be posted to the 2nd Commando unit.

I trained very hard and on the day of the fitness test I passed it all, with better results than I had at any other time. However, when I got to the 10-kilometre mark of the 15-kilometre pack march, my ankle started to seize up. I had never felt that amount of pain in my life. But I finished the march, with five minutes to spare.

When I got home that evening I was unable to get out of my car due to the pain, and the next day I was unable to put any weight on my leg. On the Monday when I returned to work, still unable to bear weight, I went directly to the physiotherapy department to get a set of crutches. I saw one of the staff members, so I put in some leave for the week so that no-one would see me in this condition, and I went home.

For the next week I did everything I could to try and recover, from using ice and heat packs, to stretching. After a week I was able to walk, though I was limping very badly. I hid it the best I could from my bosses. I had to convince them that I was fit enough to be put on the next course, which I managed to.

When the course began, however, the staff realised straight away that I was injured and that I should not be in the course. But I didn't want to give up. They would have to kick me out if that was going to be the case!

After three weeks of emotional turmoil, I was eventually pulled out of the course and told to come back in six months when I was fitter. But something had changed inside me, between the moment I had broken my leg and now. At the time, I had no idea what it was.

A few days later I was told by one of the staff that regardless of how much I wanted to pass, I was never going to due to my injury. A week later I did the Special Forces Close Quarter Fighting Course and Subject 2 for Corporal, and was then posted to the School of Infantry in Singleton.

My ankle hadn't recovered from the break. Would it ever? Physically, I was not done for yet. Mentally, I was just hanging on the edge. It wouldn't take much to tip me over.

FIFTEEN

SINGLETON

Returning to Singleton was hard for me, as the last time I was there was in the early months of 2008, just prior to breaking my leg on the parachute course. I marched into the School of Infantry (SOI) RSM's office to find out where I was going to be working while waiting to see an ankle specialist, as it would take time to fix the grinding in my ankle. The RSM, who I knew from 1 RAR, made me feel really comfortable and told me that I was going to be helping out at the Training Support Platoon (TSP). TSP provided the SOI enemy and infantry demonstrations, such as contact drills, for the PTEs doing their Initial Entry Training (IET) prior to being posted to a Battalion. The RSM gave the TSP SGT a phone call, letting him know that I was there and to come down and pick me up. The RSM and I had a long chat about past days in 1 RAR and what I'd been up to over the last eight months.

When the PL SGT from TSP arrived, I noticed that he was an old friend from 1 RAR who I had also been deployed with on RTF 2 to Afghanistan. I said goodbye to the RSM and went over to the TSP offices. Once I arrived, I had a long chat with the PL SGT and the boss. I was allocated a room in the accommodation block, issued all the equipment required, such as an enemy uniform, and then told to sort out my room and return the next day. Normally the accommodation for the rooms would cost around $150 a fortnight. However, as I was married, I came under the status of 'Member with Dependants Separated' so I didn't have to pay for the accommodation, as I was already paying for a house in Sydney where my wife lived.

The next day when I arrived, I was allocated a Section and was told that I was going to be acting Section Commander until my surgery. As I was posted to Singleton in a 'pool position', meaning that it was not an official position, I was unable to be promoted to CPL. This didn't worry me too much, as when I finished the reinforcement cycle I would drop rank back down to PTE and have to work my way back up again. My good friend Tim Aplin was an infantry SGT and was about to be promoted to WO Class 2. However, when he finished his reinforcement cycle, his rank went back down to PTE.

I was very unhappy with my life overall and didn't understand what was going on in my head. I had the motivation to keep pushing myself physically regardless of the outcome, as I was so focused on getting my ankle fixed and finishing off the reinforcement cycle. I had to get my green beret, which I had dreamt of and worked so hard for, for so long. Every night I was still drinking very heavily, though I hid it well and no-one suspected how much I was drinking. The boys would go out a few nights a week. They would always ask me if I was keen on going out but I mostly declined the invitation. I would go to the gym and punish myself physically. I thought that if I put all my energy and negative thoughts into the time I spent at the gym, I would be able to release those thoughts. However, once I got back to my room, which had only a single bed, a desk, a chair, a TV and a wardrobe, I would fall back into the bad thoughts and start drinking again.

While at Singleton I would drink on average around 2.5 litres of wine per night. I would drink warm white cask wine — it didn't worry me that it was warm. All I wanted was to be able to relax, to stop my mind going around and around, going over thoughts over and over. I wanted to drink until I was so drunk that my memory was wiped.

I kept this secret from the blokes I was working with. I was doing it behind closed doors, when everyone was either in bed or out. The period I was posted to Singleton I averaged three to four hours maximum of sleep per night. As my wife was still posted to Sydney and was living in a house in Sydney's southern suburbs, I would drive three hours home every Friday night, spend the weekend with her and drive back at around 2000 hours on Sunday night. I was so exhausted, but the first thing I would do was start drinking as soon as I got back.

I was getting sick of being apart from Shelly all the time, but we supposed that eventually we would both be posted permanently to the same location again, in Sydney, and be able to live the best we could as husband and wife. The problem was that when I was home I was too afraid to leave the house. Just around the corner from our house was the main street, which included a number of shops. Shelly would want to go and have a coffee or breakfast in the main street, but I didn't want to leave the house. All I wanted to do was sleep and drink. Some Saturday nights we would go to our favourite restaurant, have a few drinks there and then come back home to the spa. However, for me to get the confidence to go out I would have to drink nearly a litre of wine and then drink at least another bottle over dinner, sometimes more. Sunday would come around far too quickly and leaving Shelly at our house alone to go back to Singleton was harder every time.

There were a few good things that I can say I enjoyed at Singleton, and they were mainly the blokes who I spent time with there. A few of the blokes who I hung around with used to go shooting at my mate's uncle's property. We would go hunting for foxes and rabbits. We would always go up in my mate's Holden Rodeo ute, which was a three-seater. It was a two-hour drive to the farm, and one time we decided that we would stop at the RSL halfway there and have a feed, as we would be shooting well into the night. When we got out of the ute, we noticed that we were all wearing black T-shirts, which was a slight embarrassment as no-one had noticed it before and it obviously wasn't planned. There was a group of thugs in Singleton who would pick on the Army people. They called themselves the 'Eight Ball Gang', which we thought was a ridiculous name, so we decided to call ourselves the 'Black Shirt Ute Gang', or the BUGS for short. We all thought this was very funny. As the Eight Ball Gang was apparently a serious gang who thought they were all very tough (even though they would only pick on an Army bloke when he was on his own) we would say that our gang, the BUGS, were serious also. We would say, 'BUGS,' then pause and then say, 'Serious,' in a serious voice. I used to enjoy those times.

A lot of the staff who were posted to Singleton were great to be around, especially the CPLs who I knew from the Battalions. To be posted to a training establishment is a very hard thing to do, as you have to teach people how things are done, by the book. It puts a lot of strain on a CPL's own life and detracts from his personal time, as his time is mostly dedicated to the PTEs who he is constantly teaching.

To all the blokes who I served with, especially five in particular (you know who you are), I thank you for making my time at Singleton a bit easier.

...

As I had arrived at Singleton in late October, I couldn't see the ankle specialist until after Christmas in mid-February 2010. So in February I received a referral to an ankle specialist in Sydney.

Sitting in the waiting room a few weeks later, I was very nervous about what he was going to say. Once in the room he made me take off my shoe, then he bent my left ankle up and down, feeling and listening to the grinding sound it was making. He told me to put my shoe straight back on. I was really worried at that stage, as the examination had only taken about 10 seconds and he already knew what the problem was. Was it bad? Was it good? Those few seconds, before he told me his diagnosis, felt like an eternity.

He told me that I had two options. The first was that he could fuse the ankle, meaning that screws and pins would be inserted into my leg and down into my ankle, and that my ankle would be locked at a 90 degree angle for the rest of my life. The second option was an arthroscopy. He then told me that due to the impact of the parachute incident and the impact that I had put on it during my recovery, it had forced my leg bone to compact on the ankle. He explained that the grinding I could hear and feel was my leg bone grinding on my foot bone. The simple operation meant that the doctor would make two small cuts at the front of my ankle. In one cut he would insert a small camera and in the other cut a bone shaver would be inserted. The bottom of my leg bone would be shaved in order to make a gap, which would allow me to bend my ankle back and forth without the two bones rubbing together.

I made the decision straight away that we would give the arthroscopy a go, due to the fact that if I did the fusion, that would be the end of my military career. The date for the surgery was booked in for six weeks later.

Just prior to seeing the ankle specialist, Shelly had been deployed to Afghanistan. Although I was extremely happy for her, as this was what she had wanted and had worked so hard towards for such a long time, it was extremely hard on me. One of the reasons I joined the Commandos, other than being part of the elite in the Defence Force was that I would be able to deploy overseas on a more regular basis. The blokes who I had done the CSTC with were already going overseas, and here I was waiting for an ankle operation that may not even work. I was stuck at Singleton playing enemy for IETs. I was so, so jealous of those being deployed. For some reason being posted to TSP is a punishment, and here I was after passing the second-hardest course in the Army with flying colours. But at that time, I felt like I needed to be punished because I had fucked up, and broken my leg in two places and dislocated my ankle. It was all my fault and I deserved to be punished. So for the six months that Shelly was away I stayed in Singleton in my small room, drinking, with my mind feeling like it was turning into an uncontrollable tornado that was growing bigger as time went on.

The tasks at TSP were very demanding, and at the start I was required to spend a lot of time outfield. This was hard, due to the fact that I could not fall back on the alcohol at night and, as I had been drinking so much for such a long period of time, I would get withdrawal symptoms every time I went outfield. Up until then I'd had a very successful career in the Army, during overseas deployment and courses back in Australia. I believe this was due to the fact that I performed well under stressful environments. But now, when I was given even the smallest task to conduct, my mind felt like it was a gathering storm. When outfield, especially at night, we were given tasks, such as attacking the PTEs positions every few hours. Although I could have allocated these tasks to the Section members under me, I went out on the majority of the tasks, as I couldn't sleep and I didn't want to deal with the nightmares I was having every night. When outfield, I was unable to drink the alcohol that I had been using to help me sleep and avoid the nightmares, which I would get anyway. I found this very hard because by the time we came back from being outfield, which averaged around a week at a time, I was very sleep deprived, even more so than I was when I was not outfield. I couldn't figure out what was going on with me. I understood that it was the fact that I was injured. In the back of my mind I knew that I was never going to be able to do the parachute course again, even though I was telling everyone that my ankle was fine and all that was required was the arthroscopy, then after that I would be good to go. In my mind, I knew that was not the case at all.

...

In March of 2010 I was in Sydney Private Hospital, waiting for my arthroscopy to be done. Shelly was due to have ROCL during my recovery period, and we had been trying to organise to meet up and spend 12 days in Koh Samui, Thailand. However, the issue for me was whether the doctor would sign a permission form saying that it was okay for me to fly so soon after surgery. Some areas overseas are out of bounds for Defence Force personnel, for example, during my entire nine and a half years of service no-one was permitted to go to Bali. My leave therefore had to be signed off by my boss which, luckily, was granted.

The arthroscopy was a success, and a week after the operation I flew to Thailand to meet up with Shelly. The trip over there was a pain, as I was still unable to put weight on my leg and required crutches. However, I was treated well when passing through Customs, and while getting on and off the planes.

I arrived in Thailand the day after Shelly arrived. I got a taxi from the airport to our hotel, where I met Shelly in the lobby. It was so great to see her — I had missed her so much. A little golf buggy picked us up and took us down to our room. The hotel that Shelly had organised was right on the beach and we had our own pool.

That first night was the best sleep I'd had for so long. I finally had Shelly back in my arms and nothing could take her away from me, at least for the next 12 days.

I had taken my computer with me, as at that time I was doing online units through the Open University. If I finished I would receive a degree in Security, Terrorism and Counter Terrorism. The idea was that if something happened to me during my military career, such as if I was injured overseas while serving as a Commando, I would be able to fall back on my degree, and still work overseas in the same environment that I had worked as a Commando, but in the private sector.

In Thailand, most mornings Shelly and I would get up at around 1000 hours, go down to the dining area and have a buffet breakfast, then head back to the room to get changed into our bathers, then go and lay on the lounges at the beach. We would then head back to the room, get changed and go down the street and get some lunch. I found a place near our hotel that made the best chicken fried rice I had ever tasted. I was a frequent visitor to that place over the next 12 days.

In the evenings after a swim in our pool and a lie-down, with me sometimes working on my university studies, we would walk down to the beach where all the restaurants were and have an evening meal, looking over the water. We went out on boat trips and to different islands in the area, where we went snorkelling and relaxed on the beach.

However, after a time the symptoms I had been having after breaking my ankle while at Singleton started to return. Our holiday, which we had hoped would be a getaway from all the pressure we were under, started to take its toll on both of us, and by the end of the holiday we started to argue a fair bit. There were a lot of tears from both of us. We still loved each other unconditionally, but because of the way I was feeling mentally, and the fact that Shelly was about to return to Afghanistan, the holiday started to turn into a bit of a disaster. I was so unhappy, but it had nothing to do with Shelly. It was the frame of mind I was in. *What's wrong with me?* I thought.

The day we were leaving for our different destinations, Shelly checked her itinerary to confirm her departure time. She wanted to ensure that she would make it to the airport with time to spare, as we were flying out at around the same time. We thought we still had most of the day together, but all of a sudden Shelly was in a panic. She realised that her plane was leaving in 45 minutes! We quickly packed her bags and I rang the front desk to organise a taxi asap. We got up to the front of the hotel just as the taxi arrived, and we barely had time to say goodbye. Before I knew it she was in a taxi, leaving for the airport. I was so devastated. We would not be together for another four months, and within five minutes she was gone. I packed my gear, and about an hour and a half later I left for the airport. The first thing I did was go to the information desk and ask whether Shelly had made it onto the flight. One of the ladies came over and told me she remembered Shelly arriving in a panic, and that they had got her onto the plane in time. I was still very upset by the fact that we had not properly said goodbye, but I was extremely happy that she had made her flight. I flew back to Australia without any issues. I went straight back to Singleton to start my rehab in order to get back to full fitness, finish off the reinforcement cycle and receive my posting to 2nd Commando Regiment.

Once I returned to work, I was put in charge of the rehab section. This Section was comprised of all the members who were not Medical Class 1, meaning they were unable to be posted to a Battalion and unable to go outfield. Every day we would do rehab PT with all the IETs who were injured and were unable to be put into a training PL. Throughout the day a lot of administration was required to be done at TSP, so I would usually sit in front of the computer for the remainder of the day, writing up reports and doing general day-to-day administration. I hated the fact that I had to sit in front of the computer every day, though most afternoons I would go and do another PT session prior to the end of the day's work. After we had knocked off I would usually go back to my room, relax for a little bit, then at 1700 I would have a meal at the mess, which was provided as I was classified as Married with Dependents Separated. I would then head back to my room for an hour or so, go to the gym or pool, and smash out another PT session. Once I had completed that, I would slip back into my normal night routine of drinking as much wine as I could. Everything was going okay with rehab, except that first thing in the morning I struggled to walk the 200 metres to work because my ankle hadn't warmed up yet.

...

On 22 June I was on guard duty and, while watching the television in the guard room, I found out that three soldiers had been killed in Afghanistan in a helicopter crash. The members were from 2nd Commando Regiment, and straight away I had that feeling in my gut that I knew the people who had been killed. It was the worst feeling.

Twenty minutes later I walked into the mess hall, and noticed a few blokes who I did my Commando course with. They were pulled aside by a senior officer and told something in secret. I went up to the only Captain who had passed the CSTC that I was on and asked him what the issue was. I could see the look of sadness on his face. He looked at me and said that it was Tim Aplin. My eyes welled up and I nearly fell over. I was so shocked.

I walked over to the area where the staff were sitting and sat down. The blokes sitting at the same table asked what was wrong and I stated that one of my friends was among the three Commandos killed in the chopper crash that morning. After a minute or two, I went straight back to the guardroom.

I instantly blamed myself for his death. Back when we were on the parachute course I had always jumped out first. Then I asked Tim, who had never jumped out first, if he wanted to swap spots, which he agreed to. I broke both bones in my left leg and dislocated my ankle, and he landed safely. I thought that maybe if he had jumped first, he would have injured himself and therefore been safe back in Australia instead of in the helicopter.

A few days later, a service was being held at the 2nd Commando base in Sydney. A bus was organised to transport people to the service who knew the three soldiers that had been killed. A week later, the military funeral of Timothy James Aplin was in Brisbane and I attended the service. I still blamed myself. The only way I could make it better was to finish off my SF course, and get back overseas and finish off what I had started, because no matter what anybody said his death was my fault.

After a while I started to get back into reasonable shape, in regard to fitness. I could do more push-ups and pull-ups than I ever could before. My ankle, however, was becoming more and more painful every day, and the grinding that I had prior to the surgery was coming back. But I kept this to myself.

I saw one of the doctors after I passed the BFA, and he upgraded me from Medical Class 3 to Medical Class 2. All I had to do was complete a 15-kilometre pack march and he would upgrade me to Medical Class 1, and I would be able to get back in to the reinforcement cycle.

After completing the BFA, I was able to go outfield again. Once again, this began messing with my head, as I was going through alcohol withdrawal symptoms. I could not fall back on the alcohol to get me to sleep, so I would be up most nights doing the majority of the tasks required again. Every day I was sent outfield, the tornado in my head grew and grew. The blokes who I was working with could see that the pressure was mounting up on me and being passed onto them.

I found out when the next lot of IETs were going to do their 15-kilometre pack march, which was going to be two weeks down the track. So I began to do a few practice pack marches. I started off with a five-kilometre pack march, then a 10-kilometre march, then I did a 15-kilometre pack march. I had no issues with the pack marches other than a lot of soreness in my ankle the day after, and the walk to work was even more of a struggle. When the day of the march came, I completed it in time and had a piece of paper signed off by the PTI to say that I had passed. I took it to the doctor just prior to lunch.

The doctor who had upgraded me to Medical Class 2 was away, so I had to see another doctor. He was an old grumpy bloke who I had never really got along with. In fact, none of the blokes got on with him because he treated us as though we were recruits, not members of the Defence Force with years of experience and operational service. He was a civilian doctor employed by the Defence Force. I told him that I was in here to be upgraded to Medical Class 1, as I had completed the 15-kilometre pack march. He told me to take off my shoes and socks, and he bent my ankle back and forth a few times. He then looked back at his computer.

He told me that my ankle was in extremely poor condition and that I had severe arthritis. I stated to him that I was fine and that the other doctor had told me that, once I had completed the pack march, I would be upgraded to Medical Class 1, meaning I would be able to re-join the reinforcement cycle. He then said that I should not have been upgraded to Medical Class 2 and that, with the severity of the arthritis in my ankle, I would never be able to serve as an infantry soldier again.

He also said that there was a strong possibility that I may be medically discharged. I stood up immediately and told him that he had no idea what he was talking about. I stormed out of the office, slamming the door behind me.

As soon as I got outside the RAP I broke into tears. I headed straight over to the work car, as I had to go and have an ammunition clearance on my equipment because I had been outfield the previous week. Once I got back to the area where the clearance was going to be done I rang Shelly, who had returned from Afghanistan two months prior. When she answered the phone I burst into tears and was unable to speak, let alone put a sentence together. After about five minutes of her trying to calm me down and reassuring me that it was going to be okay, I was eventually able to explain to her what had happened and that I had been caught out. I had always known that my ankle was getting worse, however I didn't care about the pain or the long-term effects. All I wanted to do was finish the reinforcement cycle and be presented with my green beret. But with my ankle, and all the stuff that was going on in my head, I gave in at that point and told Shelly, 'I think it's time to tell the truth.' I couldn't keep fooling everyone anymore, especially myself.

After the clearance had been completed, I went back into the RAP and explained to the nurse that I would like to see the doctor again and that I had calmed down. She had seen and heard my reaction when I stormed out earlier that day, and told me to take a seat and that she would let the doctor know that I was back to see him. While sitting there I had a million things going on in my mind. I had decided, with a lot of regret, that it was time to wave the white flag. I had to give up. I had to tell the Army psychologist the truth, and not what they wanted to hear. I would tell them everything that had been going on, especially the thoughts that had been running through my head since the parachute incident. This was the increased anger, nightmares, flashbacks, loss of emotion, intrusive thoughts, triggers, increased anxiety, alcohol abuse, hyper vigilance, lack of sleep, fear of going to sleep, fear of being in public, suicidal thoughts, depression, frustration, the need to control everything, the lack of identity, and many other thoughts and actions that had been affecting me.

I stated to the doctor that he was correct about the fact that my ankle was bad and that it was getting much worse, and that I had been having problems mentally. I requested a referral to the Army psychologist.

I went straight to see the psychologist, and explained to her with tears welling up in my eyes what I had been going through. She listened to me and then asked whether I considered going on medication. This was something that I never thought I would do, whatever happened to me. When she suggested the medication, I broke down into uncontrollable tears and all the emotions I had been holding back since the parachute incident came out. After about 45 minutes, she said that she would write up a summary of our session and send it straight to the doctor.

By the time I left the psychologist, I was an emotional wreck and was absolutely exhausted. I rang up the TSP PL SGT and stated that I was going to be at the RAP for a while, and asked if he could get someone to sort out handing back the weapons we had used the previous week. He said that request wouldn't be a problem. I could tell he sensed the uneasiness in my voice. Something was not quite right.

When I arrived back at doctor's room, the paperwork for my ankle had been completed and I had been downgraded to Medical Class 3. He also received the summary from my session with the psychologist, and he booked me in to see a civilian psychiatrist in Sydney in two days.

I returned to the TSP office and explained to the boss and the PL SGT what was going on, and requested leave for the remainder of the week so I would be able to go back to Sydney that day and be with my wife. The leave was approved. I packed a few things and headed straight back to Sydney. It was so good to be home and be back with

Shelly, even if it was just for a couple of days.

Two days later, sitting in the civilian psychiatrist's waiting room, I was shitting myself. After a short wait I was called up. It was time to find out what the hell was going on. I explained to the civilian psychiatrist all the stuff that I explained to the Army psychologist two days prior. I did a survey, where he asked me numerous questions about how I had been feeling over the last month and how I had been feeling since the parachute incident. He then stated that he had diagnosed me with alcohol dependence, major depression, anxiety and PTSD.

What in the world was PTSD? He explained to me a bit about PTSD, then wrote me up a script for medication. He then down-classed me to Medical Class 403. He booked me in for another appointment in two weeks, and also booked me in to see a psychiatrist.

I asked him what Medical Class 403 was, and he stated that I would be medically discharged and that I would not return to work. My Army career was effectively over. It was November 2010.

I rang Shelly and told her my diagnosis, and in a way we were both a little relieved because it was an answer as to why things had been tense between us. I went via the chemist on the way home, picked up my medication and returned home to wait for Shelly. I needed to be with her asap.

I rang work and explained to them the diagnosis, and they said I would have to come in next week to fill out some paperwork, but until then I should rest up and spend time with my wife. It was at this point I stopped doing my university studies. I had completed and passed four units, but there seemed to be no point in continuing with them. My career in that field was over. If I couldn't deal with day-to-day activities, I would be unable to work in the same field as an independent contractor, especially overseas in a hostile environment.

SIXTEEN

PTSD AND DISCHARGE

My military career was over. I would never return to work. I would never wear my uniform again.

I had another appointment booked with the doctor in a couple of weeks, but other than that I had nothing to keep me occupied, and I didn't go out and look for something to do. I just hid in the house all day, and in the early hours of the afternoon I would start drinking. Even though I was on medication, it was doing nothing for me. I even felt like I was getting worse. I still felt scared and uneasy going out in public, I was just as angry, I slept just as bad and I felt even worse knowing that my Army career was over. On top of this, it had been confirmed that I was suffering from a mental illness, which was the last thing I expected.

Every day, Shelly came home to see me half intoxicated, which would have been very hard for her to see. What I hated seeing when she got home was the fact that she was still in uniform. I was so jealous that she could go back every day to the job I loved so much. Obviously, with every job there are days when you wish you could instead lie in bed all day. There had been many days over the last nine years when I was annoyed with my job, wanted to quit, or just wanted to stay in bed and go in late, but now I was unable to go to work at all. I wished that this was not the case, but I was too unfit to be a member of the Defence Force and to handle weapons, and for me to even just be around Army personnel was not the best situation either. So, as much as I hated being on sick leave, it was the best situation for me to be in.

Although I could have occupied myself a lot better, I was very sick and unable to make good decisions. When I saw the psychiatrist who had diagnosed me, he increased my medication, then told me that he would be on holiday for two months from December 2010 to January 2011, and to book an appointment with him in February. He said to keep busy and to stay off the alcohol as much as I could. Asking me to stay off the alcohol that was blocking all of the things going on in my head was a big ask, and seemed like an impossible task.

The two months the psychiatrist was away was when I needed to talk the most because I was in my most vulnerable stage. I had just found out that my military career was over and that I had a few different types of mental illness. I also felt that I had been cheated somehow, as when I was first diagnosed with PTSD it was just before Christmas.

Shelly's holidays started mid-December, and we drove down to Lorne to spend some time with my parents for a couple of weeks. We then planned to fly to Perth to spend Christmas, New Year's Eve and the rest of her holidays with her mother.

While in Victoria with my parents, all four of us went for a drive to Geelong. I was sitting in the back with Shelly. My father allowed a truck to pull out in front of us when the lanes were merging, even though he had plenty of time to get in front of the truck, which was travelling at a very slow speed. I argued with my father about this, to the point where I started shaking, sweating and then burst into tears and cried out, 'What is wrong with me?' After a while, I calmed down. Other than a few angry outbursts, this was the first time Shelly and my parents had seen how emotionally unstable I was, and how easy it was for me to get into that state. It scared the hell out of me, as I didn't know where it had come from and at that point had little information about PTSD, depression and anxiety.

The flight over to Perth was hell, with me suffering a lot of anxiety. This I kept from Shelly the best I could, as she was going through enough dealing with all my problems. We were picked up by her mother and taken to the two-storey apartment she was renting on the Swan River, which had a beautiful view of the city. Not long after we got there, we went to the bottle shop and bought a lot of alcohol. I had planned to do a fair bit of drinking over the holidays. We celebrated Christmas and New Year's Eve with just the three of us, and the two dogs. We drank a lot of alcohol, ate a lot of food and had a pleasant time. I was happy that we hadn't made too much of a big deal out of it. I only had to deal with two other people, which didn't really worry me.

Over the coming days I continued to drink very heavily. One night, Shelly's brother and his fiancée come over for dinner. Everything was going well until I cracked the shits over something that was said. It was no big deal, but due to the state I was in I reacted badly to it. The situation annoyed me, because I got along well with Shelly's brother and his fiancée. I went downstairs, and after a little bit Shelly came and told me to stop being silly and come back upstairs.

For some reason, I completely lost it and started packing my bags. I had made the decision that I was going back to Victoria. Everybody came down and tried to talk me out of leaving, but it just made things worse. I left the apartment with my bags and then I went to an area near the river where I knew they wouldn't be looking for me. From there I rang the airport, changed my flights and rang a taxi to take me to the airport. Shelly rang my phone over and over, but I was so upset and angry that I didn't even answer.

When I got to the airport I had to wait there for three hours. I cried the whole time, as I didn't know what the hell was going on and whether my marriage had just ended there and then. I still loved Shelly with all my heart.

I rang my parents at about 0100 and told them what had happened and asked if they could pick me up from the airport at around 0700. There was no hesitation in their answer that of course they would be there. I then rang Shelly, as I thought it only fair to let her know that I was safe and what my plans were. She told me that she had already rung the airline to see if I had changed my flights. She knew that I would soon be boarding a plane back to Victoria. When I was talking to her, I was still very upset and told her we should talk in a couple of days.

The whole flight, I was holding back the tears. Every now and then I would get up and go to the bathroom and cry. Every time I sat back down, I had the immediate feeling that I was about to cry again. I got off the plane as quickly as I could, picked up my baggage and rang my father, who was parked around the corner, to let him know that I was out the front, ready to be picked up. As soon as I got in the car I burst into tears and cried the whole way to Geelong, which is about an hour's drive.

When we arrived in Geelong, Dad suggested that we get some food, so we went into a little souvlaki shop and had a bite to eat and a chat. When I got back into the car again I began to cry, all the way back to Lorne, which was another hour's drive. Mum had decided she wouldn't come, as she thought that I would need some time alone with Dad, but when I finally did get back to my parents' house and opened the door to see Mum, I started crying more than I had before. They had set up the spare room for me, which I went straight to and spent the next two days in, only coming out when I had to go to the toilet.

After talking to Shelly, we agreed that she would spend the rest of her holidays in Perth with her mother and that I would stay down in Lorne. I would then drive back to Sydney prior to her arriving back so I could pick her up from the airport, and we would go from there. We would talk most days, trying to figure out was going on. We knew that the issues were from my illness and that it wasn't going to get any better until I got some professional treatment.

...

I saw my psychiatrist in January 2011. I had been at the appointment for about five minutes, telling my psychiatrist about what had happened since I had seen him previously. Almost immediately, he said he thought it would be best for me to be admitted to Saint John of God hospital to conduct a PTSD course. He also stated that even though the course wouldn't start for another week, he wanted me at the hospital immediately so I could get some rest prior to participating in the course.

I didn't understand what he meant by 'get some rest', but once I was checked into the hospital I felt as though a weight had been lifted off my shoulders. When I went home that afternoon, Shelly and I sat down and I explained to her what my psychiatrist had recommended. Although she didn't want me to go away again, she understood that it was something I had to do for myself and for us. The worst thing was that Shelly had put in her military discharge papers almost six months ago and that in four weeks time we were to pack up our house. She was going to Perth while I waited for my military discharge, and afterwards we were going to figure out where we would live, either in Victoria or Western Australia. We had arranged it so that while I was waiting for my military discharge, we would meet up every month. I would fly to Perth, she would come to Sydney, and on some occasions we planned to meet halfway, in Adelaide. But the day after I saw my psychiatrist, I packed my bags and headed to Saint John of God hospital (SJOG) in Richmond, located in the outer suburbs of Western Sydney, almost where the country meets the city.

The St John of God website said it was a place of 'beauty and tranquillity'. When they say beauty and tranquillity, they mean it in a big way. The hospital was set on a huge area on a hill overlooking the outer suburbs of Sydney, with beautiful gardens, walking tracks and a lot of grassy areas, where you could take out a blanket and lie in the sun for the afternoon. To me, it was the perfect place for a hospital of this type.

There were many different wards in the hospital. Mine was the PTSD ward, which was mainly full of Vietnam veterans. Every four weeks, a PTSD course was conducted. There was a group staying there who had just finished their course and were leaving in a couple of days. They were a mixture of policemen, nurses, public citizens and Defence personnel.

The Vietnam veterans would come in when they were down and out. For most of them, it was a place they had been to many times before. What I didn't understand about the Vietnam veterans was that if they were not eating, sleeping or in an appointment with their psychologist or psychiatrist, they would be in the common room watching war movies with the volume turned up to the maximum. I didn't understand why, if they had been traumatised by their experiences while overseas, they were constantly reminding themselves of it by watching these movies. I never did discover the answer to that. They had completed their PTSD courses and were staying in the hospital to get some counselling and some rest from the outside world. At the time I found this a bit odd, but I would later understand how important it was to recharge.

For the next week I was left to do my own thing; I was able to go outside and utilise the grounds, lie in the sun, walk, catch up on my sleep, watch DVDs and basically just relax. I was able to do this in there, as I felt safe for some reason. At the same time, I was also detoxing from my reliance on alcohol. I had pill parades in the morning and in the evening, where I would go to the office area and collect my pills.

The following Monday, when the three-week PTSD course was due to start, the other members who were attending the course checked in to the ward and were settled in, ready to begin the next morning.

After breakfast, we all met up in the group room for the first time. We were given an introduction by the people running the course, in regards to their background. We then went around the room, stating our name and our background. For me it was James, Army nine years, currently serving. There were four police officers in the course, who I developed incredible respect for. I realised that their sacrifice allows the rest of us to feel secure.

We then agreed on our group rules, which was very important to do, as a lot of things that would be said during the sessions would be the first time anyone had ever spoken about their trauma. They had to know they had total confidence in the group. The main rule was that what was said in the group would stay in the group, which is why I can't share any of the other participants' stories. We also came up with other rules, such as mobile phones were to be turned off during the session, no judgments, everyone was to be honest and show respect.

After a quick break and a cup of tea we got into the nuts and bolts, and the actual dirty parts of the course. The first thing was to discover what PTSD actually was, as although we had been diagnosed with PTSD we still had very little information about it.

PTSD is a disorder that is anxiety-based, caused by an external event. For me, that event was working in the hospital in Iraq, serving in combat zones in Afghanistan and when I broke my leg on the parachute course.

The acronym TRAP explains PTSD:

Trauma: assault or abuse, natural disaster, war, vehicle accident, armed robbery, witnessing death or injury.

Re-experiencing: intrusive thoughts and memories, nightmares, night terrors, flashbacks, triggers which may include anniversaries, people, places and sensations.

Avoidance: of thoughts, feelings, sensations, people and places.

Physical Tension: sleep difficulties, irritability, outbursts of anger, concentration difficulties, hypervigilance, exaggerated startle response.

Other symptoms include feelings of excessive guilt, depression, low self-esteem, low sense of identity, alcohol or drug abuse, relationship difficulties and disillusionment with authority. (Based on information from the Diagnostic and Statistical Manual of Mental Disorders, 4th Edition, 2000.)

After a big morning, we went and had lunch in the dining facility. It was set up like a cafeteria. The other option was to buy lunch at the shop on the grounds. I hated it in the cafeteria, as there were people everywhere. People were in front, beside and behind me. It was also very noisy, as many different conversations were going on at the same time. There was also the sound of chairs scraping on the ground and noises from the kitchen. As soon as I would finish I would get up and get out of there asap.

After lunch we talked about anger, as anger is a big issue for people who suffer from PTSD. It's a way of letting out all the negative energy that has been built up inside of you; it feels like a pressure release valve exploding. The acronym for this is Subjective Units of Distress (SUDS). An easy way to explain what this means is that your head space is compared to a bucket of water, divided into 10 parts. Most people without PTSD have about 3/10 of their bucket, or head space, full of water. When something happens, such as a minor traffic incident, you get angry and another 2/10 of water is placed in your bucket. This is a total of 5/10 of water in your bucket. The average person with PTSD usually has around 7/10 to 8/10 of their head space bucket full off water, so when an incident occurs the added water causes the bucket to overflow. This can result in an angry outburst.

This is a way of explaining why people affected by PTSD have moods that are so unstable. When the smallest thing happens they can fly off the handle, and worst of all they mostly blame the closest person to them. The loved ones have to walk around on eggshells all the time. Most of the time it's not the fault of the loved one, but is a result of the unstable mood of the person suffering from PTSD.

Anger for us is like an iceberg — you can only see what's above the water. Anger is often the first thing that is noticed, however there are many things underneath the surface that ensure the anger is always there. They are emotions such as vulnerability, sadness, a feeling of being alone, powerlessness, helplessness, guilt, frustration, grief, a feeling of being overwhelmed, feelings of failure, unworthiness, shame, feeling lost, feeling inadequate, feeling neglected, broken, afraid, misunderstood, in denial, threatened, useless, depressed, hurt, let down, feeling anxious and undeserving.

We were given a set of rules to help us manage anger, which are:

It is okay to feel angry but
don't hurt others,
don't hurt yourself,
don't hurt property,
DO talk about it.

Just prior to being knocked off for the day, we were given a book which we were encouraged to write things in, which is how this book was started. This included things such as goals that we would like to set, an activity schedule so that we had structure when we left, an area to write the names and numbers of the health professionals that we were dealing with, our key support people and our emergency contact people and their numbers. Also in the book there was a place to write about relapse prevention, meaning that if we noticed what our early warning signs or triggers were we could do something about it prior to getting to that extreme point. It also had a list of 150 pleasant things we could do and think about, and also an area where we could write down pleasant events that we had previously experienced and would like to do in the future, as well as relaxation techniques. We were also encouraged to write down what we were feeling so that when we were talking to our psychiatrists or psychologists we could talk to them about it.

Some of the things I wrote included:

I just want to get out now, I feel trapped, I need to get out of the Army. I hated it so much but I used to love it so much. I just want to die. What's the point? Please put me in a situation where I can die. I don't want to be alive.

I feel that I can't get away and whatever fantasy dream that I may have is all bullshit. How am I going to avoid all the shit things in my shit life? I wish it would end right now. I wish the TV in this shit place was not always so loud. How the fuck am I supposed to relax? I wish I would just drop dead. I don't care how, I just wish it would happen now. I want more medication. I don't care where I get them, I just want this shit to stop now. I hate myself and if I can't get back to the way I was then what's the point of all this hard work? Everything pisses me off. Everything. How the pen touches the paper, how everyone always talks to me. FUCK OFF!!! Why do I laugh sometimes when all I am doing is hiding what is inside? I hate everything and would be better off dead. I fucking hate this place. I wish I was FUCKING DEAD.

<u>Thoughts</u>

- I hate myself.
- I feel insignificant.
- I feel like I have failed in life.
- I feel I don't deserve to be alive.
- Why did I survive when others didn't?
- I feel that if I can't be in the Commandos I'm no good.
- I feel like I'm getting in everyone's way.
- I feel like I am holding everyone back, such as my wife.
- I feel like I don't deserve to be treated for PTSD.
- Why should I get special treatment?
- Why should I be on sick leave?
- I feel I am weak and emotionally fucked.
- I don't know how I will get out of this hole that I am in.
- I feel like my career within the Army was worthless.
- I feel like what I have done in the Army was worthless.
- I don't know if I want to accept this change. I will live with it and have a shit life.
- I don't want to let go of my dream of being in the Army.
- I hate when I see people doing things that I cannot do, e.g. running.

- I hate and I am jealous of people that are doing their dream job when I can't do mine.

When looking back on some of the things I wrote I feel a bit shocked. However, I still feel a lot of things I wrote down and can understand why I was feeling this way.

...

Over the next three weeks, we explored in detail the reasons why we were suffering and those things that could help us. We discussed the different types of self-talk, such as black-and-white thinking, crystal balling, catastrophising and self blame.

We also talked about how important family and friends were for our recovery, and also discussed relapse prevention. Triggers could be things such as anniversaries, people and noises. For me, my alcohol intake was an issue, which we all know is a depressant.

We talked about timeouts. For example, if we were having a conversation with a family member or a friend and it got to be heated, we should have a timeout, a 10-minute break, and after 10 minutes we could return and finish the conversation without saying things that we would regret later. We were given a way to talk to family members and partners so that it wouldn't come across as confronting. It was:

I feel___when you___because___and instead___.

An example of this would be:

I feel sad and upset **when you** talk about the Army **because** I am jealous because I cannot be a part of it anymore **and instead** could we talk about something different?

We also focused a lot on the fight or flight response, which is a physiological reaction that occurs in response to a perceived harmful event, attack or threat to survival. And for people with PTSD, when they are put in a situation they can be adversely given an adrenaline rush, their sensors detect that there is a threat or danger, heart rate rises, they get tunnel vision, muscle tension, shaking, and then they either react to the situation or get away from the situation as quickly as possible. For example, if I was at the pub and I was challenged, I would not back down and I would fight until I felt that there was no longer any threat to myself or the people I was with. In regards to the flight response, when fireworks were going off in the vicinity of the Lorne aquatic and angling club not long ago, I ran as hard and as fast as I could to get away from the area, which was more like a really quick limp due to my fused ankle, and I hid in an area where I felt safe.

...

After three weeks, the PTSD course finished and I returned home to help Shelly go through our possessions and figure out where it was all going. I had rented a storage shed in Sydney, as I didn't know how long I was going to be staying there prior to my discharge. Shelly took the majority of the stuff but I kept a few things, such as my huge comfy leather chair.

When Shelly left for Perth, I broke down again and was admitted to 1 HSB hospital at Holsworthy Barracks. Three days later I was sent back to SJOG to do the depression/anxiety course. I was happy to be in a different ward, as being around Army and ex-Army personnel made me very uncomfortable. During the three weeks I was at SJOG, I felt more comfortable than I did in the PTSD ward.

I was the only soldier in the whole ward of about 20 people. In this ward there were a lot of everyday people. There were mothers and fathers, teachers, doctors, real estate agents, police officers and nurses. It was a course that ran all the time. There were always groups of people coming into the ward at various times, which was the same as the PTSD ward.

Two days after I was admitted to the depression/anxiety ward,

Shelly and I decided that too much damage had been done to our marriage. We agreed that we should separate. I was devastated. If I wasn't where I was, in a controlled and stable environment, I can guarantee I would not be here today.

...

The depression/anxiety course included lessons such as the personal skills lesson, which dealt with communication, assertiveness and relationships. We would talk about our beliefs about emotions and our increasing vulnerability to negative emotions. We would do mindfulness sessions, as well as lessons on understanding depression, anxiety and stress, self-talk and problem solving.

We did art sessions, where we would paint and draw, and even paint plaster moulds. This I thought was a bit silly at the start, though I really enjoyed it as it was very relaxing and kept me focused on a task.

We were educated about the medication we were taking. It was explained to us what the side effects and long-term effects were. We looked at sleep management, communication, relationships, addiction, self-esteem, mood management, goal setting and future planning. We also participated in yoga, which a lot of people recommend. I found it difficult though, due to my ankle injury and the fact that my back and neck had started to play up. Tai chi was also recommended, however I haven't done any yet at the time of writing this book. Every night we would do a relaxation session, where we would go into a darkened room and lie there and listen to CDs, with the intention that we would go to that place in our mind where we felt safe and happy.

When the groups finished we were encouraged to utilise the large grounds of the hospital to exercise because, as they say, 'healthy body, healthy mind'. I had recently bought some new walking shoes, which helped my ankle a little bit, and I began walking every morning and every evening. This helped immensely. I also used to take a blanket out and lay down in the sun on the grounds and listen to my iPod.

The worst part about doing the depression/anxiety course was that I began smoking again, which became a habit of 30 to 40 cigarettes a day. I hadn't smoked since the day after I put in my application for the Commandos, back in 2007 while I was in Afghanistan. The worst thing about starting up smoking again was the fact that although I knew all the dangers of smoking, I didn't care at all as I didn't care about my life in general. My mindset was that I felt like I had nothing to live for.

Once I was discharged from SJOG, I was readmitted to 1 HSB. I hated it there more than anything because every day I was reminded of what I couldn't have anymore. I would stay in my room all day with the curtains around my bed so that I could cut myself off from the world.

After about two and a half months of being there, I moved into a house in the western suburbs of Sydney with a person I had met at SJOG. After living there for about a month or so, I received a letter that had my discharge date on it. It was set for 13 September 2011. I was upset, sad and angry — about 40 emotions hit me at once. I had known my Army career was over, but now that I had a set date it seemed real.

Something that started happening to me during this time was that every time I'd relax, such as when I started to fall asleep, my body would jump like when you get that falling feeling. The jumping would happen for maybe 30 to 45 minutes every night. After a while I was too afraid to go to sleep, as I knew that every time I went to bed or relaxed the jumps would start. I talked to my psychiatrist about it and he said it was due to the PTSD. I asked if there was any medication I could take but he didn't have any for me, so I began to self-medicate. I would drink even more alcohol at night time, and also started over-medicating myself. I would have more Seroquel every night, to the point where I would sleep well into the next afternoon. I still had the jumps but it helped me deal with them a little better.

The next couple of months leading up to my discharge date was hectic for me. I had so many appointments with the Department of

Veterans Affairs and my discharge counsellor, and I was doing all my final medical and dental checks and needs assessments. I was experiencing more jumps when I relaxed. I was also having what felt like mini fits, where my body would go into a spasm like an epileptic fit for five to 10 seconds.

One good thing that happened to me during that time was that I got myself a dog, a Maltese/Silky Terrier cross. I called her Joey. Other than my close family, she is the best thing in my life. She is my psychologist, my psychiatrist, my GP and my best friend 24 hours a day, seven days a week. I love her more than life itself. At the time of writing this, she's two years and three months old and weighs 2.3 kilograms. A perfect lap dog, except she takes up most of the bed.

...

Everything was starting to get too much for me and I didn't care about anything anymore. One night after an argument with my housemate, I decided that it was all over for me. I rang a few friends and said goodbye. The majority of them had their phones turned off as they were on courses, overseas or at work. I also called my parents for their bank account details so I could transfer my money into their accounts. After a while of them telling me that I could do it the next day and me insisting that I needed the details now, they eventually gave up the numbers. Then I said goodbye.

I put on my 1 RAR jumper and a pair of pants that I'd worn on my three deployments, got out my medals and a couple of photos and sat them in front of me. I also got a very sharp pocket knife and put it into my pocket just in case the original plan didn't work. I took out around 150 of the strongest anti-depressants and anti-anxiety tablets I had, sculled two bottles of wine and took the tablets in big handfuls. I then sat there and waited for the tablets to take effect.

My phone rang a couple of times but I didn't hear it. My housemate, who I thought was fast asleep, did hear it. They woke up and came out into the lounge room and saw what I had done. That was when they called 000.

The rest I can't recall. I was told the police arrived first, as the western suburbs was a rough area and they usually came before the ambulances. They took the knife from my pocket and walked me out to the ambulance, which had arrived shortly after. In the ambulance I was biting my wrist, trying to cut my veins with my teeth, as I must have realised that my suicide had not been successful. As a result, I was secured to the bed in the ambulance and at the hospital with large zip ties.

I woke up at some point the next day and was moved to the psychiatric ward, so I could be assessed and to figure out where I would go from there. My parents had been called not long after I was put in the ambulance, and they had left Lorne straight away to be with me. The date was 12 June 2011.

I stayed in the psychiatric ward for a couple of days, then I was released back to 1 HSB. I was so annoyed because, firstly, I wasn't trusted to live away from the hospital and, secondly, I had to see what my family was going through.

My sister had travelled from Melbourne to Sydney by train. She had arrived in the western suburbs late in the evening, which I wouldn't recommend anyone to do. When she arrived at the train station she rang my parents, who had no idea that she was coming, and they went and picked her up. She had come up because she was worried about me, but also to look after my parents, which I thought was incredible. She made sure they ate their meals, drove them to and from the hospital and supported them in any way she could. For this I will never be able to thank her enough. I don't have the courage to bring the subject up again with her, so I will say thank you now for what you have done for our parents and for me.

I know a lot of people say that suicide is the weak way out, but unless you have been in that situation before, which I hope to hell you haven't, you will never understand how much sense it makes.

...

After a few days at 1 HSB, my parents and sister drove back to Victoria and I was released back to the house I was renting. It was so great to be out of there and back at home, as the Army base was an uncomfortable place for me.

I returned home semi-happy, however my discharge date was fast approaching. I was asked to come in at about lunchtime and have a 'discharge party', where there would be a few other people who were being medically discharged. We would all have cake and tea and celebrate our discharge, and be presented with our certificates saying thank you for your time and service in the ADF.

That was the last thing I wanted to do. I didn't want to eat cake and drink tea with people I didn't know, and be presented with a piece of paper that said thanks for everything by some stranger that I had never met. No thanks.

Even though it was the last thing I wanted to do, I probably should have done it because the reality of being discharged didn't settle in for a long time. I should have gone so that I could have had that separation, despite not being in the right frame of mind.

At this time I was getting so depressed that I would have a 'Seroquel party', as I will call it now. Seroquel was a drug that helped me get to sleep at night and, along with my other medication, it would assist me to calm down and sleep. However, I was taking 10 times the normal dosage and I would sleep for two days. That way, I didn't have to deal with feeling depressed. All I had to do was take a few tablets and it would make the pain go away, however temporary that was.

My discharge date came and went, and within a week I started to feel more depressed. Once again, I prepared to take my own life. I had more than 200 tablets this time and my housemate was not an issue.

However, at the last minute something come over me and I didn't do it. I decided I would go down and spend a week with my parents in

Lorne, then come back and do it once and for all, no stuffing around this time. But when I returned to Sydney after seeing my parents I realised there were a lot of things in Lorne that I could be doing, such as fishing and working on the house I owned there. So I decided to leave Sydney and move to Lorne.

Within an hour and a half of arriving back in Sydney, I packed up the car and drove to Lorne. I slept for a couple of hours about halfway back, then finished the drive. I arrived in Lorne relieved but emotionally drained, and I cried myself to sleep. I shut all the curtains in the house and ignored the world for a couple of days. Every now and then I let Mum and Dad know I was okay, but other than that I was shut off. My mother did some ringing around and found a fantastic psychologist and a great GP in Lorne, and a great psychiatrist in Geelong. When I told the psychiatrist about the jumps and the mini fits I was having, he said it was because my body was used to being always alert. It was telling me to focus and concentrate every time I relaxed, and the mini fits were a continuation of that. He prescribed me some medication, which almost immediately limited the amount of jumps and fits I was having. Even though they didn't stop completely, it was still a hell of a lot better than it was previously. I was so confused because I had been telling my psychiatrist in Sydney this for months, and in the first session with my new psychiatrist I had it sorted to the point where I could live with it. This just confirmed for me that I was in the right place.

SEVENTEEN

PREPARING FOR THE CHALLENGE

'If your dreams do not scare you, they are not big enough.'
— *Ellen Johnson Sirleaf*

When I arrived in Lorne in September 2011, fishing and being on the water was the only time I felt 100 percent. So the priority was to buy a boat asap. I started looking at the boat magazines and figuring out what model of boat I needed. I was going to be fishing in the open ocean 90 percent of the time and the boat ramp at Lorne was not set up like other ramps. The launching and landing facility was off the beach between the rocks. If the tide was low, when returning from fishing the boat had to be dragged up to the harder sand using a snap strap, so the car and trailer wouldn't get bogged in the wet sand.

I decided I would need an aluminium boat, as aluminium is lighter than fibreglass or steel. It would need a steering wheel at the front and a windscreen, and need to be about four to five metres long. I looked around the boat shops in Geelong and Melbourne, but I couldn't find one that suited my needs.

While looking for a boat during the day, at night I would go fishing off the pier or at the beach in the areas surrounding Lorne. I was dreaming that soon I'd have my own boat and would be able to go out and catch those fish that I couldn't catch from the pier. These were fish like the bigger snappers, bigger sharks and flathead.

A few days after returning from Melbourne, my father started talking to the local tradesman in Lorne who were into fishing and boats, and asked them to put the feelers out to see if anyone in the area was looking to sell a boat. One of the tradesmen he asked said he would make a phone call, as he knew of a person in Anglesea, about 25 minutes from Lorne, who had a boat for sale. We organised to look at the boat that afternoon.

When I first saw the boat, I knew it was the one. It fit all my specifications, even though Dad said I should buy a boat with a centre console, meaning that when fighting a fish I could move all around the boat instead of just fighting it from the rear, avoiding the possibility of having to start up the boat and chase the fish. His opinion changed, however, when we took the boat out on the water.

The boat was a 4.55-metre 1994 Quintrex Fishabout, with a wider hull that made cutting through the waves easier. It came with a 2001 60hp 2-stroke engine with only 120 hours of use. It had a nice canopy that folded up neatly on the top of the windscreen, a fishfinder, a radio and a 65-litre underfloor fuel tank, plus all the safety gear.

Two days later, the owner took Dad and I to Geelong for the test run. As the owner was doing the prep for the boat he was showing me how to do it, which I think helped make the sale. We motored around for a while and then I had a drive of it. Then we stopped the engine and drifted for a bit. The owner talked to me and Dad about the boat and its history. We shook hands over the sale while drifting, then brought the boat back in and loaded it up on the trailer. He said he would start the paperwork and I could pick it up in a few days.

Now I had to get my boat licence, which I was booked in to do the next day. I had been studying the book for a few weeks and knew it from front to back.

The next day when I arrived at VicRoads in Geelong, I fell in a heap. The pressure had started building before I even got to Geelong. When I walked into VicRoads my anxiety went up tenfold, and by the time I was sitting in front of the computer ready to do the test I was sweating, shaking and nearly in tears. My mind was blank.

I did the test and failed by one question. I walked outside, rang Mum and told her I failed, while crying my eyes out. But Mum had it sorted. She'd cut out an advertisement in the *Colac Herald* a week prior. The advertisement was a boat licence and personal watercraft course in two days time. A presenter would explain the rules and regulations in a public speaking forum. If anyone had questions or didn't understand something, the presenter could answer them. This seemed okay to me, but I was going to be there in a group. Mum gave me his number and I called him straight away. I explained my situation and he stated that he was in the Army a long time ago and understood a little of what I was going through. Dad said that he would come with me for support, which would allow him to brush up on the rules, as he'd had his boat licence for 10 years now.

The course was held at Colac's RSL. When I got there I didn't want to walk in, but it turned out the course was upstairs and nowhere near the Army memorabilia. We arrived early and introduced ourselves to the person running the course, and took a seat at the back of the room.

The course went really well. Everything was explained in a way we could all understand. I came out of the course 10 times more confident than I had been before I walked in, and when I retook the test I passed.

I picked up the boat the next day, on 3 November 2011. I paid for it, the previous owner and I shook hands, and I took the boat to VicRoads in Colac to sort out my licence and registration. I returned to Lorne, happy as Larry. I owned my very first boat.

Every day that the weather was good, I went out on the water. I went with my dad and my mates, but best of all I would go by myself, as much as I could. Out on the water nothing could get to me, mentally or physically. I was on top of the world. But when I got back to land it was a different story.

One time I was out fishing with a friend, and the weather was perfect and the ocean looked like glass. I said to him, 'Do you think I could make it from Lorne to Tasmania by boat?' He said, 'No!' That was all I needed. I decided that I was going to cross Bass Strait in my boat. What I also needed was something to keep me occupied because

I had booked in for an ankle fusion in March 2012, and needed to keep myself busy while I was on crutches and in plaster again. I was so worried that my mental state would suffer big time, because the last time I was in plaster was when everything started to fall apart.

I rang up the general manager of Quintrex with half a plan. I asked if they would be willing to fit out my boat with all new equipment and after the Challenge was completed, Quintrex could use a slogan like, 'If a 1994 Quintrex boat could cross the Bass Strait, what could you do with a new Quintrex?' He told me to write up a plan and send it to him. I started typing up the plan, but then I thought, *Why do this for them? Why not do this Challenge for people like me, who suffer from mental illness?*

...

I started looking around on the internet for companies that raised money and awareness for mental illness. The first one that I found was Beyond Blue, based in Victoria. Beyond Blue became known to a lot of people through the former premier of Victoria, Jeff Kennett. I went to their website and read through their fundraising guidelines. One rule was that they wouldn't put their name to any dangerous water activities. There was no way I could talk them into backing the Challenge I had planned. I checked out a lot of other organisations, but nothing really jumped out at me.

I went outside for a smoke and noticed Mum on the front deck. I told her I couldn't find an organisation that would be able to support the Challenge. She asked if I had looked up Black Dog Institute. I went back to the computer and looked up their website. The first thing that got me excited was their logo. It was a hand in the shape of a peace sign, but the shadow of the hand showed a dog's head. The way I think about the logo is that when you see a person walking down the street you think they are fine, represented by the peace sign, but you cannot see the problems they are carrying around, represented by the shadow.

The Black Dog Institute was perfect. I filled out an application to fundraise and sent it in. I was still very worried I would get knocked back due to the risks of the Challenge, but in the fundraising guidelines nothing was stated about not supporting water activities. So there was still hope. My proposal to the Black Dog Institute included the following:

Ex-Australian Soldier Battling a Different Challenge

My name is James Prascevic and I am 33 years of age and currently living in Lorne, Victoria.

I am a qualified plumber and on 23 April 2002 I enlisted in the Australian Army, The Royal Australian Infantry Corps.

On 13 September 2011 I was medically discharged from the Australian Army, after serving nine and a half years, due to Post Traumatic Stress Disorder (PTSD), Major Depression, Anxiety and Alcohol Dependence. This included severe arthritis in my left ankle, after breaking my leg in a training parachuting accident.

While in the Army I completed six-month tours of Timor (2003), Iraq (2005–06) and Afghanistan (2007) and most of the Commando/Special Forces Selection and Training Courses (2008).

Since my discharge, I have purchased a boat. I love the freedom of being on the open water and have loved fishing all my life. When I am in my boat fishing, the only thing I worry about is the end of the rod tip. I feel like I have nothing wrong with me, mentally or physically.

My Idea

My proposal is to drive my 4.55-metre Aluminium Quintrex motorised boat across Bass Strait solo, from Victoria to Tasmania without stopping or assistance (route to be advised by RAF navigator — see below).

I have the support of Margaret Bowling (world record holding ocean rower), xxxxxx (Royal Air force Navigator and ocean rower) and xxxxxx (ex-British Army soldier/experienced ocean rower) who have agreed to help in various ways. I also have the endorsement of Victorian and Tasmanian Marine Safety, Victorian Water Police and Victorian Boat Safety.

The purpose of this trip is to raise awareness of my condition, which also presents an opportunity to profile the work of Black Dog Institute and fundraise for the Black Dog Institute. Although there are many organisations I could fundraise for, Black Dog Institute is my preference.

I am seeking Authority to fundraise on your behalf and a Fundraising Toolkit.

What I need from the Black Dog Institute

In closing, if this is successful I plan to continue to raise awareness and take on other challenges (for example, completing my book).

I look forward to hearing from you with an approved Authority to Fundraise on your behalf and a Fundraising Toolkit.

James Edgar Prascevic

...

Now it was the waiting game. In the meantime, in between fishing, I had covered the inside of my boat with marine carpet, which matched the floor. I did it with such precision. I was so proud of myself as the boat looked like a million bucks. I also got into contact with Margret Bowling, who holds a world record for the first Australian woman to row across the Atlantic in a crew of 16. She had been on polar expeditions and transcontinental bicycle races.

I talked to her on the phone and she told me about some of her adventures and about when she rowed across the Bass Strait. She advised me of how to advertise my Challenge and how to approach sponsors, and also put me in contact with a person who could help me with a route. Margaret told me to call her at any time if I had any queries, and for this I would like to thank her.

I also contacted, James 'Cas' Castrisson and Justin 'Jonesy' Jones, two Australians who made history by completing the longest unsupported polar expedition without assistance. They have also paddled 3318 kilometres across the Tasman Sea, another world first.

They gave me some advice and encouragement via email. I also started to read their books *Crossing the Ditch* and *Extreme South*, and watched their documentaries *Crossing the Ditch* and *Crossing the Ice*, which got me pumped up and excited about my Challenge. Other inspiring books I read were Jessica Watson's *True Spirit* and Jesse Martin's *Lionheart*, which were about when they both sailed around the world solo and unsupported, e.g. they couldn't pull into a marina and repair their boats or have fuel or food given to them during the trip.

A couple of weeks later, I received a phone call from the Black Dog Institute and was asked a few questions about my Challenge, what research I had done and what safety precautions I was going to take. I explained to them some of the safety equipment I would take, such as an Emergency Position Indicating Radio Beacon (EPIRB), a dry suit, radios, chart plotters, a Global Positioning System (GPS), a satellite phone and life jackets. They said that if I kept them up-to-date and sent them a risk management assessment prior to leaving that they would support me. They sent me the approval and all the information I needed that afternoon, and I was ready to go.

Next was the harder part of the Challenge for me, which was getting sponsors and advertising the trip. However, I had one thing going for me that would help set me up for the whole Challenge: my sister. What she had studied and aced at university was exactly what I had to do now, so I organised to stay at her place. She was unbelievable and helped me set up everything that I needed, and was the first person to donate a sum of $500 to the Black Dog Institute. I said to her that her help and knowledge in this area was more than enough and that I didn't want a donation from her, however she knew that the money was going to a good cause. Her help was incredible, as administration was not my favourite area.

Firstly, we set up an Everyday Hero page, where people could see my story, what I was doing and how they could donate money. Next, we set up a Facebook page. On the page I would update it with information about sponsors, photos, videos, facts about PTSD and depression. I named the page 'Ex-Australian Solider Battling a Different Challenge'.

The only problem was that only a few people close to me knew why I had been discharged from the Army. This was the point that I realised if I was going to do this I would have to tell anyone willing to listen what problems I had. Shit. I contemplated it for a while, until I decided that if I wanted to help others I had to bite the bullet. I had to tell them the truth and that my ankle problem was not the only reason I had been discharged. So my first post on Facebook said:

To everyone out there, this is something that has been hard for me to say to you all. Most of you know I was medically discharged from the Army. However, I have told most of you it was due to my ankle, after breaking it on the Basic Parachute Course. The other reasons I was discharged from the Army were for Post Traumatic Stress Disorder, Major Depression, Anxiety and Alcohol Dependence. I have been living in hell since about July 08 but kept it all to myself and lost everything close to me. I spent about 6 months in hospital and 7 weeks in, as I say now, a 'nut house'. I have decided to help people out there like me, including civilians, by raising money for the Black Dog Institute (they help out people with depression). How am I going to help? I am going to take my boat across Bass Strait. Not that hard, however my boat is only 4.55 metres long. I hope you can all like this page I have just set up and pass it on to your friends. I only just started it 20 minutes ago, but I will update it regularly with how much money I have raised, the re-fit of my boat, a bit of footage and what sponsors are willing to help out. I know this may come as a shock to some of you, as it did to me. But trust me, if you don't speak up sooner it will only get worse. Much, much worse. Cheers.

This post on Facebook was one of the hardest things for me to do. But it was received well by my friends, with encouraging words such as, 'You're so brave,' and 'Well done for speaking up where others can't or won't.' I had about 200 people following my page by the first afternoon. I was off to a good start.

My sister and I then put together a media release and a template to send to potential sponsors. She said that I first had to figure out what I needed and then send out proposals to three companies. The plan was that hopefully at least one company would jump on board and I would not lose valuable time if a company said no, which a lot did. She also told me to write down the reasons why I was doing this Challenge in big writing and hang it up near my computer, so that when I got angry or fed up with what I was doing I could look back at the points I wrote at the start. This would give me the motivation to keep going and not give up. The points were:

- To prove to everyone that I could do what I set out to do
- To prove to myself that I could do what I set out to do
- To raise awareness and money for the Black Dog Institute
- To raise as much awareness for PTSD, depression and mental illness as I could
- To show to people that they should not be afraid to speak up if they are feeling down
- To make people aware that mental illness should be taken seriously (even though you can't see it, it's still there)

The first sponsor I needed was a company that made stickers. I contacted a sticker company in Geelong, Victoria called Signific. In the proposal I sent them, I requested that they provide me with stickers that would advertise the Black Dog Institute, and for them to make a donation to the organisation. I also offered to mention Signific in a video documentary of the Challenge.

...

On the morning of 30 August, I had woken up to see that two soldiers from 2nd Commando Regiment had been killed in a helicopter crash and three soldiers had been killed by a member of the Afghan National Army. Five members of the Australian Defence Force had been killed while I was asleep. As it was early afternoon by the time I had my breakfast, I decided to go to the Lorne Aquatic and Angling Club and get drunk. I had no tolerance left. I needed a day off, as well as a chance to drink away my sorrows and drink a toast to the five soldiers who had just been killed. It was Australia's worst death toll since 18 soldiers were killed on 12 June 1996, when two Black Hawk helicopters collided during a training exercise. It was also the worst death toll from overseas since the Battle of Long Tan on 18 August 1966, when 18 Australian soldiers were killed.

While down at the Aquatic Club and almost three parts pissed, I had received a phone call. I didn't look at the number at first, but when I did I realised it was my mate in Sydney who I had been on the Commando courses with. I had continued a friendship with him after I broke my leg. As soon as he started talking I knew that it was bad news. He said that it was not 100 percent confirmed, but he was almost certain that one of the soldiers that had been killed in the helicopter crash was our good friend Merv (Mervyn John McDonald).

I had been so shocked — another close friend killed in a helicopter crash. He was engaged, and recently I'd been meaning to see him when he got back. I'd been very down at the time, and this was the last message he sent to me in response to me writing to him about how I was feeling down in the dumps:

I remember thinking of you as a bloody machine on selection! Yeah xxxxxx is an amazing person, best part of my life! Sounds like you're down in the dumps bro, what happened to your leg? Sorry to hear about you and Shelly. Where in Victoria are you? Planning on getting married in Victoria, Yarra Valley in Feb/Mar next year, let me know your address so I can send you an invite mate. Cheer up mate, and realise some things happen for a reason. I am totally jealous of your fishing photos, maybe one day I'll have a boat. :) Stay cool, bro!

I had gotten absolutely hammered that night, and in a week I had put on six kilograms due to my intake of alcohol and food. It took a lot of fighting to get back into the mood of sitting at the computer and continuing on with what I was doing. However, I decided that what I would do was put Merv and Tim's names on the port and starboard side of my boat. They would be watching my flanks. And I decided I would take a beer with me on the trip, and when I got back I would cheers to the both of them.

The media release I wrote included information about my background in the Army and the purpose of the Challenge, as well as the lines, 'While I'll be alone on the water, I am taking the memory of two mates with me. My port side is being watched by Mervyn McDonald and my starboard by Tim Aplin. Both died while serving in Afghanistan.'

Then I sent out all the proposals. In total, I sent out 53 sponsor proposals to different companies. This was not as easy as I thought, as I had to find out exactly who to send it to. It was hard when I had to ring the companies and explain I was asking for a donation. You could here in their voices that they had more important things to do. However, in saying that, there were a lot of people interested in my story who were happy to talk. I had a lot of companies who wrote back with a reply along the lines of, 'Good luck with your Challenge. However, at this stage we are unable to help due to such and such.'

The knockbacks were very disappointing, but I knew from the start that I had to expect a few companies to say no, especially when times were tough for a lot of people. The funny thing is that what I asked for were mainly small and not very expensive things from the companies. For a donation of something such as a fishfinder/chartplotter, which retailed at $900, after they subtract the money made from the unit and then write it off as a tax donation, to me it was a very good investment. Possibly they thought that if something bad happened (a lot of people said I was crazy to even think about going through with the trip) they didn't want their name associated with me. If I looked at it through their eyes, I probably would have sent back a rejection letter, too.

The first 'happy to support your cause' letter was from RFD Survitec Group, who specialise in safety and survival equipment. They donated a Kannad Marine Sport Emergency Positioning Indicating Radio Beacon (EPIRB), a life jacket and a Kannad Marine SafeLink SOLO Personal Location Beacon (PLB). The PLB is small enough to fit in your pocket, so if you get into trouble and you don't have a chance to get your EPIRB you will have the PLB with you.

Shortly after that, Signific responded to my request and were more than happy to help. Also, GME donated a G142CFD fishfinder/chartplotter combo. The Lorne Aquatic and Angling Club also said they would help out however they could.

The Melbourne Boat Show, held at the Melbourne Convention and Exhibition Centre in Docklands (better known to Victorians as 'Jeff's Shed', because Jeff Kennett was premier of Victoria when it was built) was coming up, so I rang the Boating Industry Association of Victoria (BIA) who run and organise the show. They allowed me to have my boat on display for the five days of the show. This donation was worth thousands of dollars. Some companies spent more than $50,000 to have their product displayed at the show. While there, the sponsors I picked up were Fusion, who gave me an MS RA5O FM marine stereo, speakers and an iPod jack, Bundoora Boat Upholstery who made me a custom canopy, with stronger and lighter bars and clear sides. Lowrance donated a LVR-250 Marine VHF DSC Radio, and Anchor Right donated a Sand and Rock Combination Anchor (SARCA) and $100 to the Black Dog Institute.

On the first evening of the boat show, I noticed a crowd hanging around the Suzuki stand. I decided to go over and have a look. When I got there I saw Paul Worsteling (from IFISH TV show and the owner of the Tackle World fishing stores), his wife Cristy and their son Jed. I waited while he talked to people, signed autographs and had photos taken with his fans. Then it was my turn. I was so nervous, as I was such a big fan of him and his show.

I put my hand out and introduced myself, and he said, 'Are you the bloke planning the Bass Strait crossing?' I was shocked as to how he knew, but he said that Cristy was following my Facebook page. I asked him if he could come over and have a look at my boat when he had time, to which he replied he would.

When Paul arrived at my boat, he said that he had come to have a meeting with Suzuki, but also to see my stand. I had goose bumps everywhere and I couldn't take the smile off my face. We talked for a while, got some photos together and then he gave me his email address. He said to send him my home address so he could send an autographed jacket/life jacket combo. He told me to keep him up to date with the Challenge and wished me well. I went out for a smoke and took in what I had just experienced.

When I went back inside, a man from Suzuki was looking at my boat. He introduced himself as the National Manager of Marketing and Sales for Suzuki. He said he had five minutes to talk. After about 20 minutes he gave me his card and told me that when the boat show was over to send him a proposal of my Challenge via email.

At this stage, the engine I had on my boat was covered up with a sign on it saying, *CAN YOUR ENGINE STAND UP TO THE TEST?* I needed a sponsor for the engine, as I only had a 2-stroke engine, which used too much fuel. If I used this engine I would properly not be able to carry enough fuel, as it would overload my boat.

The boat show was very tiring for me and I was lucky I was staying at my sister's place in Melbourne. The first couple of nights, when I went to bed I cried myself to sleep because all the people, noises and explaining my story to everyone who walked past was so mentally draining. My psychiatrist and psychologist told me I would be mentally drained and that for the week after the show finished I would be very tired.

After five days and a successful boat show, gaining sponsors, potential sponsors and raising around $400 for the Black Dog, I was exhausted. For the next week I had nothing left in me. When I got out of bed I would have breakfast at lunchtime, then I would sit in my chair and sleep until dinner, then go back to sleep again at around 2000 hours. I felt like I did the week after I finished the CSTC.

A week later, I got back into it and sent out the information to the people I met at the boat show. The main thing on my mind was whether I could get a Suzuki engine.

I took my boat to Bundoora Boat Upholstery. One week later I picked it up and the canopy looked fantastic. It had clear sides, which I could take off if required, and if the canopy was not needed I could lay it down on the windscreen nice and neat, like the old canopy. The boat looked so much better. While the boat was having the canopy fitted, I contacted Breakwater Marine in Moolap, Geelong. I asked if they could rewire the entire boat and install an anchor light that I received from Quintrex, as well as a new switchboard and an antenna for the Lowrance radio. They were happy to help out — they also gave me a compass, two new seats and pedestals, and a new steering wheel. I also picked up two 75-litre and one 50-litre fuel tanks, donated by Geelong Boating Centre (GBC) in Belmont, Geelong. Also during this time, a friend from Colac lent me a satellite phone. Once I got the boat back to Lorne, I fitted it with the new equipment.

I bought some metal strapping and two doormats. With the help and guidance of my uncles, I cut the mats into six pieces, put them under the metal strapping, secured the strapping over the fuel tanks, and fastened them to the side of the boat and to the floor. I also placed wood at either end of the tanks to ensure they wouldn't move a millimetre. The tanks were spread out around the boat for even weight distribution.

Fernwood Fitness at Waurn Ponds donated some money so I could buy new fuel lines that would burn for 30 minutes until they melted, and a three-way tap that I installed just below the fuel filter. This tap fed the 65-litre underfloor tank and also an extra fuel line two meters long that could be connected to the red fuel tanks attached to the floor. This gave me the capacity to carry 265 litres of fuel. That should be enough fuel, shouldn't it?

...

I received an email from The Scuba Doctor in Rye, Melbourne, saying they would lend me a dry suit for my trip. I also got an email from The Bridge Hotel/Motel in Smithton, Tasmania, offering me accommodation while I waited for the right weather to begin the Challenge. The plan was to leave from Tasmania and arrive at my home in Lorne, Victoria.

Now I had to get over to Tasmania. Easy — I would take the Spirit of Tasmania. The plan was that Dad and I would go over to Smithton, with my car towing the boat. Then, on the right day, I would leave from Tasmania and Dad would come back on the big boat with my car and trailer.

But this was where I came unstuck. It was early October when I rang up the Spirit, but the size I required was booked out until mid-November and I wanted to have the Challenge completed by the end of October or early November 2012. Also, it would cost $3000 dollars to get there and back, and that was just the car and trailer, not including Dad and myself.

I rang up two other shipping companies that carried freight from Victoria to Tasmania. One was booked out until the end of January 2013, and the other was a similar cost to the Spirit and Dad and I still had to get over there, either by plane or on the Spirit. It was just too much money. At that stage, I hadn't even raised that much money for the Black Dog. I was stumped.

Dad suggested I leave from Lorne, which sounded good. If it took two weeks waiting for the right weather it didn't matter, as I was at home. However, I would still eventually have to get my boat back to Victoria. I rang up the two shipping companies and we talked about the possibility of getting the boat back, but in the end the price was always a problem for me.

Then it hit me: I knew the boat could cross the Bass Strait, so why not come back in my boat? I would leave from Lorne when I had the best possible conditions, stay at The Bridge Hotel/Motel in Smithton, refuel and fix up anything if it broke on the way across, then come back to Lorne when the conditions were good again. Perfect.

I contacted The Bridge and they were happy with that. I also contacted the local council in Smithton and organised to have my boat moored at the marina. I had everything sorted, except for the engine.

It had been a few weeks since I sent the email to the National Manager of Marketing and Sales for Suzuki, so I gave him a call. His secretary said he would call me later, as he was in a meeting. The phone call did not come. What had changed since the Boat Show? Had they decided it was too much of a risk to put their name to? During this time, Signific put the stickers from all the sponsors on my boat. At least that was something — the boat looked awesome!

Two days later I found out about the engine. I received an email stating they were happy to loan me an engine. I took the boat to Richardson Marine in Warrnambool, Victoria and had the engine fitted. The conditions of the loan included that I get someone from the Coast Guard to look over my boat, and that I also send them a risk management assessment of the Challenge. I told them that I had met some people from the Victorian Volunteer Coast Guard at the Melbourne Boat Show, so I would ring them and get them to do an inspection and a write-up of the boat, so I could send Suzuki a copy. I rang the Coast Guard and organised an inspection in Rye, Melbourne, which enabled me to pick up the dry suit at the same time.

I went out fishing a few days before I had to take the boat for its inspection. While motoring along it didn't feel right, even with the new Suzuki 60hp 4-stroke engine. I stopped and had a look at the engine. At first I thought it might have had some seaweed around the prop, but there was no seaweed. I then opened up the inspection openings in the floor and noticed that the underneath was full of water. I turned on the automatic bilge pump, got out the manual bilge pump, and started to pump the water out, but it kept flowing in. Shit, there was a hole in the boat. I turned around and headed straight back to the boat ramp, put the boat on the trailer and undid the bungs. The water poured out — the entire boat under the floor was full of water.

I washed the salt water off the boat and engine at the Aquatic Club, and went home and filled the boat up with water to see where the water was coming from. Straight away I could see where the leak was. It turned out the trailer was not the right size for the boat, and when launching and landing the majority of the weight was being put in one place on the port and starboard sides. The aluminium had worn so thin it had caused the plastic slides on the trailer to wear through the hull.

I rang up a friend in Colac who specialised in welding aluminium and explained the situation. He said to bring it down to Colac the next morning and he would weld it up and check over the boat. I had to remove everything, including the floor and the underfloor fuel tank. I was up until after midnight pulling the boat apart.

The next day, the hole was welded up, and other spots where the hull looked thin were welded and made thicker. Adjustments to the trailer were done at the same time to avoid the same problem happening again. Once back in Lorne, I put the boat back together. As the underfloor fuel tank was out I took the opportunity to drain the tank, making sure there was no dirt there, or anything else that may be an issue later, which resulted in another late night.

The next morning I went to Melbourne and picked up the dry suit from The Scuba Doctor. Then I went to the Rye boat ramp to meet with the person from the Coast Guard who was going to inspect my boat. When he arrived he went over the whole boat and I showed him all the safety equipment I had. At the end of the inspection he said to me that the first time he was told about my Challenge he thought it was a joke. But after the inspection, and after talking to me, he had total confidence that the Challenge could be completed. A week later, he sent me the results and I forwarded them to Suzuki, the Black Dog Institute, and all my other sponsors.

The report included a list of the items I required for the trip, a list of the modifications I made to the boat and the details of my experience in the Army. The report also included the following:

This report represents xxxxxx personal opinion, yet would seem to indicate that you have taken all legal requirements into account and have further added to those requirements to augment the safety of the venture.

[...]

On Saturday 13 October 2012 at 1200 I met James Prascevic, xxxxxx Street Lorne Vic 3232 with his vessel, a 1994 white aluminium 4.55 m Quintrex Fish-A-Boat powered by a Suzuki 4-stroke, outboard of 45 kw rating, at the Rye public boat ramp with a view of inspecting this vessel for all the legal equipment required by Transport Safety Victoria.

James is proposing to take this vessel on a promotional journey from Lorne, Victoria to Smithton, Tasmania as a fundraising venture for the Black Dog Institute.

The hull has recently been inspected and had some repair to weak aluminium areas and some reinforcing, and appears to be in sound condition.

[...]

The proposed journey is from Lorne via the east side of King Island to Three Hummock Island then on to Smithton, a total of approx. 140 miles in straight lines, and we should allow at least 15% for drift, etc., making about 160 miles.

James reported an economy of approx. 50 litres per 70 miles, but this is not confirmed and seems a little optimistic. I think 1 litre per mile would be very conservative and what I would allow. That would mean 160 miles is 160 litres, then add one third, 52 litres = a total of 212 litres. He proposes to take 265 litres, so that is very conservative.

[...]

When first hearing of the proposal in this size vessel I thought it sounded a little foolhardy, but after inspection of the vessel and its extra equipment, plus the preparedness of the operator, I am prepared to say this may be accomplished in relative safety.

I also forwarded on my risk management assessment. It read:

Risk Management For James Prascevic Crossing The Bass Strait

This risk management outlays the risks and ways that I have used to overcome or solve the risks involved in the Challenge.

My name is James Prascevic and I am an ex-Australian soldier battling a different challenge from my previous Army days. I am preparing to take on the Bass Strait solo in my 4.55-metre Quintrex aluminium boat, 1994 model between Lorne, Victoria and Smithton, Tasmania and return in order to raise funds for the Black Dog Institute. Once I arrive in Smithton I will say at the Bridge Hotel/Motel where I will check over the boat, refuel, get some rest and wait for the right weather conditions to return to Lorne.

I am planning on doing this trip mid-October 2012 (weather permitting).

My 4.55m Quintrex aluminium boat has been fitted with the following:

- 1 x new Suzuki 60hp 4-stroke engine
- 2 x new registered emergency position-indicating radio beacons (EPIRB)
- 1 x new Lowrance VHF-250 marine radio and new VHF aerial
- 1 x new GME G142CFD fishfinder/chartplotter (which is also attached to the marine radio so the VHF gets the GPS info for the Emergency Distress signal, if required)
- New anchor light
- Port and Starboard lights
- New canopy with side protection
- Anchor with 3 metres of chain and 50 metres of anchor rope
- Electric and manual bilge pump
- Bucket with lanyard
- 2 x hand held orange smoke signals
- 2 x hand held red distress flares
- 1 x Red star parachute distress rocket
- Satellite phone
- 2 x approved personal flotation devices
- 2 x waterproof buoyant torches
- 1 x pair of oars/paddles
- New fitted compass
- First-aid kit
- 10 litres of water
- Assorted food

- 265 litres of unleaded fuel

- New 2.5-kilogram fire extinguisher

- New 1-kilogram fire extinguisher

- A spare battery for the boat

- Jumper leads

- Assorted tools

- A strong LED spotlight that plugs into the boat (in case of the Challenge going into the night. However, the Challenge will be done during daylight savings, so it will most likely not be needed.)

On my person I will have the following:

- Drysuit/hood

- 1 x registered Personal Locating Beacon (PLB)

- 1 x hand held Garmin GPS

- Knife

Other Points To Note

- I have an approved boat operator's license and I have a lot of experience on the open water, as I have lived in Lorne, Victoria, most of my life and have always fished in the open water.

- I have the backing of the Victorian Volunteer Coast Guard, who will look over the boat prior to leaving.

- I will have all the relevant phone numbers, such as the Victorian Volunteer Coast Guard and Water Police, King Island personnel and Tasmanian Coast Guard, etc. programmed into my satellite phone.

- I will have a person in Lorne that I will have regular contact with every half hour. I will update them on my location, weather, heading, fuel left, conditions, etc. They will have the relevant numbers of the Coast Guard and Water Police, to keep them updated if required and notify them if I miss a scheduled check-up.

- I have replaced all the fuel lines with commercial grade hoses and the underfloor connections are double clamped. I was told by the sales person that the boat will burn for 30 minutes before the hoses will melt.

- The boat has been professionally re-wired by Breakwater Marine.

- The boat has been stripped and filled with water to check for any leaks.

- This trip to and return will only be done when the weather is suitable.

- The boat is fitted with a new Suzuki 60hp 4-stroke engine.

- If the weather turns bad on the trip, I will return to my start point or the nearest safe spot.

Bad Weather

If the weather is bad or looks like it will turn bad, I will not go. If while on the trip the weather turns, I will either turn around and/or head to the nearest shelter point or land base. I will also notify my contact at Lorne of the changes in weather and route.

Breakdown

In the event of a breakdown between Lorne and King Island, I will try to fix the problem by any means. If I cannot fix the problem, I will call the escort boats for help or the Coast Guard at Warrnambool, Geelong, Melbourne or King Island with my satellite phone and or my marine radio. In the event of a breakdown between the southern tip of King Island and Smithton, I will try to fix the problem by any means. If I cannot fix the problem I will call the Tasmanian Coast Guard or King Island with my satellite phone or my marine radio.

Fire

In the event of a fire, I will try by any means to put it out. I will then contact the above personnel if possible, depending on where I am on the trip. If I cannot put the fire out, I will activate my EPIRB and PLB and get out of the boat. I will then get back to the boat, if possible, and stay with it, or get into the survival position and wait for rescue.

Capsize

In the event of a capsize, I will try to get back to the boat and stay with it if it has not sunk. I will activate my PLB (attached to me) and if possible I will activate my EPIRB (attached to boat). If the boat has sunk I will get into the survival position and await rescue.

Leak Or Hitting A Submerged Object

In the result of hitting a submerged object, such as a sea container, floating wood, etc., resulting in a leak, I will start my electric bilge pump and try to carry on to the closest land point. If that fails. I will use my manual bilge pump and try to continue on. I will also notify my contact in Lorne, and the Coast Guard and Water Police, etc. If the boat has a leak, meaning it will sink, I will activate my EPIRB as well.

...

I started doing sea trials so I could determine how much fuel I would use, to see if 265 litres would be enough. I also wanted to see how the new engine would handle the extra weight, if the red fuel tanks attached to the floor were in the correct place, and if the boat would sit evenly in the water while both stationary and moving.

I loaded the boat up with a bit more weight than what I intended to take. Almost every day I took the boat out, going to Apollo Bay and to Anglesea and back. I went out in deeper water and on rough days, but on those days I didn't want to go out too far, as I didn't want the Challenge to finish before it had started. I was very impressed with the Suzuki and very happy that 265 litres would be sufficient. The normal rule in regards to fuel when boating is that you use one third to get to your fishing or motoring and cruising spots and have two thirds left in the tank to get back. This allows you enough fuel if the weather gets bad. I figured I would use up to 200 litres, so I felt good knowing I would have at least 65 litres spare. I was happy with that. Now all I had to do was wait for the weather gods to favour me.

EIGHTEEN

THE CHALLENGE

By this time I had been in about 10 newspaper articles (mostly the *Geelong Advertiser*), on the radio five times, on *The Project* on Channel Ten and on the SBS television show *Insight*. I had approximately 1000 people following me on my Facebook page. I had so many encouraging words coming my way that I felt like I was spreading the word, and possibly inspiring people to speak up about their mental health issues, and even seek help. That is why I had wanted to do this Challenge in the first place, apart from having a ball crossing the Bass Strait twice in my boat.

I had been told by essentially everyone I knew to expect some or even a lot of criticism. A lady from Apollo Bay, who obviously didn't read the article and didn't have any idea about boats, responded to one of my articles. I won't name her, but I would like to say thanks to her, as it gave me even more passion and drive to complete the Challenge.

Her response read:

Sea at Risk

In response to the article in The Echo (June 7/12): are you kidding? Many questions are raised about this proposed solo adventure in a tin boat across Bass Strait. Firstly, would anyone be prepared to sponsor such a dangerous attempt? Who will be responsible for the costs when he goes MIA? The fact that he states that a satellite phone, new outboard and other navigational and safety gear is needed, leaves one to questioning: A. Does he have the knowledge to operate such equipment?; and B. Does he honestly believe he can cross Bass Strait, renowned to be one of the roughest stretches of water in the world, in an open 4.5-metre craft? It seems a ridiculous proposition to me. Risky to the extreme. I suggest Mr Prascevic refers to the internet blog of Father Adelir Antonio, who attempted to set a world record for a clustered balloon flight. His proposed solo challenge is just as ludicrous. Whatever happened to the good old-fashioned sausage sizzle fundraiser?

I was furious and so upset. Did everyone feel this way? Was I the only one who thought the Challenge could be completed? I talked to a few people who had read her response and they thought the same as me, which made me feel a little better.

I wrote a response to her straight away and was going to send it to the paper there and then, but my mother had advised me not to do anything I would regret. I didn't want my sponsors or followers to think I was unprofessional. So I delayed sending my response. I read it over and over again, and asked Mum to read it.

Eventually, I sent my response back to the paper and gave them a call to ask their opinion. The editor said it read very well and that it would be in the response column the next day. I trusted him, as he was a supporter of my cause (I was usually wary of the media, but in this case I felt he could be trusted). My response read:

Well Planned

In response to xxxxxx letter (The Echo, June 21/12): No, I am not kidding. If you or anyone else would like to ask me any questions, feel free to do so. Firstly, yes, people are willing to support/sponsor me (15 sponsors was the end in total) in this important cause. Secondly, I will be responsible for the costs if I go missing, not you, so don't worry about that part! Do I know how to operate my equipment on my boat? Yes. I have served almost 10 years in the Army, and after six months of the hardest training, I was four weeks away from becoming a fully qualified Special Forces soldier (Commando) when I broke my leg. I am able to operate a satellite phone, which I used many times while serving my country overseas in

Timor, Iraq and Afghanistan, and I am qualified and competent in many more things than you may think. What you don't know xxxxxx, is that this trip has been in planning for almost a year and I still have four months until I plan to go. I did not wake up one morning and decide that I might go for a drive in my boat to Tasmania. This trip has been planned in every detail and I will only go when I have the perfect weather window. If I am not happy with the weather, I will wait. The equipment I need I have, but to have newer equipment would be better, don't you think! If you don't want to help me, please host a sausage sizzle and raise $50 for depression, which affects one in five people in Australia. These stats only include the people who have spoken up and it does not include the effects it has on their families and friends. Thanks for the feedback. I don't suppose you would like to make a donation at my Everyday Hero page. If anyone else would like to donate, the address is www.everydayhero.com.au/james_ prascevic and anyone who thinks they can help me out can email me at urabus_45@hotmail.com. By the way, I am also a qualified plumber and have completed a number of university units, so I am not the dumb infantry grunt that people may think I am.

There was another response to her argument, which read:

Brave Soldier

Regarding xxxxxx letter on James Prascevic: I take it she does not approve of someone trying to dig themselves out of the depression hole. Jim has suffered immensely from physiological and psychological pain for the past two years as a result of serving his country in the armed forces. I could not even imagine the amount of courage and intelligence needed to become a modern day soldier. Imagine being dropped into a strange country and having to navigate the terrain there under the cover of darkness, all while being under the threat of enemy attack and IEDs. I don't think it would be any challenge for him to find his way or for him to summon the courage to do the journey. You seem to have forgotten, this crossing is going to be done for the Black Dog Institute to raise money and awareness for mental illness, which seems to be in epidemic proportions. When you complain about the cost of the rescue mission (not that it's going to happen), think about the Sydney to Hobart sailing race and how much money was spent on these affluent people who sailed into a big Tasman Sea storm. These people were not sailing for any other cause apart from prize money and glory, unlike Jim who is making the crossing to help others. So get back in your box.

After these responses were published, a lot of people told me not to worry about the woman's comments, especially the part where she said, 'Who will be responsible for the costs when he goes MIA?' The fact she said 'when' really annoyed me. And to compare me to a person who attempted to set a world record for a clustered balloon flight is just ludicrous. But I wasn't going to let it get to me. The fact that someone else took the time to respond to her comments in support of me made me feel great.

...

It was 26 October. Looking at the Bureau of Meteorology website and other weather sites, 29 October looked like it was going to be the day. I watched the weather for the next three days, checking for updates every five minutes. They only updated them at 1600 hours each day, but I was still checking. During this time I had packed the boat and was ready to go, and was checking and rechecking all the equipment. I changed the batteries in my torches and in each GPS, and fuelled the boat up to the maximum capacity of 265 litres. Everything was ready to go. The morning of the 29th came and the weather was perfect — well, as perfect as it was going to get in Bass Strait. I, my mum, my dad and a mate took the boat down to where I was to launch, behind the pier at Lorne at 0700 hours. I did a quick radio interview, got into my dry suit, put the PLB in the pocket, put on my life jacket, wetsuit booties and strapped a diving knife to my ankle. The weird thing was that I wasn't nervous at all, and hadn't been even in the few days before. I just wanted to get it done. I knew I could do it and I knew my boat was capable. The boat had been stripped to the point where there was nothing in it and then put back together again. I felt as though I was one with the boat.

I did a radio check, said my goodbyes and was off. Next stop: Smithton, Tasmania.

I left Lorne on Monday 29 October at 0700 hours to pretty good seas. Winds were five to 10 knots south-easterly. I was pushed off course a bit due to the wind and the way the swells and rolls were coming in, and almost ended up in Apollo Bay. Eventually, I got out into the open ocean and got some good weather, and was able to get back on course to King Island. About two hours out from King Island I was going straight into short chop, which was really annoying and uncomfortable.

Once I arrived at King Island I went along the east side, which was sheltered from the wind. I stopped the engine, had a toilet break, checked over the boat, had a feed of sandwiches and had a mental break. I then continued in a southerly direction down King Island. My plan was to go all the way to the southern end of the island, then go in a straight line to Tasmania. However, once I got about halfway down I realised the weather and sea conditions were as good as they could get. So I cut across at the halfway point of the southern side of king Island, then turned and headed for the north-west tip of Tasmania.

At one stage, a pod of about 20 dolphins escorted me for an hour or so, which was great. Although it was only a pod of them, their presence helped with the feeling of isolation. It was as if they were escorting me on my trip. I talked to the video camera a lot, which also made me feel not so alone in the middle of nowhere.

To get to my destination at Smithton in Duck Bay I had to go between two islands — Hunter Island Conservation Area and Three

TOP: The gruelling PT sessions on the CTSC.
BOTTOM: More of the PT sessions on the CTSC.

At my wedding — my sister Clare, my father Peter and my mother Denise.

TOP: At the Melbourne Boat Show 2012.
BOTTOM: Leaving Lorne on 29 October 2012.

TOP: Arriving back in Lorne on 3 November 2012.
BOTTOM: The Challenge completed successfully.

A cheers to Merv and Tim, who were with me in spirit.

TOP: Lily at about three weeks of age. She and Shelly kept me sane just that little bit longer.

BOTTOM: Joey — my best friend, psychologist and psychiatrist.

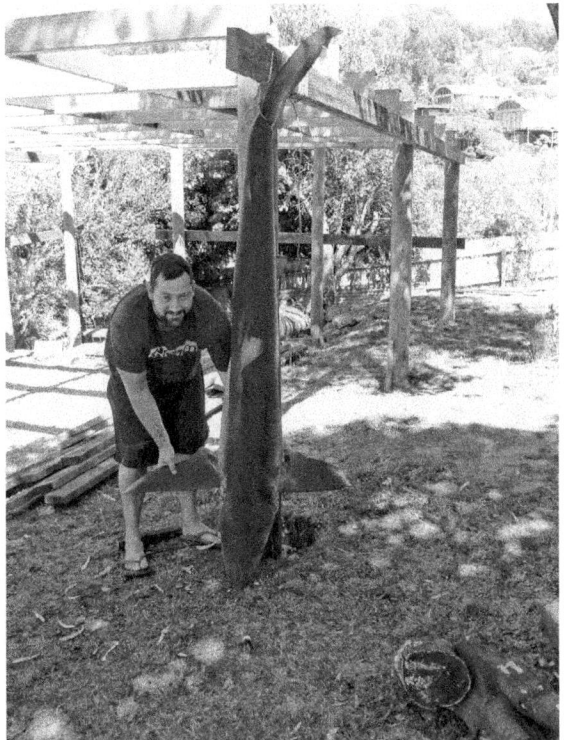

TOP: My new boat, the 27-foot yacht *Nari*.

BOTTOM: My passion — shark fishing. A Blue Shark.

TOP: A Bronze Whaler Shark.
BOTTOM: A Mako Shark.

Hummock Island State Reserve. Once I got past them, all I had to do was locate the entrance to Duck River. This was the hard part. I couldn't find it anywhere. After a few phone calls to the locals, getting bogged twice as it was low tide, and losing daylight fast, I eventually found the entrance to Duck River. The river felt like it went forever, but was maybe only two kilometres. I got bogged again and was filmed by WIN News as I was pulling my boat up the river. I had organised to meet up with them for an interview, scheduled for two hours prior.

I tied my boat to an oyster boat, and had the interview with WIN News. Steve, the interviewer, then took me to The Bridge Hotel/Motel. By this time it was 2130 hours. I made a phone call to my relieved parents, then went into the bar area of The Bridge. I sat down and ordered a beer. There were a few locals there and, being a small town, they could tell straight away that I was not from the area. They asked where I was from and I told them that I had just arrived from Victoria. They promptly replied, 'Are you the bloke that came across Bass Strait in the tinny?' I replied, 'Yes.' They said, 'You are not paying for any beer tonight,' so I had a few free beers with them, which tasted like heaven. I then went back to my room, had a long shower and went to bed. I was stuffed and fell asleep pretty soon, even though I was still on a high.

...

The next day I woke up at about 1300 hours, had a pub meal, moved my boat over to the local marina, which could only be accessed at high tide, and went back to my room and slept until the evening. I had pizza for dinner, had a few beers at the bar and was in bed by 2200 hours.

The next day I woke up feeling refreshed. I went to the local service station and organised to have my boat refueled. I did a few repairs on the boat and got it ready to leave, as I didn't know what day the weather was going to be suitable. With the boat ready to go, I went back to my room, updated my Facebook status and relaxed for the rest of the day. Looking at the weather websites, Saturday 3 November seemed like the best day for me to return to Victoria. The good thing was that because it was on Saturday, a lot of my family and friends could meet me when I arrived back at Lorne.

...

On 3 November, I headed home. I planned to leave at 0400 hours, however I slept in and didn't leave until 0615.

There was short chop on the ocean until I got away from Tasmania, then big swells and waves three times the size of the boat, coming from three different directions. I had so much fun. I felt like Lieutenant Dan from *Forrest Gump*, when he was on the shrimp boat in the big storm.

While continuing on between Tasmania and King Island, out of nowhere on the port side, the left side, a large wave started to break. I immediately turned the boat into the wave and accelerated to get over it before it broke on the boat. I was successful, however the wave behind it was bigger and started to break as well. Once again, I accelerated into the wave. As I got to the top of it, the wave broke as the engine was going through it. The boat come through the wave and then went on a 90 degree angle, straight down on the other side. The front end of the boat up to the windshield was buried in the ocean, turning the windscreen into what looked like a giant diving mask. The boat bobbed up and down on a 90 degree angle for what felt like an eternity (but in reality was probably only a second or two) and then flattened out, with water gushing in from every side. I immediately turned on the bilge pump. Everything in the boat was saturated but there was no structural damage, so I was able to continue.

From then on, my eyes felt like they were the size of dinner plates. I didn't even have the confidence to blink, as I was too worried about rogue waves. I must have had help with this from Merv and Tim, because I was so lucky to get through that set of waves, which had come out of nowhere.

Luckily, there were no more rogue waves. After another half hour of travel, the large waves that were coming at me from three different directions turned into big swells coming from the south. The only way I can explain the way they looked is the way a farm at the bottom of a hill looks — like an endless grassy plain.

Eventually, I got to King Island and did the same as on the way over. On the final run home I was pushed way past Apollo Bay, to the west, and had to motor into a strong easterly wind in short chop, which made the last hour of the trip very uncomfortable.

Approximately 10 minutes from home, while travelling along the coast, I used up one of the tanks of fuel and had to change the hose over to a new fuel tank. While I was doing this I heard a voice saying, 'Congratulations James, we have been trying to catch you for the last five minutes.' It turned out to be the Commodore of the Lorne Angling and Aquatic Club, who was there with another member with a large Australian flag. I got a massive fright, as it was the last thing I expected. The only voice I expected to hear was my mother on the satellite phone. It was good to see a friendly face, and when I shook hands with him I knew then that I had completed the trip. The Commodore told me to follow him, as he would escort me into Lorne.

When we got to the point where I could see the Lorne Pier, I noticed straight away the *Welcome Home James* banner painted in my favourite football clubs colours — Essendon, red and black. I rounded the pier and all the people at the Aquatic Club were clapping and cheering, which I was a bit embarrassed about, but I had a large smile on my face all the same. I then looked up at the pier and noticed nearly 20 members of my family standing there, clapping and cheering. I went under the pier directly below where my mum was standing. She had been the one doing the schedule check-ups, where I would ring her every hour and give her my position throughout the trip. She looked relieved that I had made it home safely.

I went around and landed my boat, and was greeted by another

20-plus family members and friends. As I stepped out of the boat, my dry suit got caught on one of the lures attached to one of my fishing rods, and I nearly fell over. It felt so good to be back on land again. I had known that I could complete the trip from the moment the idea first entered my head, so I was not as excited as I thought I might be, but I was very relieved that it was all over.

My family and friends came over and gave me the mandatory hugs and handshakes. I then grabbed the stubby of beer that had been with me the whole time, opened it, tapped the end of the stubby on Tim's name, said cheers and drank half the stubby. I then walked over to the other side, tapped the stubby on Merv's name, said cheers and drank the rest. Two mouthfuls and it was gone. They were with me, I was sure of it.

My uncles loaded the boat up onto the trailer. I then gave a little speech, thanking everybody who came down. Then we all went to the Aquatic Club, where the boat was washed and we all had a few drinks to celebrate my homecoming. After a couple of hours at the Aquatic Club, the crowd thinned out and a few of us went back to my house, where we had a barbecue and a couple more beers, and I was asleep within the hour. I was very tired for the next few weeks.

...

While out fishing during summer, a man from *Trailer Boat Magazine* came to see my boat at the boat ramp. He started taking photos, and he asked me a few questions about the stickers on the boat. I explained the purpose of them, then I gave him my contact details, as he was interested in writing a story.

In the 292nd issue of *Trailer Boat Magazine*, February to March 2013, an article titled 'Therapeutic Waters' appeared. It began, 'A soldier employed in a war experiences a range of emotions, and occasionally none at all. Sometimes, after service, these emotions continue, while new ones develop. How do I know? Former soldier

James Prascevic told me about it when I meet at Lorne boat ramp on Victoria's great Ocean Road.'

It went on to detail my military career, the parachuting accident during Special Forces selection, suffering from PTSD, and the details of the Challenge. I was very happy with the story, especially the fact that I had a two-page spread in a magazine that I'd been reading for as long as I could remember. The only thing I was a little disappointed with was that he didn't mention my return trip — that I had made the Bass Strait crossing twice. Despite this, the magazine, along with magazines such as *Modern Boating Magazine* and *Fishing World Magazine*, which also had stories in them about my trip, were going straight to the pool room, so to speak.

It still hadn't sunk in that I had completed a return trip across the Bass Strait in my 4.55-metre boat. But I never had any doubt when I started to plan this trip in February 2011 that I could not achieve it.

By doing the Challenge, I had originally decided that if I could make a difference in one person's life then it would all be worth it. However, in doing the Challenge I had put all my focus into it and had neglected myself.

An analogy they use at the clinics I have been admitted to is the same as what you are told during the safety briefing in a plane. The airline personnel tell you to put your oxygen mask on before you help others. What I had been doing from the start of the Challenge up until this point was putting all my emotions and feelings to the back of my mind, and in a way putting the oxygen mask on others before I put it on myself. This, eventually, led to disaster.

NINETEEN

THE BREAKDOWN

After the Challenge was complete and I had finished doing all the media follow-ups, such as articles in *Fishing World Magazine*, *Trailer Boat Magazine*, *Modern Boating Magazine* and the *Geelong Advertiser*, I decided that I would set up a webpage, as my intention was to complete more Challenges. The webpage was named Different Challenge.

The next Challenge I had planned to do was to make a documentary about my military career and the Bass Strait trip, and take my boat down the Murray River, starting in New South Wales and finishing where it meets the ocean in South Australia. My plan was that I would stop at major towns and cities along the way, and in a public speaking forum I would show my documentary, talk about my military experiences and talk about depression, PTSD, and other mental health issues.

What I had been doing for the previous six months was the exact opposite to what I'd been taught — I had been putting the oxygen mask on others before myself. I decided that I needed a bit of a break, and over the Christmas period I focused on myself. During this time, all the emotions and feelings I had blocked out during the preparation of the Challenge were starting to re-emerge. Now that it was over, I had nothing to think about other than what I had put to the back of my mind. I started to feel the way I had been previously, when I was admitted to hospital back in February 2011. I was starting to jump more at night time. The jumps and the mini fits were happening again, which scared the hell out of me. I hated the fact that I knew they were happening, but I had no control over them.

My psychiatrist recommended that I do a second PTSD course, as the first course I did was very close to when everything was happening to me, such as losing my career and separating from my wife. I was told back in February 2011 that there would be a good chance that I would do either the same PTSD course, or a more in-depth course when I was a bit more stable. I agreed to participate in the 12-week PTSD course, which was run two days a week from 0830 to 1500, which included a live-in week of five days. I talked to my parents, my psychologist and my GP, and they all agreed that it would be a great idea. I was excited to be doing the course, as I had it in my head that there would be a good chance that a light bulb moment would happen and this would cure me.

About five weeks prior to starting the course, everything started to unravel for me, as I was still suffering heavily from PTSD and major depression. The suicidal thoughts that had been in my head had started to get stronger and stronger, and over a period of about one week I started to plan to take my own life. Without getting into too much detail, I had it planned even to the point of how my body would be found without having to put other people through the traumatic event of seeing a dead body.

The day I had planned it for was the day that I had an appointment with my psychologist. I rang her up and asked for an earlier appointment, as my appointment was late in the day and I knew I had to stop myself from carrying out my plan. She stated that she had no earlier appointments. I said that it was fine and that I would see her later in the afternoon.

When I arrived at my appointment, I was in tears. I explained what I was planning and how I was feeling. She told me that I should have told her how I was feeling earlier in the day when I rang, and that I would have been able to see her immediately. We talked for a few minutes and it was decided that she would ring my psychiatrist to organise a stay in the Geelong clinic. I went home and packed my bags and within an hour I was checked into the clinic, where I would feel safe and be able to recharge my batteries.

There are so many things that are said about suicide, that those who attempt it are taking the easy option and that they are weak. In my opinion, it's not until you have been in that situation that you truly understand it. You believe the only option is to not exist anymore. If you understand this, you will understand why people attempt or succeed in taking their own lives. Even though I hope no-one out there ever gets into that situation, if you do you must utilise your support network. In my case, it was my psychiatrist, my psychologist, my parents and, of course, my dog.

Being in an ordinary hospital was hard, as it brought back memories from when I was working in the hospital in Iraq. However, being in a clinic and surrounded by people who understood what I was going through made me feel a lot more comfortable. I had my own room, with a television and my own bathroom. This suited me, as I lived only with my dog Joey, and when I wanted to I could go into my room, close the door and shut myself off from the world.

My psychiatrist came to see me every morning. We would have a good chat about how I was feeling. I also tried some new medication. It was an antidepressant that was supposed to stabilise my sleeping patterns and change the nightmares I had every night into dreams. Changing medication and adding to existing medication is good when you are in a stabilised environment where you can be monitored. If there were any adverse side effects of the medication, I would be in the right situation to deal with it.

It was decided that I would spend two weeks in hospital, then go back home and spend two weeks there before beginning the PTSD course. My psychiatrist and I agreed that I shouldn't rely too much on the hospital. For the things I'd learn on the PTSD course I'd need to be in my normal living conditions, trying out the methods that we had been taught, seeing whether they could help me through the days, weeks, months and years to come.

In the end, I spent two weeks in hospital relaxing and catching up on sleep. I also did some classes at the clinic about mindfulness and breathing and also wrote 'The Challenge' chapter of this book. I went home feeling awesome. I felt refreshed and ready for the PTSD course, starting in two weeks.

Returning home and seeing Joey was the highlight, as that was the longest I had been away from her since I had got her, almost two years ago. She was so excited when I got home that she nearly licked my beard off. It was great to be home because I was able to go out fishing in my boat again, which helped a lot. I spent a lot of time with Joey, as I felt bad for being away from her for so long, though having Mum and Dad next door made it okay because they had looked after her while I was gone.

...

On 20 February it started — my second PTSD course in two years. I was shitting myself. I was hoping that there was going to be no Defence personnel on the course and that the other people would be the same as those in the PTSD course in Sydney, being mainly police and nurses. I still did not like being around Defence personnel or hearing about their experiences, as it reminded me of how I so desired to still be a serving member of the Army.

When I arrived, we were all given a brief by the head psychologists of the clinic. We then had a talk by a former ex-Army member, who had done the course previously. Then we were introduced to the staff, which included six psychologists who would be giving us lessons over the next 12 weeks. We were also allocated a psychologist that we would talk to once a week in addition to the course. It then came time to find out the backgrounds of the people in the course. This was when my worst nightmare came true — all the people in the course, six men and one woman, were ex-Army and Navy personnel.

When all the introductions had been made, we made up a set

of rules, which included confidentiality, punctuality, no judgments, respect, honesty, and that it was okay to take time out but return to the group once you have calmed down. We also made a list of group expectations. These included developing an understanding of PTSD, gaining tools to deal with it, mutual support, sharing what we had learned with others, being able to communicate better with other people (especially family), feeling more comfortable with people, increasing tolerance levels, stop blaming ourselves (be self-nurturing) and stop blaming our friends.

Once we finished compiling the rules and the group expectations, we finished for the day. I drove back to Lorne and when I got home I was absolutely exhausted.

The next day I was up early again, which is not that early for most, but when you don't sleep and haven't slept much over the past weeks, getting up at 0630 hours is very hard. I arrived in Geelong by 0830, ready to start the day. The first session was an introduction to goal setting. The goal setting acronym is SMARTY, which stands for S= specific, M= measurable, A= achievable, R= realistic, T= timeframe, and Y= your reward. The idea is that if you make a SMARTY goal, you will have more success in achieving your goal. For example, if you wanted to lose 10 kilograms in a month, when you write it down using the SMARTY format you would see that it is not achievable because it is unrealistic.

We then had an introduction to the signs and symptoms of anxiety. We watched a DVD called *You're Not In The Forces Now*. This DVD is presented by ex-Australian soldier Nic Fothergill, who was drafted during the Vietnam War from 1967 to 1968. After many years of suffering from PTSD, he eventually became a psychologist and worked for Veterans' and Veterans' Family Counselling Service (VVCS). In this DVD he explained how the Defence Force changes the way you think, especially after being exposed to war-like situations. If you don't speak up about the problems you are having when you return home, there is a high probability of suffering from a mental illness, such as PTSD and depression. Although this DVD was made up directly for Vietnam veterans and their families, it was still relevant to those of us who served in Timor, Iraq and Afghanistan. This DVD, which is available for free from VVCS, is well worth watching. I would recommend it to anyone who has served overseas and is suffering from a mental illness, as well as their families. My parents watched it, which I believed helped them a lot to understand what I was going through.

For the next few days I was totally exhausted. Although it had only been one and a half days of group sessions, the lead-up and the anxiety that was building up had hit me all in one go. I rang up DVA and asked them whether it was possible for me to stay in the clinic on the Wednesday night of the course, which would save me having to travel back and forth. Almost immediately DVA responded, saying that I would be allocated a certain amount of money towards a motel room, which I felt took a lot of pressure off me. I found a fantastic motel in Geelong called The Rose Garden, which was only a five-minute drive to the clinic. When I explained to the owner of the motel my circumstances, they supported me thoroughly. Although I found it hard to sleep much at night due to the nightmares, when I eventually got to sleep it was very hard for me to wake up because of the medication I was taking. Usually, Mum would have to set her alarm and come over to wake me up so I could get to the clinic on time. When I explained this to the owner of the motel, she said she would be quite happy to personally wake me up in the morning. So with that all sorted, I felt a bit more pressure taken off me.

The following Wednesday, we started off with a morning check-in and were told what the plans for the day would be. We also had a check-in of our SUDS. SUDS stands for Subjective Unit of Distress explained in detail in the PTSD and Discharge chapter, when I did my first PTSD course. After that we would have a coffee or tea, and I would go out and have at least two cigarettes in a couple of minutes. Then we would start the day's sessions.

That week, two human-sized cut-outs of people were displayed in the room. One was in the shape of a civilian and the other was in the shape of a military figure in the kneeling position, wearing webbing and holding up a rifle. Most of the people there were intimidated by the military figure. However, I was intimidated by the civilian figure, as that was what I was now even though I still didn't want to accept that I could never be in the military again. To see that figure every day for the remainder of the course was going to be hard for me. They would not be taken out of the room, although after the first break we did hide them under the couch, without much success, as the staff found them almost straight away. Apparently this was not the first time they had been hidden. The reason the figures were there was to try and get us comfortable in a situation we were not comfortable in, and to show us that there was nothing to be frightened about, as we were in a secure environment.

The first session for the day was an introduction to managing addictive behaviours. This was the first of six sessions focused on alcohol and the effects it can have on your mind and body. The other sessions we had were on addictions such as smoking, caffeine and overeating, which continue to affect or worsen the effects of PTSD and depression.

We were given a worksheet titled 'Stages of Change'. It starts with the contemplation 'that maybe what I'm doing is not so good for me', then the decision 'that I'm going to quit'. It then moves on to the action 'I'm actually doing something about this now', and then to maintenance, such as 'I'm still not using'. From there you go on to the long-term change of 'I haven't used for ages', or you can relapse with 'I used again' (or in other words, 'fell off the bandwagon'). From there you can go back to being addicted to the thing you decided to quit. For example, I could go back to drinking a cask of wine a night, which is a lapse, or I could decide, 'Okay, I have relapsed. However, I'm going to start the cycle again to see if I can get to the point where I have made a long-term change, where I haven't drunk for a long time and will continue to stay sober.' In this case, perhaps you should reconsider your SMARTY goal, which is so important to do when setting a goal of changing addictive behaviours, especially when they have been long-term issues.

After lunch we had two lessons on understanding PTSD, then from 1400 to 1500 we did a review of the day. We then did a mindfulness session, which involved some breathing and grounding techniques. Grounding is a way to distract yourself from the thoughts that are going on in your mind. The way we were taught grounding is that you sit up in your chair with your arms either on the armrests or resting on your legs, with your feet firmly on the ground. You then close your eyes and focus on where your body is touching the chair, where your feet are firmly touching the ground, and at the same time you are doing long, slow deep breaths. Using the breathing and grounding methods, you can focus your mind on what you are doing at the time and not on the negative thoughts.

We were given a cartoon picture of a man walking his dog in a park. There was a caption above the dog's head and all he could see were the trees that were in front of him. However, the man could see the trees, plus a variety of other things that were on his mind and not relevant to where he was. What the dog was seeing was the idea in the grounding and the breathing, which would hopefully result in us being able to shut off our thoughts and have that feeling of freedom. We were given a CD that had relaxation tracks on it, which I put on my phone so I could listen to it at any time I wanted to. We were encouraged to do a minimum of five minutes of relaxation a day. We were told to listen to at least one track of the CD, which would cover the minimum five minutes.

When we finished up for the day, I was relieved I only had to drive five minutes until I got to the motel room. I thought this was going to be very good for me, as I didn't have to travel. However, I was in a new bed and unfamiliar surroundings. It was strange not having Joey there, not being able to feel her cuddling up to me at night time. I missed her a lot. I couldn't sleep very well at all, and probably managed on average around three hours per night for the entire course.

The next morning, after our check-in and review, we started to talk about trauma awareness and how we measured it, which went up until lunch. In this course, the families of the veterans involved were very important, and on Thursdays the families would come in at 1130 and do a session with a psychologist. They would then join us for lunch, and then we would all join up as a group and do the final session of the day. As I had separated from my wife, my parents came to learn how to help me. They came every week and did everything they could to get the most out of it, and I thank them so much for their support. The first joint group session was fun, as we did a family tree. I had always wanted to do one, but I'd never really got around to it. I was happy that my parents were there with me, but I really wanted to be doing this with my now ex-wife.

At the time, I didn't really care whether I lived or died. During question time in the family group sessions, the staff pushed us to answer those questions and talk about them. One week, I was asked what I wanted to work on in my relationship with my parents. I was stumped. I got a bit emotional, and that was when Mum said to the group that she and Dad knew I didn't want to live, and the only reason I was doing the course was for them. To see what it was like for them after I had tried to commit suicide was so hard. I felt so selfish, and that if I was to do that to them again I'm sure it would nearly have killed them. But they understood that I was fighting a losing battle, and they would try to accept the fact that I wanted to end my life.

With the day finished, and the review and mindfulness finished, we parted company and I went off to have a session with my allocated psychologist. Once that had finished, it was straight back to Lorne, back to seeing Joey, to have a few days rest. It was only the second week of the course and I was exhausted. Getting home and getting the welcome home treatment from Joey, which was about a thousand licks on the face, always cheered me up. I was so happy to see her that her feet barely touched the ground for the rest of the night, as she was cuddled up in my arms.

...

On the Fridays and Saturdays after the course I would be too tired to do pretty much anything, but by the time Sunday and Monday came I would be out fishing in my boat for the sharks that were around Lorne during that time of year. It was at this time, over the space of a few weeks, I caught my first Blue Shark and Bronze Whaler Shark. I was so pumped up, but little did I know that this was nothing compared to what was about to happen. While out shark fishing with a friend, we had the surprise of our lives when a 4.2-metre Great White Shark came up from the dark waters and circled my boat for 40 minutes, which I filmed on my GoPro. It was the best experience I have ever had and I don't think I will ever be able to top it, in terms of fishing. I said to my friend as the shark was circling the boat, 'I don't care if we don't catch any fish today, this is the best day ever.' Even though having the Great White Shark swim around the boat was likely a once-in-a-lifetime opportunity, ever since, I've had my GoPro with me every time I go out in the boat.

The next day I rang up Channel Ten and they sent a film crew to Lorne. They used some footage from my GoPro, and also interviewed my friend and I. That night, the story was on the Channel Ten news. It would have been the first story, but there were some serious fires in the country, so it was the second story. They also talked about the Bass Strait trip that I had completed and why I had done it. We were also on *The Project* that evening.

...

Often on Monday nights, my anxiety levels were so high I could not relax, and Tuesday was always a bad day for me. This course, even though it was only going for two days a week, felt like five days of intense work.

On the Wednesday I was back on the course again, and over the next three weeks we focused on cognitive behavioural therapy, exposure to areas we were not comfortable in, such as busy supermarkets, shopping malls, football games, even to the point where we walked down the main streets during busy times. We also focused on anger therapy, mindfulness and avoidance.

Cognitive behavioural therapy looks at the behaviour of how we are feeling as sufferers of PTSD, depression and anxiety. We were given sheets to fill out called 'Thought Records', for when we felt like we were in a vulnerable situation.

An example is:

THOUGHT RECORD				
Date, time, situation	Physical reaction	Behaviour	Emotion(s)	Thoughts
12/09/2012	heart racing	speeding	anger	I'm going to be late
0830	sweating	avoid talking to people	anxiety	I may not fit in
Driving to the Geelong Clinic	rapid breathing	swore at slow driver	nervousness	People are going to judge me
Delayed by slow driver	hand trembling			I have the worst luck with bad traffic

After filling out many of these thought records, it would come up with a pattern of how our physical reaction, behaviour, emotions and thoughts would be. Once you could see it on paper, you could start working on those particular issues. For me, after all the thought records were completed, the pattern was that I had no confidence in myself anymore and that I felt as though I wasn't worth anything. Now that I had that realisation, I could work on my thoughts and train myself to think in a different manner. Although it would not be overnight, I now had something to work on.

During the cognitive behavioural therapy sessions, we were told that the average person has between 60,000 and 80,000 thoughts a day, and that a lot of these thoughts are recycled. For example, for me thoughts of failure constantly go around in my head. We were encouraged when we had those thoughts to balance them out with some positive thoughts. An example of a positive thought using the thought record above would be: 'I may be late, but the people on the course will understand, as people are delayed by traffic all the time.' Another positive thought was that I could have simply made a phone call to let them know that I was going to be a bit late, and I could catch up on what I missed later in the day.

We also did classes on trauma awareness and understanding PTSD. It was explained to us by a psychologist that our brain works the opposite from those of people not suffering from PTSD. I, as a PTSD sufferer, react immediately. For example, while in traffic, if a driver cuts me off I automatically go into the angry stage without thinking that maybe the driver didn't see me or that it was a close call.

We also looked at healthy living — the idea that if you eat a healthy diet and exercise regularly, and get the right amount of sleep, you will feel better in yourself and feel better overall.

It was suggested that I make up a happy box, something that I could go to when I was feeling down and out. The idea was that it would be things that would make me happy. My box included fishing and boating magazines, photos of my boat and my dog, shells that I had collected on the beach, some of my favourite DVDs, a bottle of lavender oil and some tactile objects, which included smooth stones and clay that I could play around with and make shapes with. The most important thing in the box was my favourite treat — a packet of white chocolate coated raspberry bullets. Your happy box could contain anything you wanted. It needed to be accessible so that if you were feeling down you could go straight to your box and utilise the things you had in it. I continue to use my happy box all the time and would recommend it to anybody.

Another thing we concentrated on was anxiety and exposure. We were given a card that we could use when our anxiety was high, such as when we were in a stressful environment. The rule was AWARE, which stood for:

Agree to accept the anxiety

What the anxiety is (rate the SUDS)

Act as if the anxiety is not there

Repeat AWA, and

Expect the best

Basically, when you were in a stressful situation such as a supermarket, you had to understand that when you went in there your SUDS was going to rise. Accept that you are aware of them and do the best you can to focus on controlling your SUDS, bringing them down. This method will work, but it will not work until you have done it many times. As with all methods you are taught, they take practice and time to work.

...

The course was going very slowly for me. We eventually got to the dreaded week five live-in phase of the course, where we stayed at the clinic for four nights. This was because the next part of the course was going to be very emotional and hard on us. I had no issues with going into the clinic to stay for the week, as I had been in there previously and felt very comfortable. However, all of the other members in the course were very uneasy about staying in hospital. Little did I know how quickly this was going to change!

During the weekend prior to the live-in week of the course, I had planned to go out with some friends to the pub with the intention of getting absolutely blind drunk. Prior to going to the pub, I drank 10 beers, six Smirnoff Double Black cans of vodka and had about 15 vodka and jelly shots. When we got to the pub, I started drinking double vodka and soda waters and doing shots, and after a while of enjoying myself listening to music and playing pool, something in my head snapped and I felt a massive wave of emotion pour over me. I started crying in the middle of the pub. I quickly went out the back entrance. My mate's wife, who had noticed my change in temperament, followed me out. As soon as I got outside, I started to cry even more. I walked over to an old derelict shed and started punching, kicking and headbutting it, trying to get my rage and emotions out.

By this time, two of my male friends had come out and noticed me doing this. Their first reaction was to jump on me and get me to the ground before I could do any damage to myself. As they lay on me I was trying to get away from them, but was stuck lying on the ground until I calmed down. However, what they didn't realise was that where I was lying, right next to my hand, there was a sharp piece of glass, which was a broken piece of beer bottle. I had a little movement under my body, so with my right hand I picked up the glass and cut myself three times across my left wrist. This was not a suicide attempt, but just a stupid thing that at the time I felt I had to do to stop the pain that was going on in my head.

As soon as I cut myself I stopped struggling, as the pain in my head had now subsided. My friends asked if I was okay, as I had stopped struggling. They slowly got off me and I sat up, now a lot calmer. That's when my friend's wife noticed the blood pouring from my wrist. Immediately, my mate took off his overshirt and wrapped it around my wrist, and said that we were going to the hospital. I stated to him that I was fine and that I wanted to go to another pub, as the place we were at had quietened down and I wanted to continue partying. My friends knew that this was not a good idea at all. They called a taxi and we went back to my friend's house where, after a few smokes and some water, I finally calmed down enough to have my sleeping tablets, and was asleep not long after.

When I woke up in the morning and looked down at my wrist, I straight away remembered what I had done. I remembered all of the previous night, and I remembered how relieved I felt when I cut myself. I knew that I could never do that again, that this was not the answer and was not the way to solve my problems. I now have a constant reminder of that night — three scars running across my left wrist. I realise now that cutting yourself is not the solution to dull the mental pain you're going through.

...

On Monday of week five, I checked in to the Geelong clinic, again for a four-night stay. We were allocated our own rooms and bathrooms, which was good. As they were doing renovations at the time, my room was without a TV and none of the power outlets worked, but I was okay with that because there was a TV in the common room and I had my computer. That week, we were to give a narrative of our life story, including the trauma that we had experienced. Mine was on Wednesday, which gave me time to gather confidence and listen to other people's stories, as I still felt that I did not belong there. Sometimes, or most of the time, you just don't want to accept the truth. I normally wouldn't feel that nervous talking about my trauma and my life, as I had done it a fair bit in recent times in regards to the Challenge. However, there was something different about this up-and-coming talk. That week in hospital was much more intense compared to my relaxing stay previously. The days started at 0830 and we would not finish until 1930. This, in my view, was way too long, especially for what we were doing. Listening to all the other members' stories was very hard. Everyone had a different event that happened in their life for them to get PTSD. No-one in the group had the same story, which in a way was good to know, as PTSD is not a biased illness — it doesn't discriminate against race, gender, sex or age, and can affect everyone in different ways.

By the time Wednesday afternoon came, it was my turn to talk. I eventually ended up taking two hours, until and I had to stop because we had a family barbecue scheduled. After the talk I was sweating from every pore in my body, but felt good because I was finished and had expressed a lot of thoughts and feelings that were inside me. That was the intention of the talk. This book telling you about my experiences will hopefully add to that feeling as well.

My stay in hospital was not what I thought it would be like. I hadn't been able to relax like last time. At first I had been comfortable, but in the end it was a complete switch around. By the time the end of the week came, everyone else was worried about how they would be once they got home. I was counting the seconds until I was able to go home. I could not get out the door quick enough.

Once I got home, Joey was so excited. It was only the second time since I had gotten her that I had been away from her. Then I went out fishing, and shut myself off from the world. Being able to relax in my own environment was a perfect way to wind down from the week I'd just had.

We finished on the Friday, but the next Wednesday came so quick it was like I had never left the clinic. The remainder of the course, which was two days a week for the next seven weeks, was to reiterate and to go into more detail in regard to what we had been taught. The families continued to come to the course on Thursdays, and we continued to have our individual sessions with our allocated psychologists.

By the time the eleventh week came I had nothing left in me, and the fact that I had wanted to pull out of the course many weeks prior caught up with me. I left early on Thursday in week eleven, as I couldn't stand to be in the group when the families joined us. The other people in the group had their partners with them, and I wanted Shelly there. Even though I appreciated the fact that my parents were able to come down every week in order to help me through these difficult times, which they did so well, I wanted Shelly there, too.

After I left the group early that Thursday, I went to see my psychiatrist. As I walked into his office I told him that I was struggling, which he could tell by my face and body language. He reiterated to me that if I didn't find this course hard then he wouldn't have recommended it to me in the first place. He said that I was in week eleven with only one week to go, and that a large percentage of people who attempted the course didn't finish it on the first attempt. He recommended that I be admitted to the clinic that afternoon and I stay there for the completion of week twelve, and a period of approximately five days after the course. This would enable me to let the course sink in a bit, then go home feeling refreshed and ready to put into practice what I'd been taught. I agreed with him, though I asked if it would be okay if I be admitted on the Friday, as I would like to go home and see Joey. He felt that this was okay as long as I felt safe to drive back to Lorne, which I did.

So on Friday I returned to the clinic and checked in. Again, I was given my own room and bathroom.

Week twelve of the course was a summarisation of what we had learnt, and a thank you and farewell to all the people on the course. There was a nurse who was with us from the start of the course, who I would personally like to thank from the bottom of my heart.

When the course finished and everyone went their separate ways, I returned to my room with the feeling that a huge weight had been lifted off my shoulders. Now, with the course finished, it was up to me to utilise my supports, which included my psychologist, my psychiatrist, my GP, my family supports and, most of all, myself. This meant putting into practice what I'd learnt over the course and to stop making the mistake of blocking all my emotions and feelings, and concentrating on the Challenge and working to get better.

I am grateful to the personnel who worked at the Geelong Clinic, in particular those involved in the PTSD course. I will never be able to thank them enough for their help and support.

TWENTY

THE ROAD AHEAD

'Wherever you go, there you are.'
— *Jon Kabat-Zinn*

When I started to write this final chapter, I had just finished watching *Sunday Night* on Channel Seven, where there was a story about a group of people who had been attacked by sharks. They started a club called the Bite Club. The telling of their story helped them to face and overcome their fears, so they could go back into the water again, starting with swimming with the sharks in the Sydney Aquarium. Before they dived they talked about their attack and how some of them had experienced depression, and some of them had seemed to have the symptoms of PTSD.

As I watched these people diving with the sharks, tears welled up and I began crying, seeing them face their fears. It was so brave of them to be within 30 centimetres of the sharks after what they must have experienced when attacked. I was so inspired by them, as they had faced their ultimate fear and overcame it. They all had permanent physical scars, but they were doing something that would help them overcome their mental scars. This is what I needed to do, but how?

Obviously, doing the PTSD courses were a step in that direction, and every time I talk to my psychologist and psychiatrist I am working on moving forward. However, the bad days still outnumber the good.

While driving to Colac one morning in May 2013, on either side of me were paddocks full of cows. Approximately two kilometres in front of me, there was a dip in the road. I noticed something coming towards me. It was an American military humvee. Straight away I was back in Afghanistan, looking for possible threats or anything out of the ordinary. I started shaking and knew that a panic attack was not far off. As I got closer, the vehicle came out of a dip in the road, and I noticed that what I thought was a humvee coming towards me was in fact the top sleeping cabin on a truck. I was still freaked out, and as the truck passed me I pulled over to the side of the road, immediately turned my car off and put on the PTSD course relaxation recording that I always have on my phone.

When people ask me what I do for a job, after two years I'm still telling them that I have recently retired from the Defence Force. I tell them I'm using my leave to finance myself. I hate the fact that I'm embarrassed about receiving a military pension. Something that I face every day is the fact that I don't trust myself to manage my own medication. It isn't even kept at my house — it's kept at my parents' house, and my mother manages my daily dose. I'm a 33-year-old man living next door to my parents, who give me my medication daily.

...

I had been told that sailing was very relaxing, and that I might enjoy being out on a yacht; the silence of sailing with the wind. When I read the Jessica Watson and Jesse Martin books, along with my experience from when I did the Bass Strait Challenge and my ocean fishing experiences, I knew that the water was the best place for me to be. So in June 2013 I conducted a Competent Crew Course, which would give me the knowledge and basic experience to operate a sailing boat, by myself or with others. After doing this course I knew immediately that I had found a new way to relax.

I decided to purchase a 27-foot yacht. It was named *Nari*, which in Arabic means 'my fire'; in Korean it is used towards people of higher rank; and, my favourite, in Japanese it means 'thunder'. Just being on the yacht immediately made me feel like I could get away from everything, that I could escape.

Eventually, as my health improves, I hope to again do some charity work in regards to mental health issues, utilising the yacht. Who knows, maybe a spin around the world? Another good thing about the sailing is that if I complete all the required courses, I will be able to turn sailing into a career. For example, if a person from Melbourne buys a boat in Sydney and hasn't got time, they will pay for someone to sail the boat from the place of purchase to them. With a 'yacht master' qualification, I would finally be able to get off the military pension.

When I first started writing this book, it was as therapy. It was recommended to me during my first PTSD course, back in February 2011. Now, the main reason for writing it is to let people know that there is nothing to be ashamed about in having a mental illness, and that if you do have a problem, regardless of who you are or how minor you think it is, there is always someone out there to talk to. I chose for two years to ignore my problems and I only ended up in a worse situation. I lost everything that mattered to me because of my pride.

Another positive thing that I have done is join the local gym. As everyone says to me, 'healthy body, healthy mind', so I'm trying to go down that path. I have recently quit smoking, utilising the SMARTY goal system that I learnt while on the second PTSD course. My reward has been that I'm able to afford to cover the costs for the upkeep of my yacht. I have also decided to cut back on my alcohol intake, which I will have to start another SMARTY goal plan for, as it has proved to be a major challenge.

The decision to cut back on alcohol happened in late July 2013, when I decided to spend five days on my yacht. I was going to set it up exactly how I wanted, get Joey used to the boat and, of course, sail it. On the first night, while I had the yacht tied up, I decided to have a few drinks. A few turned into about $300 worth of vodka at a club, and I ended up in the emergency room at Geelong Hospital with a gravel rash all over my face from falling down. The only memory I have is of having a paramedic from the ambulance stick his fingers down my thought to try and clear out the vomit. My mum and dad had to come and get Joey, and lock up the boat.

Even though I recommend those with a mental illness to plan projects to keep themselves occupied, I don't recommend that people suddenly take on such huge challenges as the ones I have, such as the Facebook page, the Challenge, the documentary I am currently making about the Challenge, and this book. Even though you might think it's helping you, it might actually be doing the very opposite. It might push your problems to the back of your mind until they manifest in a negative way, as they did for me in the above situation.

Although I hate the position I'm in, sometimes I feel like I'm very lucky with the amount of support I have. Yes, sometimes I do complain about the fact that my parents have to hand my pills to me, but no matter what time it is, day or night, I can always go across and talk to them. I also have my dog Joey, who is my best friend and someone to talk to when I need a chat. I am also lucky to have my sister, who is so supportive, along with her husband, who I love as though he is my own brother. I am also very lucky to have my psychologist and psychiatrist. If I didn't have these people working with me, I can guarantee that I would not be around today. I also have some very close friends, who are very supportive and who I care about more than I can say.

...

If I ever had the chance to do it all again, I would still sign on the dotted line to begin my Army career. The only thing I would change is that I would speak up when I was hurting and not suffer alone because, as I found out once I was medically discharged, there were a lot of people in the same boat as me who were doing the exact same thing. There were so many people out there who I could have talked to but didn't.

I still find it hard to accept that I'm not in the Army anymore. I'm in mourning for my career, and for my wife and all that I've lost in my life. I constantly think, *Why can't I just be posted to the Reserve Commandos in Williamstown, Victoria, so I can still be a part of the Army. I could help out the Reservists, the younger blokes preparing for the CSTC. Would that be so hard?*

Sometimes I think that someone has stuffed up and this is all a bad dream. I think that if I say the right thing to someone, it will go back to how it was. But that isn't true.

It's hard to get over the fact that my marriage and my career are over. But if I went back to both, I would be a liability to the Army and may even hurt my ex-wife more than I already have. Somehow I must let it all go, but how?

A friend of mine, Michael Hawke, recently wrote a poem for me.

Not Your Time

Mate taken out by an IED

Bushmaster?

Funny name for a ship of the desert?

Or was it APC?

Russian roulette on a convoy

Why him, not me?

Join the medics

Trying to do the right things

To understand

But sorting body parts

Back home again

Shunning the light

Craving break of day and birdsong

Wife up and leaves

Loves me

But not the Black Dog
I've brought back home
Plane Jump
Static line at 1000 feet
'You want first this time, mate?'
You say (you usually lead)
He does
You follow
And break your leg
He's redeployed
You recuperate
And now he's dead
Another bone for the Black Dog
Guilt trip and nights of dread
No control: it all gone wrong
Hey, I understand!
And weep with you
Grab my hand
And just hold on
You need to grieve
And grieve it out
Never know what it's all about
So stop asking 'Why?'
Confuse guilt with grief
Accept that it's
Just not your time

Maybe I should take the advice of the poem.

The end, for now.

A NOTE FROM JAMES' PSYCHIATRIST

I initially met James during his battle with mental health issues, which included Depression, Post Traumatic Stress Disorder and alcohol abuse. These conditions are often sequelae of exposure to extreme trauma, such as that experienced by servicemen.

Many challenges exist for people who suffer with mental illness. One of the most significant hurdles to overcome is gaining the courage to seek help. This may, in part, be due to the stigma associated with mental illness. While there have been significant movements to remedy this, there remains an undercurrent in society that mental illness is a flaw or weakness. This is not the case and often the opposite is true. Strength is required to admit one needs help, and to share one's personal information, thoughts and fears with others. Indeed, it is only by doing this that people can begin their recovery.

In addition to the perceived stigma, inherent features of these illnesses can create barriers to seeking help or engaging in treatment. Depression can be viewed as an unshakable darkness that envelops all aspects of the person's life. Features include excessive and inappropriate guilt that one's situation is warranted. Sufferers may experience a sense of worthlessness, believe that they don't deserve help or feel that the situation is hopeless. Motivation and energy difficulties create physical barriers. Post Traumatic Stress Disorder characteristically involves an intense and exaggerated fear response in response to trauma, and causes the person to be on the lookout for danger unnecessarily, with recollections of the trauma in the form of nightmares, flashbacks and an avoidance of any potential reminders of the trauma. A desire to suppress or avoid reminders of the trauma may impair ability to seek help for the condition.

Alcohol misuse often accompanies the above conditions. Although alcohol is socially acceptable and readily available, its misuse is associated with significant health problems. Alcohol may be used as a form of self-medication to block out unpleasant emotions and thoughts or to improve sleep. Excessive or prolonged use compounds depressive symptoms and enables avoidance associated with Post Traumatic Stress Disorder.

There are a variety of effective treatments available for these conditions. There is no 'one shoe that fits all' policy when it comes to treatment. Treatment often requires a team approach, utilising various professionals with different skill sets. The aim of treatment is to reduce the symptoms, distress and dysfunction. Medications are commonly prescribed to treat these conditions. There are a wide variety of medications that may be used, and medication regimens can often be tailored to assist an individual while minimising potential side effects. Medication is often combined with therapy to obtain optimal results. Therapy can take different forms and may occur individually or in a group setting. This can often involve measures that may seem counterproductive to people who need help. Therapies may involve tackling distorted thoughts, confronting behaviours, such as avoidance, and developing coping strategies. This process is often challenging and may temporarily cause some distress in order to achieve longer term gains.

I am privileged to be involved in supporting people through these issues. I am repeatedly amazed and humbled by the strength, courage and achievements by people such as James who navigate these illnesses. James' story reminds me of something I often observe in therapy, that it is often through adversity one achieves personal growth.

I believe James' story encapsulates the experience of mental illness and can provide valuable insight into what may seem a very isolating condition. For those who are about to commence their own battle with mental illness, there is support and help available, and most importantly hope. For those who have embarked on the challenge, you are not alone and there are many who share the same experience. Finally, I hope those lucky enough not to be affected by mental illness can develop a deeper understanding of and compassion for those suffering from these conditions.

Dr Raymond Bruozis
Consultant Psychiatrist
MBBS, MPM, FRANZCP

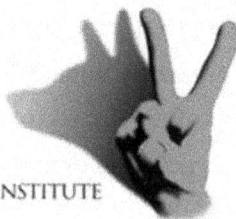

BLACK DOG INSTITUTE

If you need assistance for depression, PTSD or related issues, contact the Black Dog Institute:
www.blackdoginstitute.org.au

www.ingramcontent.com/pod-product-compliance
Lightning Source LLC
Chambersburg PA
CBHW070023100426
42740CB00013B/2586